Development of Graphic Skills

Development of Graphic Skills

Research Perspectives and Educational Implications

Edited by

John Wann
Psychology Department, Edinburgh University,
Edinburgh, UK

Alan M. Wing
MRC Applied Psychology Unit, Cambridge, UK

&

Nils Sõvik
Institute of Education, Trondheim University,
Trondheim, Norway

ACADEMIC PRESS
Harcourt Brace Jovanovich, Publishers
LONDON SAN DIEGO NEW YORK BOSTON
SYDNEY TOKYO TORONTO

This book is printed on acid-free paper

ACADEMIC PRESS LIMITED
24–28 Oval Road
LONDON NW1 7DX

United States Edition published by
ACADEMIC PRESS INC.
San Diego, CA 92101

A catalogue record for this book is available from the British Library

ISBN 0-12-734940-5

Printed in Great Britain by Galliard (Printers) Ltd, Great Yarmouth

Foreword

In the summer of 1989, the fourth conference of the International Graphonomic Society (IGS) was held in Norway at Dragvoll, the University of Trondheim, AVH under the auspices of the IGS, the Norwegian Research Council for Science and the Humanities, and the University of Trondheim, AVH. The theme of the conference chosen by the co-organisers (Nils Sövik and Alan Wing) was the Development of Graphic Skills and this encouraged the participation of psychologists and educationalists, both researchers and practictioners. One of the strengths of the IGS is its multi-disciplinary approach to the study of handwriting and, as with earlier IGS conferences in Nijmegen (1982), Hong Kong (1985), and Montreal (1987), the Trondheim meeting was well supported by those with other interests such as the computer recognition of handwriting and the physiology of movements subserving handwriting. Indeed, over 70 papers were presented at the meeting and these fell into three broad categories; development of graphic skills, handwriting pattern recognition and handwriting as a perceptual motor skill.

Encouraged by the support of the Board of the IGS, the co-organisers considered much of the formally presented material of sufficient general interest to warrant publication. Because of the number and range of topics the decision was taken to seek three separate avenues for this. Papers dealing with issues in motor control based on the analysis of adult graphic skills are to appear in a thema issue of the North Holland (Amsterdam) journal *Human Movement Science*, with Gerard van Galen, Ar Thomassen and Alan Wing as guest editors. Papers concerned with computer applications of handwriting research are being published by World Scientific (Singapore) in a volume entitled *Computer processing of handwriting* and edited by Rejean Plamondon and Graham Leedham. However, the flagship publication taking the papers directly related to the primary theme of the Trondheim conference is the present book: *Development of graphic skills: Research perspectives and educational implications.*

The development of graphic skills is a topic of undoubted interest to academics concerned with perceptual motor skill acquisition. But it must also be considered as highly relevant to practitioners and teachers entrusted with the direct responsibility for children's education. As editors, we therefore saw our role as twofold. First we would aid the authors in putting their ideas on public record and thereby stimulate further research. Second, we would help the authors draw out the many useful and practical ideas which either they had advanced or had emerged in subsequent discussion. Our goal was that these ideas should have the greatest chance of being implemented in due course. Consequently much of the material in this volume has been extensively edited and we are extremely grateful to our authors, some of whom have been put to considerable trouble in reworking their material. It is our hope that the reader will share in our opinion that the result is a book that will stand as a landmark in applicable research. To further this end, any feedback which you, the reader, would like to offer the authors would be most welcome (we would suggest that, in the first place, any correspondence arising from matters in the book be directed to Nils Sövik at the University of Trondheim's Department of Education).

The book comprises six sections: *I Development of written language; II Dynamics of development: Writing; III Dynamics of development: Drawing; IV Individual differences: The development of style; V Dysfunction; VI Remedial issues.* These sections have been selected to lead the reader from basic principles of handwritten letter formation as it has evolved in western education, through some of the features of children's developing skill, to highlights of the problems that children may display. Each of the chapters includes the presentation of the findings of one or more research studies. To assist the reader, the device of using boxed sections for procedural and methodological material has been adopted. The details provided in these boxed sections are necessary for other researchers to appraise, and possibly extend, the work. The details may also provide the teacher with useful tips for refining classroom assessment procedures etc. However, methodology does not make easy reading. Thus, it is intended that the more casual reader be able to skip over the boxed sections and pass from the introduction to the results, yet still be able to glean the essential findings of each study. Another feature of scientific papers that can sometimes make them inaccessible to those involved in education rather than research is the use of technical or statistical terms. For this reason a brief glossary has been included at the end of the book that, hopefully, will assist the reader to a better understanding of the evidence presented in support of each author's arguments.

A number of people have assisted at various stages in the production of this book including Sue Allison, Sally Clapp, Naznin Virji-Babul and the staff of the Visual Aids Department, MRC Centre, Cambridge. We thank Sheila Henderson, Margaret Martlew, Ruud Meulenbroek, David Sugden and Mary Smyth for constructive reviews on earlier versions of the chapters. In addition the following were singled out for individual mention by the various authors: N. van Kruysbergen (van Doorn); R. Browne, L. Waites (Phelps); K. Jensen (Simner); J. Bourriau, A. Gaur, J.Tait (van Sommers); A. Aubert, M-P Michiels (Vinter). We owe a special debt to Colette Wann and Joyce Wing, both for their editorial contributions to the book and for their support throughout the project.

John Wann, Edinburgh, Scotland; Alan Wing, Cambridge, England; Nils Sōvik, Trondheim, Norway.

Contents

Contributors

Sylvie Athenes (with Yves Guiard), CNRS LNF1, 31 Chemin Joseph Aiguier, 13402 Marseilles Cedex 9, France.

Cees Bruinsma (with Cock Nieuwenhuis), PPW-Pedagogiek-THP, Vrije Universiteit, Van der Boechorststraat 1, 1081 BT Amsterdam, The Netherlands.

Robert van Doorn (with Paulus Keuss), Faculteit de Psychologie en Pedagogische Wetenschappen, De Boelelaan 1111, 1081 HV Amsterdam, The Netherlands.

Annlaug Flem Mæland (with Ragnheidur Karlsdottir), Department of Education, Universitet i Trondheim, 7055 Dragvoll, Norway.

Judith Laszlo (with Pia Broderick), Department of Psychology, University of Western Australia, Nedlands, Western Australia 6009.

Frans Maarse (with Jos van der Veerdonk, Marijke van der Linden & Winifred Pranger-Moll), NICI, Katholieke Universiteit, Postbus 9104, 6500 HE Nijmegen, The Netherlands.

Joop Mojet, Rijksuniversiteit te Leiden, Faculteit der Sociale Wetenschappen, Wassenaarseweg 52, Postbus 9555, 2300 RB Leiden, The Netherlands.

Joanne Phelps (with Lynn Stempel), c/o Texas Scottish Rite Hospital, 2222 Welbourn, Dallas, Texas 75219, USA.

Rosemary Sassoon, 34 Witches Lane, Riverhead, Sevenoaks, Kent TN13 2AX, UK.

Marvin Simner, Department of Psychology, University of Western Ontario, London, Ontario N6A 5C2, Canada.

Peter van Sommers, Department of Psychology, Macquarie University, Sydney, New South Wales 2109, Australia.

Nils Sõvik (with Oddvar Arntzen), Department of Education, Universitet i Trondheim, 7055 Dragvoll, Norway.

Annie Vinter (with Pierre Mounoud), Faculté des Lettres et Sciences de l'Homme, 30 rue Mégevand, 25030 Besancon Cedex France.

John Wann (with Maha Kardirkamanathan), Department of Psychology, University of Edinburgh, 7 George Square, Edinburgh EH8 9JZ, UK.

Alan Wing (with Fraser Watts & Vidyut Sharma), Medical Research Council Applied Psychology Unit, 15 Chaucer Rd, Cambridge CB2 2EF, UK.

Tsz Hang Wong (with Henry Kao), Department of Psychology, Pokfulam Road, University of Hong Kong, Hong Kong.

I: Development of written language

On logical grounds any analysis of skill must take account of both the product and the performer. It is the match between the between demands of the task and the capabilities of the person attempting to perform it that determines the quality of performance. Thus a fitting starting point for our consideration of the development of the graphic skills of writing and drawing is to consider the product, the conventional system of signs and symbols embodied in the written word, and how the evolution of letter form over the centuries has been shaped by people's motor abilities. In a fascinating and wide-ranging survey of scripts through the ages, van Sommers *(Where writing starts: The analysis of action applied to the historical development of writing)* applies findings from studies of constraints on hand movement imposed by psychological and biomechanical factors. His argument is that there are many commonalities in the production of different scripts and these arise because people have moulded script forms to their own capabilities. This would seem to be a pre-eminently relevant point in understanding the development of style over an individual's lifetime from the starting point of a formal, taught school handwriting model that is common to most children.

Chapter 1

Where writing starts: The analysis of action applied to the historical development of writing

Peter van Sommers

This chapter deals with issues that I know are already a central preoccupation of students of visible language: The adoption of a practical, empirically-based approach to the study of drawing and writing. I am going to concentrate mainly on problems of script history rather than script acquisition — the phylogeny rather than the ontogeny of writing — and try to apply some of the findings of my research from the 1970s and early 1980s to the development of scripts during three important and well studied epochs in the history of writing: Hieroglyphic in Egypt, cuneiform in Mesopotamia, and the emergence of the Greek alphabet from Semitic scripts.

My emphasis will be on the *graphic* aspects of these writing systems, rather than for example the way they mapped onto sounds or ideas. Specifically I shall concentrate on the form of characters, the manner in which they were compiled, the direction in which they faced and the way they succeeded one another in rows or columns.

Many of the forces and circumstances that shaped these features of writing are part of what I think of as *practical logic*: (i) the impact of the media, (ii) the mechanics of the body and (iii) the operations of central coordination and control. I do not claim that these matters are the most important issues in the history of writing, or the most fascinating. They represent in a sense the "nuts and bolts" of writing's history. None the less they do provide us with interesting opportunities to see how different levels of causation interacted in the development of scripts and

Development of Graphic Skills
ISBN 0-12-734940-5

may impose some order on the apparent capriciousness of writing's history.

1.0 Three levels of structure

First I want to list three general classes of causal principle in drawing and writing. Unfortunately, the first category has no widely adopted name. Crystal (1987) terms it *graphetics*. I think of it as articulatory and economic. At one time or another I have called it *formal* or *geometric* or *mechanical*. It concerns such issues as how and where the hand approaches the writing surface, the maintenance of contact with that surface, the manner in which the hand and arm work as a stroke is made, how writers and drawers anchor one stroke to another, and so on (see Figure 1).

Within the domain of graphetics the *meaning* of script characters or geometric forms can be regarded as analytically irrelevant. It does not matter at this level whether the shape Δ represents an arrowhead, a pyramid or the letter delta. It is simply a shape to be produced by the mechanical system of the body under the direction of the nervous system and in interaction with the media. It is representationally anonymous. The equivalent in speech analysis would be that part of phonology, phonetics, that studies how speech sounds are generated and articulated, independently of what the sounds mean or even in which language they are uttered. We ask simply how forms might be physically produced independently of their communicative value.

The second level is that of representation or *semantics*. What, for example, does the symbol ᴧᴧᴧᴧᴧ *mean* in Egyptian hieroglyphic script? It represents a substance, water, and it stands for a sound "n": thus it may be used in the writing of words containing that sound, and alone for the prepositions "to", "for", etc., so pronounced.

Finally there are what I term *pragmatic* issues: How might the production of a script or a drawing relate to its context and purpose? Egyptian hieroglyphs did not stand in isolation. They

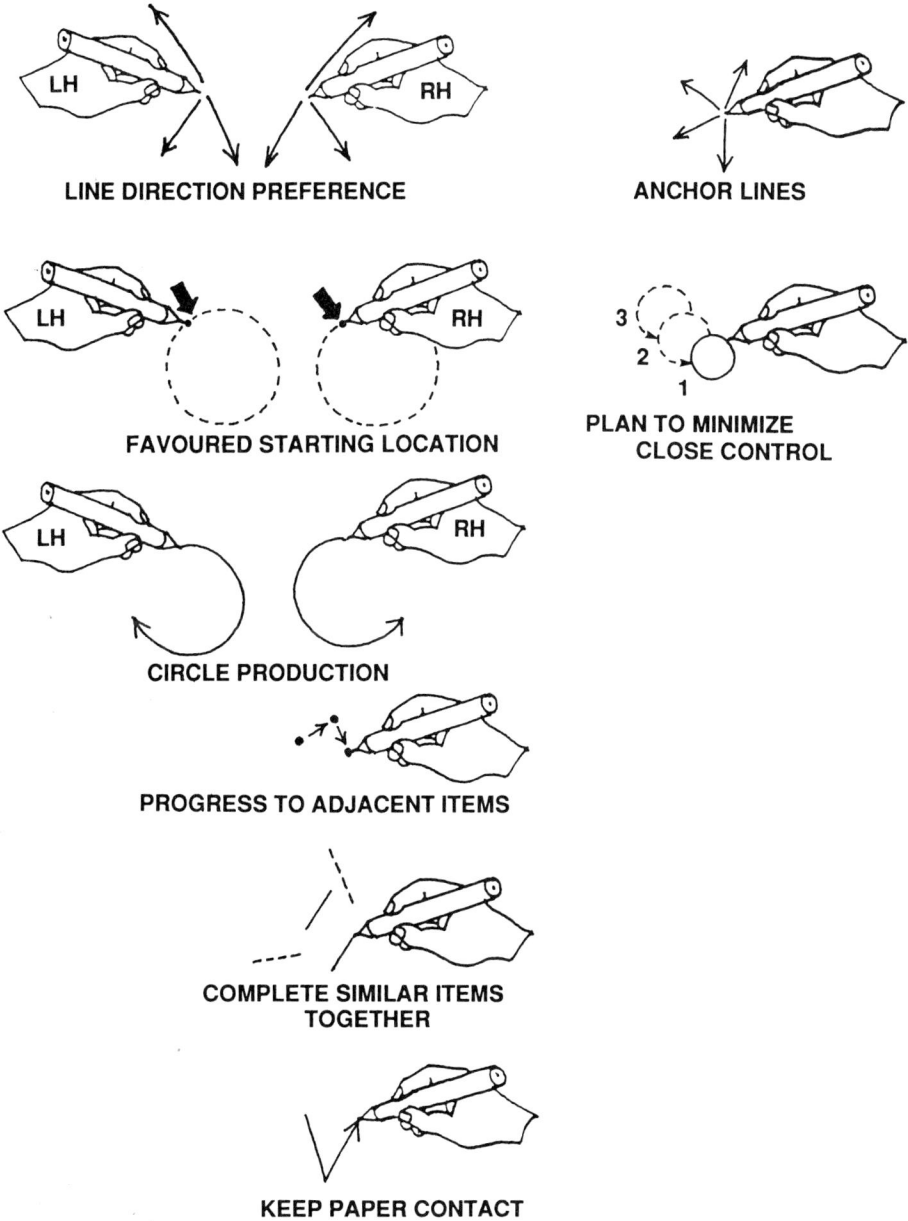

LINE DIRECTION PREFERENCE

ANCHOR LINES

FAVOURED STARTING LOCATION

PLAN TO MINIMIZE CLOSE CONTROL

CIRCLE PRODUCTION

PROGRESS TO ADJACENT ITEMS

COMPLETE SIMILAR ITEMS TOGETHER

KEEP PAPER CONTACT

FIGURE 1: *Eight principles of action arising from kinesiological, economic and planning considerations that contribute to the domain of graphetics, the non-representational aspect of drawing and writing.*

were often closely related to the paintings that accompanied
them, to carved reliefs, to the statues on which they were cut, to
the structure of the buildings on whose walls they were
inscribed. They were oriented in relation to audiences, static
and moving, human and supernatural. It is impossible to
consider them adequately outside the context of their social use.

Although I have spoken of these three levels, graphetics,
semantics and pragmatics as analytically separable, in every
practical case they compete and interact. Many of the important
transition points in the history of writing were marked by shifts
in the dominance of one or other of these sets of principles. For
example, the more a writing system came to serve secular
purposes on a large scale, the more the first category of cause
(graphetics) came into prominence, as formal articulatory
forces and principles of economy became salient. It is a theme
that repeats itself often in the history of writing. As the script
was freed from ceremonial and monumental functions and
moved towards commercial and administrative purposes and as
volume increased, several changes regularly occurred: (1)
There was a reduction in the number of characters and (2) a
diminution in their size. (3) Form became simplified and (4)
standardized. Frequently, if the media permitted it, (5) cursive
forms evolved with curves replacing angles and ligatures
joining letters. In particular cases, eg Arabic, these changes
were retarded by aesthetics or by conservative religious
principles (Gaur, 1987, p97) but this in fact often occurred long
after the scripts had already adopted many cursive qualities.

2.0 Graphetics and script development

2.1 The impact of economics: Cuneiform

One of the best documented cases of the routinization of script
production occurred in Mesopotamia. As many people will
know, Sumerian cuneiform was largely a commercial and
administrative script. Like Egyptian hieroglyphic script it
developed from a simple logographic form and (like the later
Egyptian scripts) it developed into a highly standardized and
economical script that betrayed little of its pictorial origins. I

want to comment on two developments in cuneiform, first the change from a right-to-left vertical arrangement to a left-to-right horizontal one, and second the contraction in the variety of the wedge-shaped marks used by scribes in producing the script.

The early Sumerian symbols were representations of faces, birds, oxen, trees, water, etc. Many of them were asymmetrical in form, and like asymmetric Egyptian hieroglyphs, these faced right. (I shall discuss the likely reason for this later.) These early semi-pictorial logograms were incised one beneath the other on small clay tablets with the sharp tip of a stylus. According to Driver (1976) the change from top-to-bottom columns to left-to-right rows (see Figure 2) occurred as a result of a simple change in the format of the tablets. Tablets became more rectangular and larger in size and as a consequence they could no longer sit snugly in the palm of the hand, and were placed on a flat surface. The palm grip had already brought about a 45 degree counterclockwise rotation of the tablets from the position in which they were read (Figure 2b), and the new placement rotated them a further 45 degrees, so that the tablet was virtually turned on end. Characters that previously faced right were now incised facing upward on the tablet in left-to-right rows rather than to the right in vertical columns.

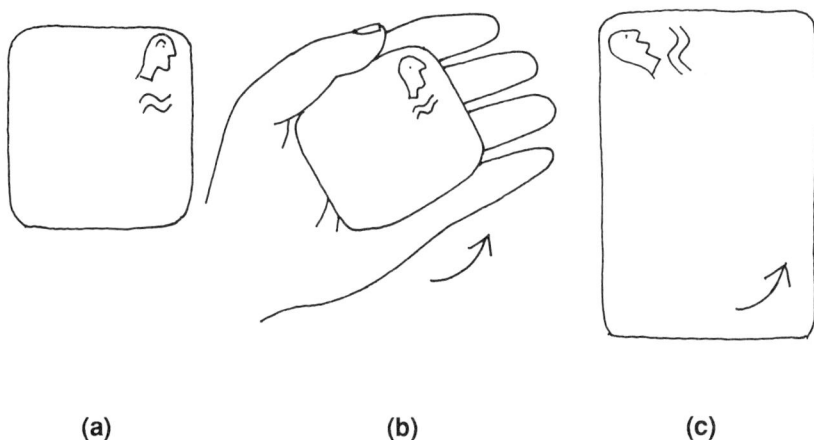

(a)   (b)   (c)

FIGURE 2: (a) Cuneiform tablet in reading position showing ideograms in columns commencing at the upper right. (b) Tablet rotated 45 degrees to the left during inscription. (c) Larger format tablets rotated a further 45 degrees. (Adapted from Driver, 1976, with permission of the British Academy).

Next there was a radical simplification and standardization of the form of the characters. Around 2500 B.C., each character, instead of being drawn with the pointed tip of a stylus, began to be produced by pressing the angular end of the stylus into the clay, making the wedge-shaped impressions from which cuneiform gets its name. Almost immediately the representational significance of the shapes began to be lost, so that today nobody could safely guess the identity of the object being portrayed in standard cuneiform except with the aid of an historic crib.

The scribes producing the early versions used a great variety of stylus angles. Driver's (1976) diagram shows eight wedge positions extending around 270 degrees (see Figure 3a). It seems likely that these were produced not just by a variation in stylus grip and hand position, but also by some modest rotation of the tablet held in the non-dominant hand. Even so, as Powell's (1981) reconstructions of the hand movements suggest, the hand manipulating the stylus would have had to move quite radically to achieve the full 270-degree range of orientations. It is hardly surprising therefore that this range quickly contracted. According to Driver, the first to go were the two most extreme orientations, the wedge pointing upwards and that pointing horizontally to the left (Figure 3b). The next casualty was a neighbouring wedge, that pointing down towards 7 o'clock. Finally (Figure 3c) we are left with four positions, two of which, the vertical and the horizontal, strongly predominated. Further contraction was probably halted as a concession to readers, that is for reasons of legibility.

It is obvious that these changes are linked to the mechanics of the hand and arm. This process of selection of certain stylus orientations can be related to the concept of extreme joint angles proposed by Rosenbaum et al (1990) in their study of hand grips and rotations. They define extreme joint angles as "... angles that deviate significantly from the joint's resting position". The idea seems intuitively right in explaining the contraction in stylus positions, although I think it needs refinement. It is possible to think of each joint having a certain range of movement which may or may not be symmetrical about a resting position. Movement within this range will follow some distinctive profile of ease or difficulty. Of course the situation may change when one changes one's grip on a writing instrument or has recourse to various additional movements of elbow and shoulder. The main point, however, is that the cuneiform system, once freed from representational constraints and routinized, followed a highly predictable evolution, given the technology of clay and stylus and the mechanical properties of the body.

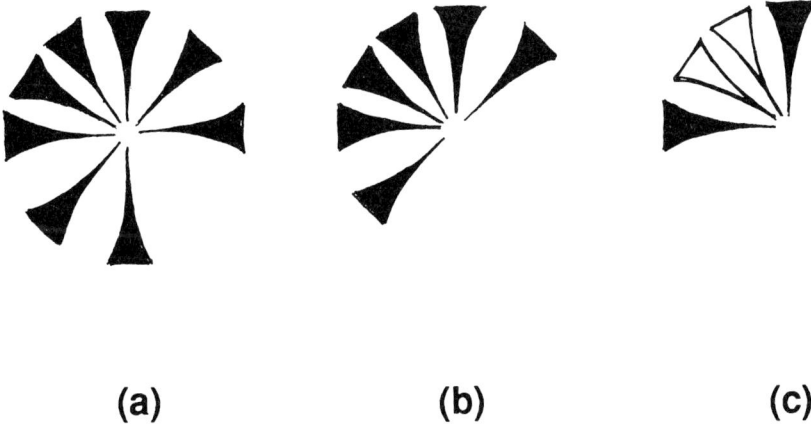

(a)   **(b)**   **(c)**

FIGURE 3: Progressive contraction of the range of cuneiform stylus impression from a range of 270 degrees (left) to four orientations (right), two of which, the vertical and the horizontal, predominated. (Adapted from Driver, 1976, with permission of the British Academy).

The actual history of any writing system's development is a matter of particularities. In the case of cuneiform it was associated with the rotation of the enlarged clay tablet and the fact that the characters were formed by the impress of the corner of a stylus rather than the trajectory of its point.

2.2 Ratings of movement difficulty

Extreme joint angle at rest, or something related to it, is not the only source of difficulty in producing writing strokes. We have also to consider movement, as Rosenbaum et al (1990) showed, and this may not simply be a matter of mechanics. Take for example Figure 4. This diagram from van Sommers (1984) plots difficulty ratings collected from normal right- and left-handed adults working, not with a stylus in clay, but with a felt pen on paper. I gave the subjects a sheet of paper covered with between 50 and 60 narrow rectangles in many different orientations. Each rectangle had a black bar at one end as Figure 4 shows, and the subjects had to make three parallel strokes from the darkened end of the rectangle and then mark on a five-point scale the degree of difficulty in making the strokes. (The study was repeated using judgements of ease which produced exactly complementary results).

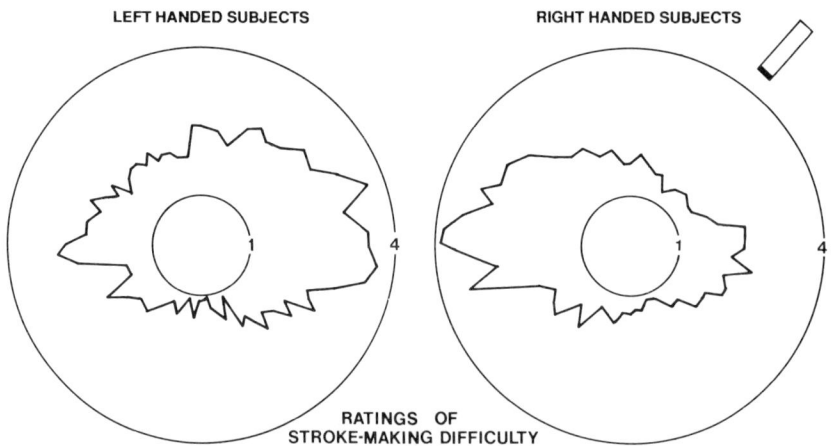

FIGURE 4: Difficulty ratings of adult subjects drawing straight lines 2.4 cm long within elongated rectangles presented in a range of orientations. Right- and left-handed subjects rated their strokes on a scale from 1 (easiest) to 5 (most difficult). The further the irregular lines depart from the inner circles the higher the difficulty rating. (From van Sommers, 1984, Figure 1.3).

Let me explain how Figure 4 is to be read. The further the irregular line departs from the central circle the higher the mean difficulty rating was for strokes in that direction. Note that there is a major region of difficulty for right-handers towards the top left. This arises in part from a problem of *scope*;

right-handed subjects do not have the possibility of extending their fingers so far from the resting position towards 11 o'clock as they do, for example, in moving up towards 2 o'clock or down towards 5. But in addition, movement to the top-left involves the coordination of two contradictory commands, one to move outwards to make the stroke, the other downwards to maintain paper contact.

A common explanation of the avoidance of movement to the top left is that it causes writing instruments to catch in the paper. John Tait (1988) has observed that the frayed tip of the Egyptian rush pen tended to fold under if driven towards the upper left. But this is probably only a contributory cause, because my subjects showed the avoidance when using felt or fibre-tipped pens, and identical tendencies were found in my Chinese subjects using a vertically held brush which can move readily in all directions. The choice of a writing instrument is probably as much a product of preferred movement as preferred movement is a product of writing instrument.

Consider next the smaller region of difficulty in moving horizontally towards 3 o'clock. For right-handers, that action too involves a complex coordination because it is produced principally by ulnar deviation (a "fanning" wrist movement) that produces a line towards 2 o'clock. That trajectory must be continually adjusted down towards the horizontal by an appropriately adjusted finger flexion. Because of the dual control this is not only awkward relative to the stroke towards 1 or 2 o'clock, but less smooth and accurate. This doubtless explains why in Chinese and Japanese script "horizontals" are commonly not horizontal but are directed slightly upward towards 2 o'clock, an effect that is documented for Chinese in van Sommers (1984, Figure 1.13g).

I do not have time to explore it fully here, but this concept of central control of stroke making can be extended into stroke *planning*, including such things as line anchoring: which line should be laid down first, and how intersections are managed. You only have to think about the absurdity of constructing the letter K in the order shown in Figure 5(b) or (c) to understand first why it is done in the way it is (a), and why such a letter would eventually come to face as it does with its upright on the left in any script that constructs letters left to right. Gaur reports that when the Greek alphabet was firmly established as a left-to-right script, "...this change was accompanied by a reversal of all non-symmetric letter signs; in other words, letters such as B, K, N, Δ and Σ acquired their present form in this process." (1987, p119).

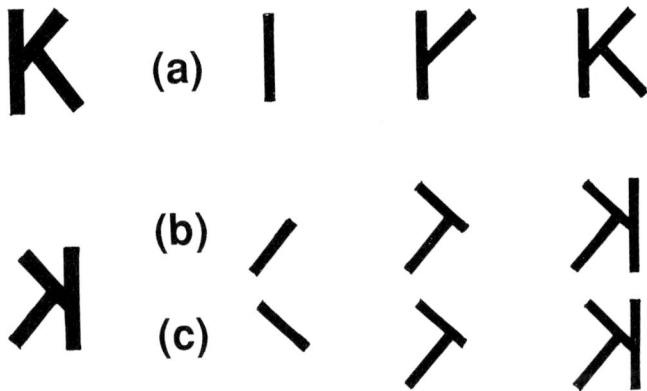

FIGURE 5: Writers who progress from left to right will prefer letters that branch rightward. (a) Each successive stroke is anchored at its left end to an existing stroke. If the letter branched leftward and writers progressed left to right they would be forced to adopt the more demanding strategies (b) or (c).

When we examine a script like Etruscan, it looks rather like Greek script read in a mirror. The Etruscans got their alphabet from the Greeks but reverted to a right-hand start. I can only assume that the script was not then used routinely enough on a large scale to achieve the left-to-right movement across letters. As a consequence, several of the asymmetrical letters have their initial strokes on the right with subsequent strokes anchored to the left.

Earlier I mentioned the reduction in size that commonly accompanied the routine practical use of script. Size reduction brought its own effects. The logic of the argument is given in this passage from Jeffery (1961, p64, letters in square brackets added), describing the development of Greek letters:."It is a well known fact that painting with a brush produces a faster and therefore more cursive script than any made by cutting; and as painted letters are written faster, they tend to become smaller, so that simplification is sometimes necessary. For a vase-painter writing letters only 4 millimetres high it was difficult to paint such shapes as closed *heta* (⊟), crossed *theta* (⊕) without blotting them; hence the first is simplified to H, and the second to dotted *theta* (⊙). In the same way tailed *epsilon* (ⅎ) becomes tailless (E) because a wider space between the cross-bars lessens the chances of blotting, and tailed *upsilon* (Y) expands to V. It is possible, in short, that these changes in the Greek letters were first made by writers with brush or pen, and then adopted by the masons.

2.3 Maintaining contact: Cursive scripts

Let us turn to another constraint: it makes economic sense for writers and drawers using instruments that leave scratches or residues (inscribing in wax, using pens, pencils or brushes, for example) to maintain contact with the writing surface as they move from stroke to stroke. This tendency is accentuated, according to my studies, as figure size gets smaller and writing speed gets faster. (These are two independent effects.) I also found that maintaining contact is more likely at some transitions than others: other things being equal, it is more probable at a right angle than at an acute angle and more likely in a change from a horizontal to a vertical stroke than the reverse.

Once a writer has started to move continuously around angles, there will be a tendency for the angles to be changed into curves. Gaur (1987) documents many examples of this rounding of letters as script development progressed. The most familiar examples occur in the transition from Greek to Roman, Σ to S, Δ to D, Y to U, but Gaur's examples of rounding include Egyptian, Aramaic, Greek uncial and Arabic. Letters were not only progressively rounded, but closed letters were opened (Gaur, 1987, p92) and of course letters were joined by ligatures. The joining of letters in cursive styles occurs in both vertical scripts (e.g. Chinese, Japanese and various central Asian

scripts) and in horizontal (Arabic and Latin). The maintenance
of paper contact between characters not unexpectedly affects
letter construction, as we shall see later in the case of Arabic.
In Egypt, according to Meltzer (1980) the cursive hieratic script
affected the non-cursive hieroglyphic script from which it was
derived when scribes used the hieratic as a draft form for the
more elaborately produced hieroglyphs.

3.0 Semantic principles in Egyptian script

Having talked of some of the practical, mechanical forces that
affected the development of cuneiform, and various other formal
constraints like planning and economy of effort affecting various
other basically secular scripts, let me turn in the centre section
of this paper to an example of semantic and pragmatic
principles in operation.

Egyptian hieroglyphs were used mainly for monumental and
ceremonial purposes, in contrast to the scripts that succeeded
them.   There were standard orientations and directions for
hieroglyphic characters to which most inscriptions conformed
(see Figure 6). Later I shall discuss the probable origin of this
orientation; at this point I want to develop an issue to which I
have already referred in my introduction: the way the context
and the meaning of the text gave rise to systematic variations
from the standard orientation.

The classic treatment of this topic is that of Henry George
Fischer (1977), who identified several motives for departing from
the standard right-facing hieroglyphs laid down in right-to-left
order, most of them linked to the architectural and ceremonial
use of the script.   We can illustrate several of Fischer's
conclusions in two of his figures. Figure 7 shows a statue that
probably stood at the left-hand side of a doorway in a temple,
while, no doubt, another statue stood to the right.   Note first the
two panels on the front on the statue. The right side faces right
in the standard way, but the left side is reversed, making the two
panels symmetrical. Sometimes this symmetry was within the
one body of text as in this case; often it was from one statue to
another, from one wall to another, from one side of an object to
another, and so on.

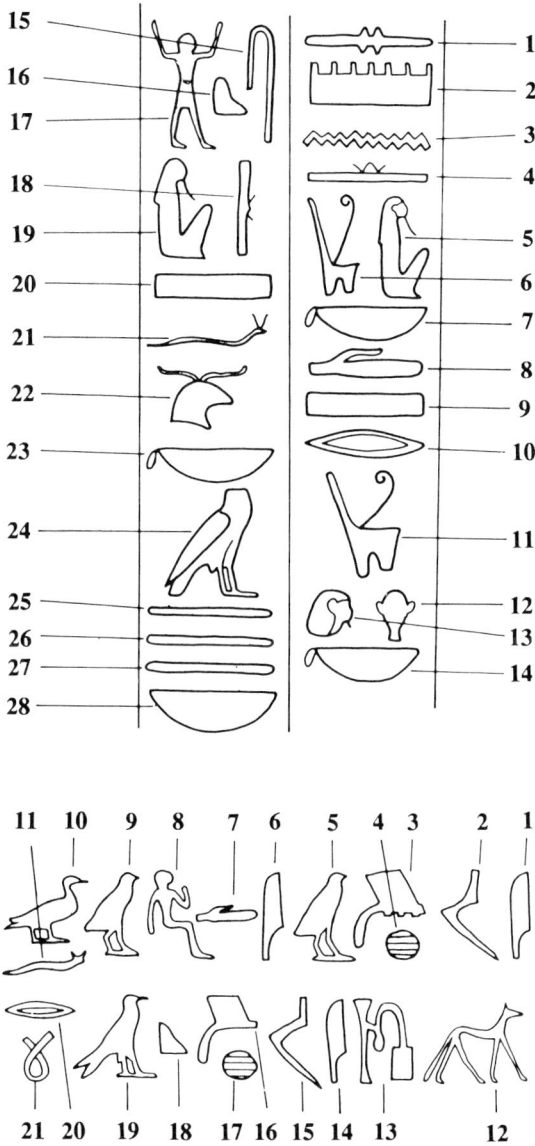

FIGURE 6: *Standard directions for the production and reading of Egyptian hieroglyphic texts. Top: vertical configuration; bottom: horizontal configuration. (From Davies, 1987, with permission of the author).*

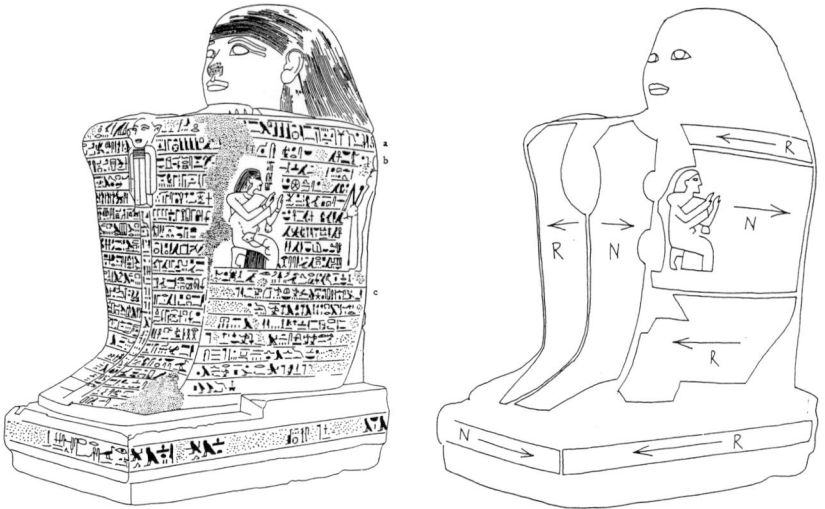

FIGURE 7: Block statue from the Twenty-second Dynasty in the precincts of the temple of Karnack. (Reproduced from Fischer, 1977, with permission of the author). (Right) Sketch of statue showing the orientation of the fields of hieroglyphic characters. (See text for explanation).

On the side of the statue in Figure 7 at the top we have a reversed field of characters which give the owner's titles and name, thus effectively *labelling* the statue. The reversal orients the script characters so that they face forward with the statue they identify. In the centre of the same side there is a hymn addressed to a divinity and oriented with the carved relief figure who utters it. Below that is another reversed field of text, in this case a hymn addressed to the audience of priests approaching the doorway outside which the statue stood, who naturally encountered it from the front. With the possible exception of the symmetrical panels on the front of the statue, in all these cases we are dealing with the relation of text to pictures, text to statue, text to architecture, text to audience.

The second example of semantics and pragmatics from Fischer's work shows contextual factors operating within the

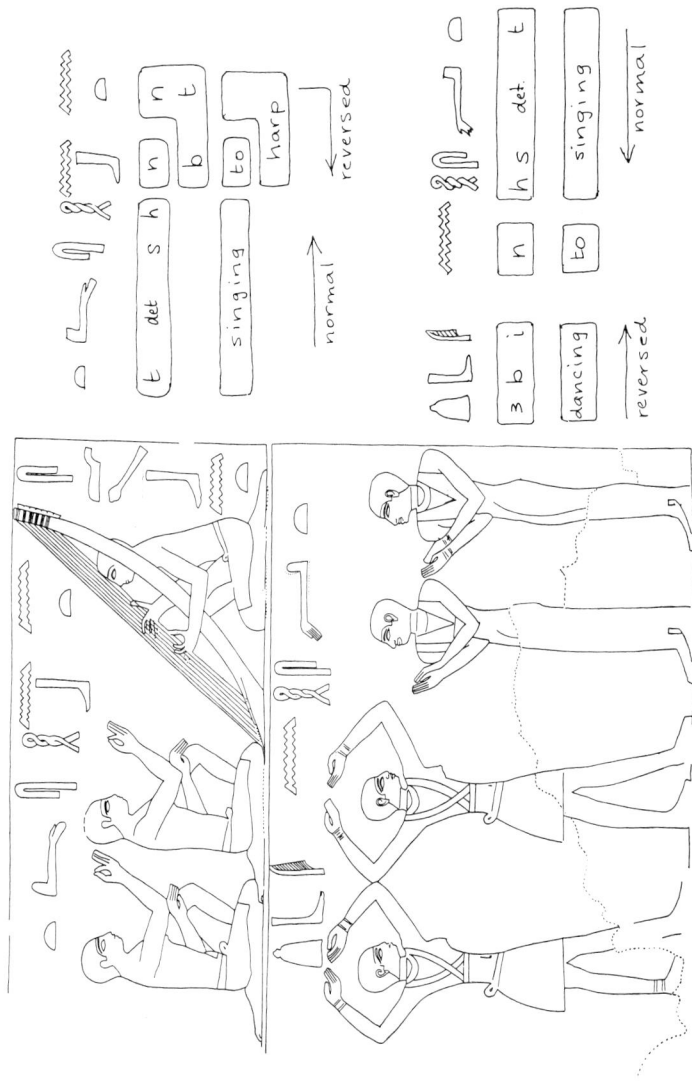

FIGURE 8: (Left) Old Kingdom scene from Saqqara of singing to the harp (top) and singing to dancing (bottom). (Reproduced from Fischer, 1977, with permission of the author). (Right) Copy of inscriptions with phonetic transcriptions, English translations and indications of the direction of facing and order of characters. Note the correspondence between the facing of the figures and the facing of the hieroglyphs.

sentence rather than on blocks of text. The upper and middle parts of Figure 8 (from Fischer, 1977, Figure 80) show several human figures juxtaposed with hieroglyphs. The top sequence of phonetic characters reads, "Singing to the harp", and the bottom one, "Singing to dancing". Not all the characters face in the standard direction. "Harp" is reversed in the upper panel and "singing" in the lower. The reason for these reversals lies in the concordance or correspondence between text and pictures. In the pictures the singers, musician and dancers confront one another, and this confrontation is represented in the direction of the corresponding phonetic characters comprising the text. It is in a sense the application at a micro level of the concordance between carved relief and text we saw on the side of the statue.

4.0 Stroke preference and starting position in scripts

4.1 The standard orientation of hieroglyphs

What about the origins of the Egyptian hieroglyphics' standard orientation and order of the majority of Egyptian hieroglyphic texts themselves? Is the rightward facing and the rightward parading of the symbols also semantic? Fischer does not think so. He believes it has practical (graphetic) origins. "The dominant rightward orientation of Egyptian writing is undoubtedly explained by the prevalent right-handedness of man; as in the case of Sumerian and Chinese, the scribe began on the side where the hand that did the writing happened to be situated" (Fischer; 1977, p6).

If Fischer is right in this assertion, how do we reconcile this claim for the *naturalness* of the right start with the universality of a left start in our own drawing and writing? If you ask a writer of the Latin script we use to draw a profile face, the great majority of us will draw it facing left. We do the same with dogs, cars, crocodiles, birds; in fact with any object or creature that has an obvious front that is drawn in profile. The front is drawn first and faces to the left. It is a very robust effect, and, surprisingly is similar for both left- and right-handers. How is it then that the main tradition for millenia in Egyptian hieroglyphics and other major script systems based historically on pictorial forms was for characters to face right and to march across or down the writing surface. *Is* there any such thing as a "natural" approach, and if so who is natural? As far as the point of commencement and the direction of facing, I believe the Egyptians did the natural thing, as Fischer suggests.

4.2 Further empirical studies of direction preferences

To explain this I need to revert again to some of my empirical studies. When I first began to investigate preferences for single short stroke production I used a tracing task, asking people to trace over lines that lay all over the page like scattered straw. The stroke production was videotaped and summarized as polar plots (see Figure 9). The results showed that people working with their right hands virtually unanimously preferred to come down from the top left rather than go up from the bottom right, and in all the other forced choices in moving along lines their preferences lay symmetrically on either side of the axis from 11 to 5 o'clock.

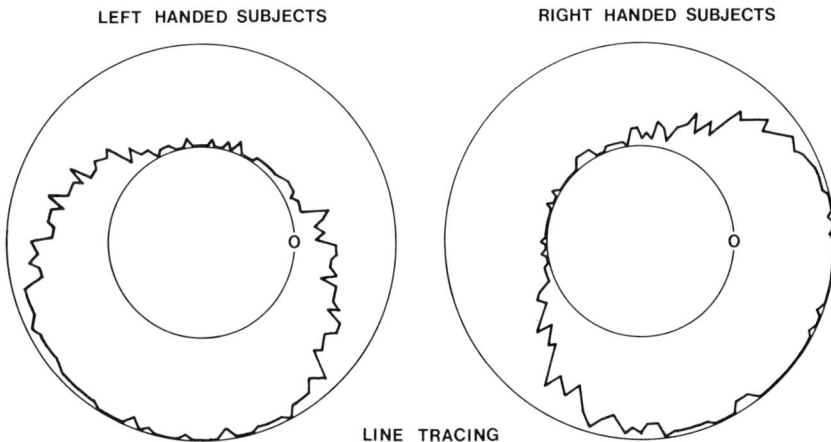

LEFT HANDED SUBJECTS   RIGHT HANDED SUBJECTS

LINE TRACING

FIGURE 9: Tracing performances of left- and right-handed adults whose native script is English. The distance the irregular lines depart from the inner circle shows the proportion of subjects preferring to trace lines in the various directions relative to the centre of the graph. (From van Sommers, 1984, Figure 1.1).

Tracing or copying lines will tell you whether a person prefers to move one way as opposed to a direction 180° from it, but not whether for example they prefer a left-to-right horizontal movement to one that rises a degree or two, or whether they prefer horizontal to vertical movement and so on. So I chose to give my subjects more degrees of freedom, asking them to draw short straight lines at random all over the page. In fact I demanded the maximum possible variation in direction and randomness in order of production. Again I videotaped the outcome and looked for biases in the performances.

This procedure had two advantages: (i) It was conservative in the sense that I demanded randomness in a search for consistency. (ii) It so happened that the outcome did not correspond at all to what might be expected if performances were governed by habit or convention, so that horizontal and vertical strokes, which are so common in conventional drawings, were not strongly favoured, especially the horizontal, which people tended to avoid.

What emerged was that the output from right and left hands were mirror images of one another, so that right handers favoured movement to the top right, bottom left, and bottom right, while left handers favoured the reflections of these three directions, namely top left, bottom right and bottom left (see top illustration in Figure 1). This symmetric relation between the canonical movements of the two hands invited some basically mechanical explanation, and this was borne out by examining the video records, which showed two common movements, a wrist movement and a finger movement. It was also supported by my finding that small children showed similar mirror-image performance on preferred stroke-making well before they began to learn to write.

At this time I had already carried out a study which is described very briefly in my book in which right-handed adult subjects were asked to rate the *similarity* of various strokes in a pair-by-pair design. A cluster analysis identified two major factors. The first included movements in two opposite directions, to top right and bottom left, that seemed to correspond to a wrist movement. There was also a bottom-right top-left factor that seemed to correspond to flexion/extension of the fingers. A study of copying errors, which I reported in some detail, identified the same canonical directions, with the exception of course of the top-left movement which is rarely used by right-handers.

4.3 Conflict and compromise

From the point of view of script evolution and Fischer's idea of natural starting points, the next step was especially significant. The question I asked was whether stroke direction preference determines starting position. After all, if you trace, copy or draw a line in a southward direction you must start in the north, or if you draw to the right you must start on the left. We can take two opposing views of this conflation of stroke preferences and starting location, either that it is happily parsimonious or that it is a case of confounding that needs to be disentangled. Disentanglement required a task that involved starting positions but no strokes, which seemed a tall order. My solution was to ask people to trace, copy and create clusters of simple dots. For the right hand all these tasks produced a result that was consistent with stroke preferences: all dot clusters started near 11 o'clock. (11 o'clock is the best position for starting the three canonical strokes with the right hand: up towards 2 o'clock, back towards 7 and down towards 5).

This outcome for the right hand seemed to confirm that starting position even for non-strokes (dots) was connected with, if not derived from, stroke preferences. *The key fact, however, was that no such interdependence existed between strokes and starts for the left-handers.* While stroke preferences for right- and left-handers were more or less mirror images, starting position was not — it was identical for right- and left-handers. Both were at 11 o'clock (Figure 10). This not only broke the nexus between strokes and starts but suggested that starts were not mechanically driven in these subjects; they should be mirror symmetrical from one hand to the other if they were. At this point I went again to pre-literate children to see whether they began with this 11 o'clock start. What I found confirmed Fischer's intuition. The starting position for right-handed pre-school children was not up at 11 o'clock but down near 5 o'clock. They started where their hands approached the paper. I had

them do other tasks like moving buttons from the edges of a
sheet of paper to the centre or vice versa and they did the same
thing, starting, if they were right-handed and illiterate, on the
right, low down. As they learned to write, the starting point for
their dot clusters migrated upwards and to the left until it
reached the adult 11 o'clock position.

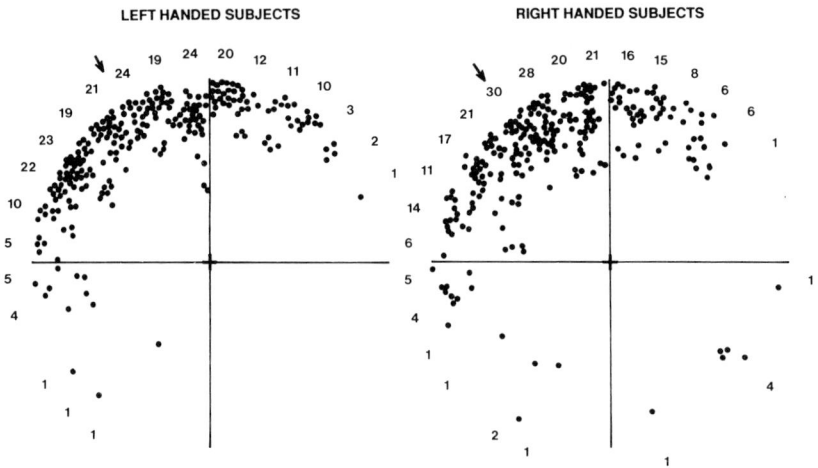

*FIGURE 10: Starting locations for 12 left- and 12 right-handed adults tracing
over a series of clusters of ten dots arranged in a roughly circular array.
Each point in these plots represents the location of the first dot traced by
subjects on each of their 20 clusters. Note that unlike the line tracing in
Figure 9, the preferred starting positions are virtually identical, centring
around 11 o'clock. This invites something other than a mechanical
explanation.*

Now recall that I had found that the pre-literate children who
preferred to start at the bottom right also preferred to move down
and across the page from top left in their stroke making, and
young left- and right-handed children showed the same mirror-
image symmetry in stroke production that adults show even
before they knew how to produce a single letter or knew which
way lines of text lay on a page. What this suggests is that
*natural starting position and natural stroke production are in
fundamental conflict, and I believe that this basic conflict or*

contradiction between where we would naturally start and which way we prefer to move our hands when we write is a key factor in understanding the history of development of script systems. It has not only destabilized the whole history so that some scripts begin on the right and some on the left, but has given rise to various compromises that only become apparent when one investigates the actual sequence of movements used by writers of the various scripts.

Consider the following major scripts: (i) Chinese, which started each page at the top right, progressed downwards, but which from the earliest times started each character at the top left. (ii) Hebrew, which started each page at the top right, progressed leftward, yet like Chinese also started each letter at the top left. It moves across the page in a sort of zig-zag shuffle. (As I shall later document, the same strategy was used by writers of hieratic scripts in Egypt when these scripts diverged from the monumental hieroglyphic scripts and were produced in volume). (iii) Occidental scripts (Latin, Greek, Cyrillic) which started top left, went right in rows and started each letter, like the others, at the top left. All these scripts adopt the same strategy for the letter, maximizing the use of canonical stroke movements. They vary only in where the line starts and which way it proceeds.

4.4 Greek alphabetic script

It might be of interest at this point to review quickly the emergence of Greek alphabetic script. Figure 11, taken from Gaur (1987), shows the historical origins of Greek script. It was derived from North Semitic scripts probably via the Phoenicians. The North Semitic script, like so many others, was written from right to left. Eventually the Greeks were to reverse this direction but for a time they wrote their script in alternating directions, line by line — boustrophedon — like an ox ploughing. The boustrophedon system has the advantage of allowing the writer to maintain close visual links between characters at the ends of lines. For people working on a large scale — inscribing on a wall for example — boustrophedon is especially appealing since a return to the right to pick up the next line is tiresome for the writers and problematic for the readers. The same would apply to inscriptions on the curved surface of a pot. It makes sense either to do a U-turn and come back or to continue as some potters did with a spiral around the whole vessel (Jeffery, 1961, p45). We do something very similar ourselves when we tuck the odd overflow word in at the end of a line in informal notes. Such consistent movement always to the adjacent element is also a quite compelling principle in drawing and is the main consideration in determining stroke order.

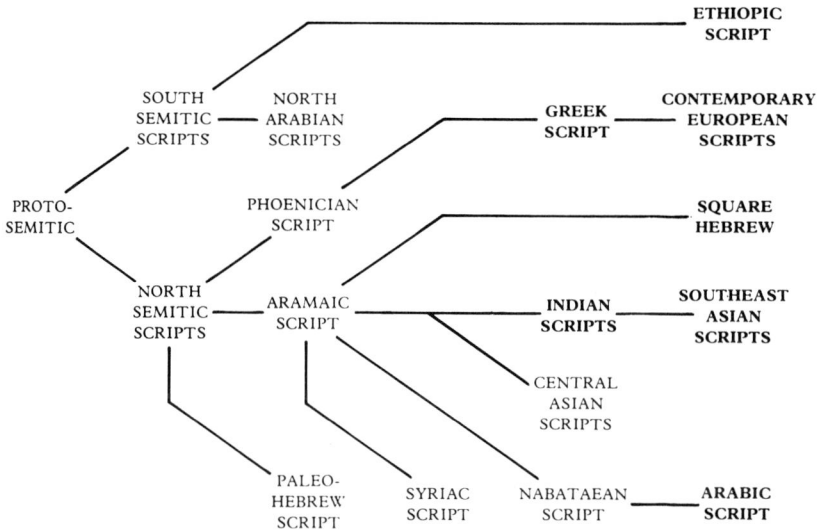

FIGURE 11: Historical origins of Greek script. (From Gaur, 1987, with permission of the author).

When one writes in this way (boustrophedon) it is usual to turn each letter into its reverse orientation, so that characters in each successive line are in a mirror image orientation relative to those in the line that preceded it. According to Jeffery (1961) this letter reversal was not in itself a major problem for Greek writers, since the majority of letters in early Greek were symmetrical, so that they remained unchanged in boustrophedon writing. It might be thought that this prevailing symmetry of letters would make the reversed lines easy to read,

PLEASE DO NOT LET ME SEE

YAM UOY.   YHTOMIT TIH UOY

NOT LIKE HIM BUT HE IS NOT

MAHW YAM UOY TAHT YOT A

INTO LIKE A PUNCHING BAG.

IF YOU EXAMINE THE HORSE'S

UOY   TAHT   WOV   I   HTUOM

WILL   BE   MOST   UNLIKELY

TAHT   HTIW   MIH   XIM   OT

OTHER ANIMAL.

FIGURE 12: English script arranged boustrophedon style. Each even-numbered line is printed right to left. All individual letters in these reversed lines are symmetrical, so they have not changed their aspect. Changes in order alone can produce difficulties for the reader.

but a simple demonstration (Figure 12a and b) shows that this is not so. The reversed lines in these two paragraphs are composed entirely of symmetrical letters, yet they are as difficult to read as normal reversed text. Kolers (1968) reported that his subjects had almost as much difficulty deciphering reversed text where order is reversed but letter orientation is normal as reflected text where both order and orientation were altered. In fact after practising on such a passage each day for a little over a week, Koler's subjects found the two transformations equally difficult to decipher. It is perhaps not surprising therefore that the Greeks, like everybody else who flirted with boustrophedon writing, eventually gave it up. They deserted the natural right-to-left progression of letters and made starting positions of lines consistent with the starting position of characters and canonical stroke making, both on the left. This is the direct antecedent of the system that we in the west use today. This sort of difficulty probably explains why, without a bridge like boustrophedon, scripts retained the right-to-left order in spite of its relative awkwardness. A complete conversion to a left-side start would render text very difficult to decipher.

4.5 Arabic script

The glorious exception to a top left start for all letters is Arabic which not only starts the line on the right like Hebrew, but does not necessarily start letters at the top left. I have two observations about Arabic: first that the progression to the left across many letters is dictated by the cursive nature of Arabic. The continuous linking together of groups of Arabic letters means that a starting position on the right necessarily commits the writer to a certain amount of leftward and even upward movement. Yet it is significant that when a cursive group is completed, the pen goes to the top of the next letter and comes down. Further, I had noticed that on many Arabic manuscripts the script does not go straight left but continually drops down in what we might call a "south-westerly" direction. This prompted me to do a computer analysis of the net direction of stroke making for different scripts. The results of this analysis are reported very briefly in my book. Allow me to describe the process more fully.

I recruited a couple of dozen people who were native writers of various scripts — Arabic, Chinese, Burmese, Thai, various Indian scripts, etc. I video-taped them writing and annotated their script for stroke direction. I then enlarged each character to approximately 50 times its original size and entered it through

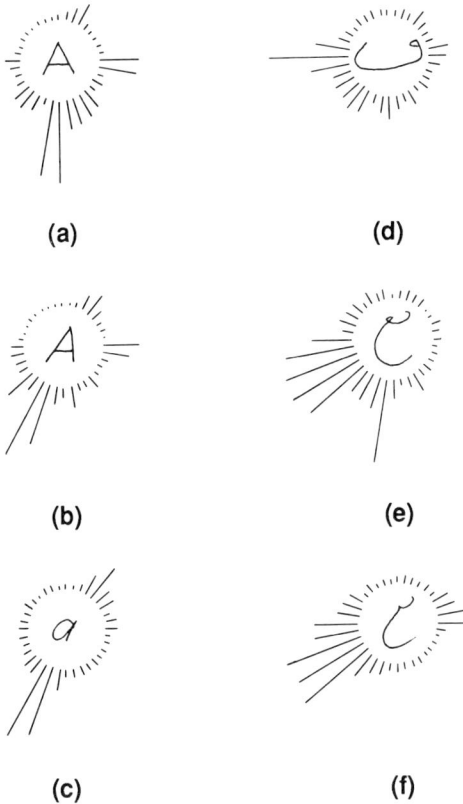

(a)

(d)

(b)

(e)

(c)

(f)

FIGURE 13: *Average direction of movement of the pen in the production of Latin (English) and Arabic script by native writers. (a) Latin upper-case letters in upright position. (b) Latin upper-case letters in italic (leaning) orientation. (c) Latin lower-case letters in italic orientation. (d) Contemporary Arabic alphabet written formally. (e) Arabic cursive script written slowly. (f) Arabic cursive script written rapidly. Note that Arabic cursive includes a preponderance of movements to the bottom left, especially when written quickly. Such direction of movement maximizes wrist movement and resembles the profile for sloping Latin letters. (Adapted from van Sommers, 1984).*

a digitizing tablet into a computer that generated summary plots showing the profile of stroke directions, that is polar plots showing the proportion of strokes or stroke segments made in different directions in the process of writing (Figure 13). (The paper in these studies was always in a standard orientation on

the table and subjects sat square on). What this analysis showed
was that my informal observation about Arabic was correct. In
spite of its start on the right and its cursive structure the profile
of stroke direction avoided the whole region towards the top left,
and as native Arabic writers wrote faster and faster (as they
were required to do in this study), the more the leftward
horizontal strokes dropped down towards obliques, resulting in a
major peak in the polar plots at the bottom left, just as we find
amongst writers of English script.

5.0 Stroke direction and order in later Egyptian scripts

I have recently extended this sort of analysis to the historical
development of scripts, and I should like to conclude with a
description of a study that uses data that are in some cases
nearly 4000 years old. I have been able to do this with the
assistance of a palaeographer who is an expert in Egyptian
scripts, John Tait, now at University College, London. What I
am about to report must represent one of the oldest bodies of data
analysed by a conventional psychologist.

In the case of later Egyptian scripts, we are dealing with two
related systems spanning two millenia, hieratic and demotic.
The hieratic was written either top-to-bottom or right-to-left, the
demotic always right-to-left (Figure 14). The traditional
instrument for their production was constructed from a rush,
which has a fibrous outer sheath and resilient centre (Tait,
1988). It was cut at an angle to form a point and that point was
customarily frayed a little to make a brush-like tip. According to
Tait this tip did not react well to being pushed upwards into the
papyrus and was inclined to turn under in the process. Later
the Greek pen, made from a firm hollow reed rather than a
rush, was introduced into Egypt. It was not necessarily any
better suited to upward movement, but there was little risk that
it would buckle in the process.

How did scribes actually compile hieratic and demotic scripts in
terms of order and stroke direction? It is not a well-documented
issue, but we are fortunate to have some direct evidence on the
topic: John Tait (personal communication) has annotated two

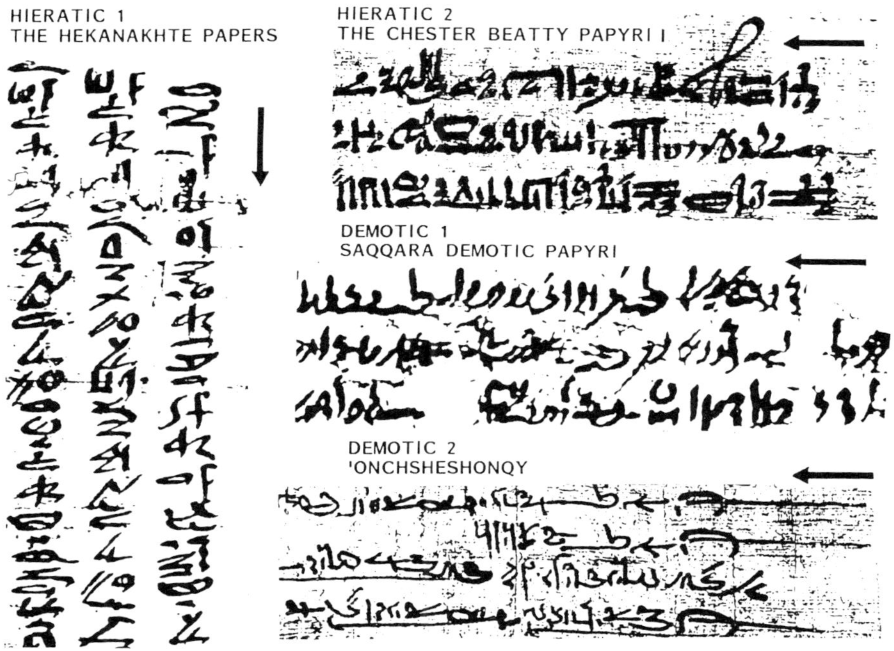

HIERATIC 1
THE HEKANAKHTE PAPERS

HIERATIC 2
THE CHESTER BEATTY PAPYRI I

DEMOTIC 1
SAQQARA DEMOTIC PAPYRI

DEMOTIC 2
'ONCHSHESHONQY

FIGURE 14: Four later Egyptian script samples. Sample 1, early hieratic, written vertically, is from the early second millenium B.C. Sample 2, later hieratic, is from the end of the second millenium B.C. Sample 3, early demotic, is from the 4th century B.C. Sample 4, later demotic, is probably late first century B.C., and unlike the other samples was written with a reed pen. Arrows indicate the overall direction of writing. The analysis of direction and order of strokes in letter construction conducted by Dr John Tait was applied to the first line of the first three samples and to lines 2 and 3 of the later demotic.

HIERATIC 1 THE HEKANAKHTE PAPERS

HIERATIC 2 THE CHESTER BEATTY PAPYRI

DEMOTIC 1 SAQQARA DEMOTIC PAPYRI

DEMOTIC 2 'ONCHSHESHONQY

FIGURE 15: Tracings of the four script samples with stroke direction superimposed. Question marks indicate where there is some doubt about stroke order. (Data provided by Dr John Tait).

samples each (earlier and later) of hieratic and demotic scripts. Figure 15 shows the traced outlines of characters from the four samples upon which I have superimposed Tait's annotations. In no case is upward movement prominent, an outcome that is consistent with the view adopted by Tait, that the writing instruments were ill-suited to it, and my own view that kinesiological and control principles in hand and arm movements strongly contributed.

In order to summarize the scribes' performance I have adopted a simple method of pooling all strokes within and across samples. Each individual stroke was processed in the following way: the starting point of each stroke was placed successively at the exact centre of a circular area and the end point of that stroke was located and marked with respect to the centre. From this we get a field of end-points for each sample that summarizes the overall pattern of stroke directions. The system does not take account of the shape of the trajectories between start and end of strokes as my earlier method did, but it gives a broad picture of stroke directions.

When all points for all samples are pooled (Figure 16) it is very clear that very few strokes move upwards (fewer than eight per cent) and virtually none terminates in the top left quadrant. Since most of the samples were written from right to left, we might expect the majority of strokes to terminate to the left of their starting points, but in fact they are almost exactly split between lower left and lower right directions.

When we examine the outcome for individual samples (Figure 17) we find some variation. The early demotic (4th century B.C.) in particular moves leftward on many strokes. We can see this when we inspect the script sample itself, which as Tait (1987) observes, seems to lean backwards to the right, and was constructed with many short strokes to the lower left.

The hieratic, both the early top-to-bottom sample and the later right-to-left, progress much as modern Hebrew does, in a sort of zig-zag, with overall line progression right-to-left, but stroke movements within letters biased towards left-to-right movement.

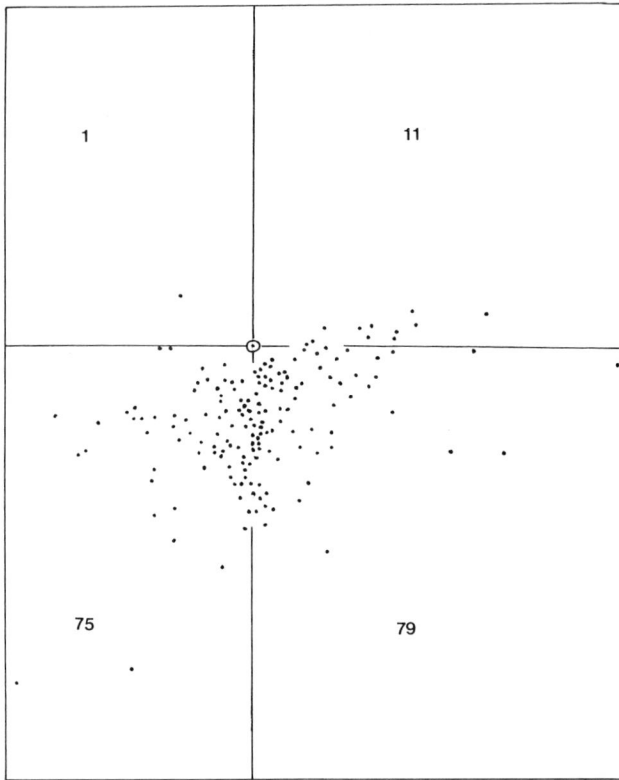

ALL SAMPLES COMBINED

FIGURE 16: Overall direction of strokes for all four samples. The centre of the figure represents the common starting location for all strokes. The terminations of the strokes are shown as points. Values show the total number of points in each quadrant of the figure.

This tendency for characters in later Egyptian scripts to be compiled left to right had actually been noted nearly a century and a half ago. Fischer (1977) refers to Möller who noted left-to-right movement in the production of individual hieratic characters (1909–12, p.7), and Brugsch who documented the tendency in demotic in 1848 (p.7).

John Tait's analysis reconstructed stroke order as well as direction. He did this by extrapolation from cursive forms on the reasonable assumption that stroke orders are similar for cursive

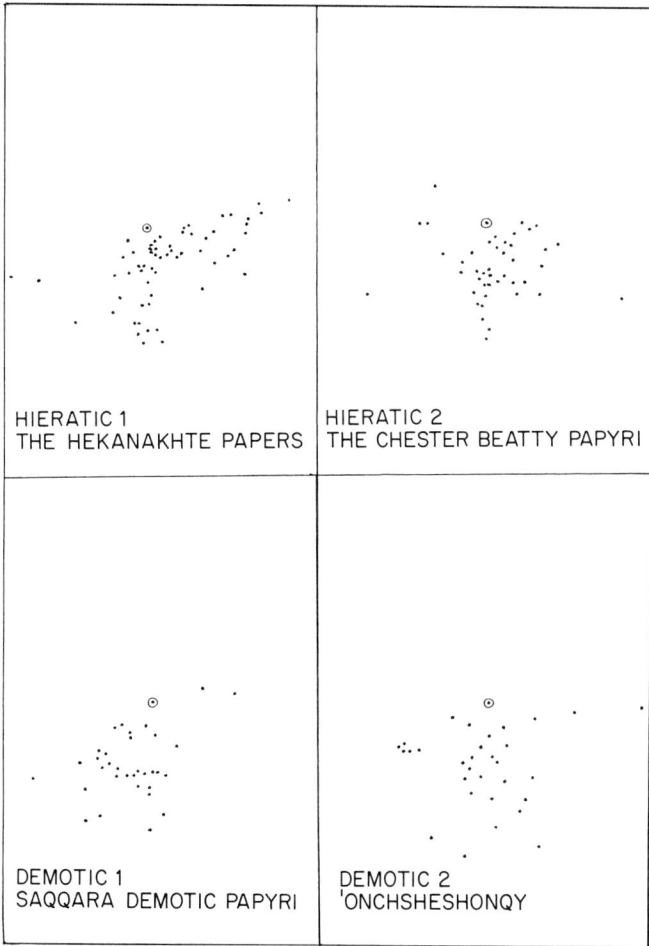

HIERATIC 1
THE HEKANAKHTE PAPERS

HIERATIC 2
THE CHESTER BEATTY PAPYRI

DEMOTIC 1
SAQQARA DEMOTIC PAPYRI

DEMOTIC 2
'ONCHSHESHONQY

FIGURE 17: Overall directions of strokes for the four samples plotted separately. The hieratic scripts include more strokes to the bottom right. The early demotic scribe in particular included many short individual strokes to the bottom left.

and non-cursive characters. Figure 18 shows Tait's suggested stroke order for several complex characters in the two hieratic samples, and we see here that with one exception, stroke order also conforms to a left-to-right progression within characters.

These data represent a test of the general proposition that in spite of the adoption of a right rather than a left start, and in

HIERATIC 1 THE HEKANAKHTE PAPERS

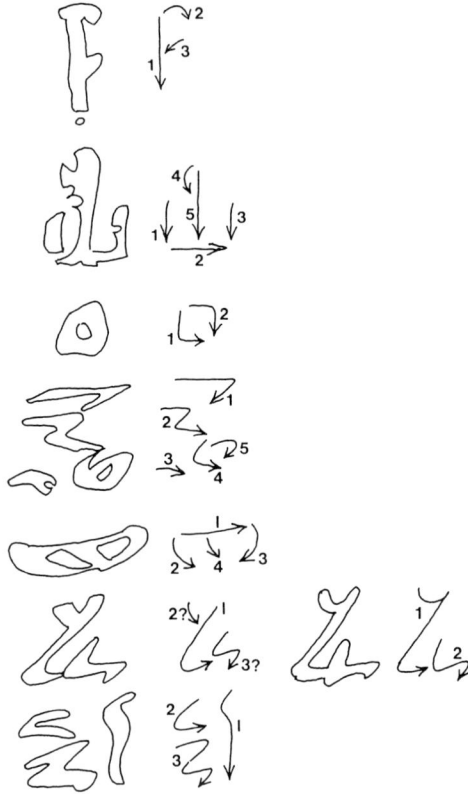

HIERATIC 2 THE CHESTER BEATTY PAPYRI

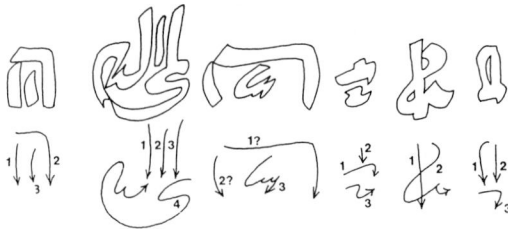

FIGURE 18: Order of strokemaking for complex characters in the two hieratic samples. (Data provided by Dr John Tait).

spite of a natural tendency to move always to the closest point on each successive element in a drawing or script, there are strong forces that operate in favour of a top left start for characters.

Like most human actions, the performances we are analysing are both multi-determined and variable. The behaviour of the pen and the scribe doubtless each make their contributions, and strategies vary. The hieratic scribes adopted a good deal of rightward movement in the more complex characters, while the earlier demotic scribe made use of simpler forms and utilized more movement diagonally down to the left in generating routine script.

6.0 Conclusion

I was tempted to conclude this chapter with a few generalities about the richness and complexity of the history of script development and the value of empirical research as a support for historical scholarship. But I might do better to provide some sort of synopsis of the ideas and empirical results I have used. First let me recall the distinction between graphetics — the formal articulatory and economic principles that deal with the issues of media, mechanics and central control — on the one hand, and on the other, representational and pragmatic principles (Figure 19a). The latter include all questions of meaning, context and use, exemplified in this paper by the work of Fischer (1977) on Egyptian hieroglyphic script.

Second, let me distinguish between the skills and constraints affecting the writer and the demands of the audience of readers (Figure 19b). In a sense writing and other communications systems develop out of the tension between the two. I have discussed a couple of examples of basic output constraints affecting script development, (i) mechanical considerations like those affecting the range of movements used in cuneiform and (ii) the coordination issues that contribute to the movement preferences of writers who use brush, stylus, pen or pencil. From mechanical limitations of the hand and arm and problems of more or less complex central control emerge certain features of action (Figure 20) including what I have termed the

A: GRAPHETICS

    Formal articulatory and economic
    skill and constraints:
    - media
    - mechanics
    - central coordination

SEMANTICS

    Representation

PRAGMATICS

    Context and use

B: BASIC CONSTRAINTS (OUTPUT)

    Hand proximity to surface edges

    Hand/arm mechanics (Scope, difficulty)

    Command complexity

    Economy of effort and control

BASIC DEMANDS (RECEPTIVE)

    Semiotic organisation

    Character contrast

    Character consistency and accuracy

    Line - tracking continuity

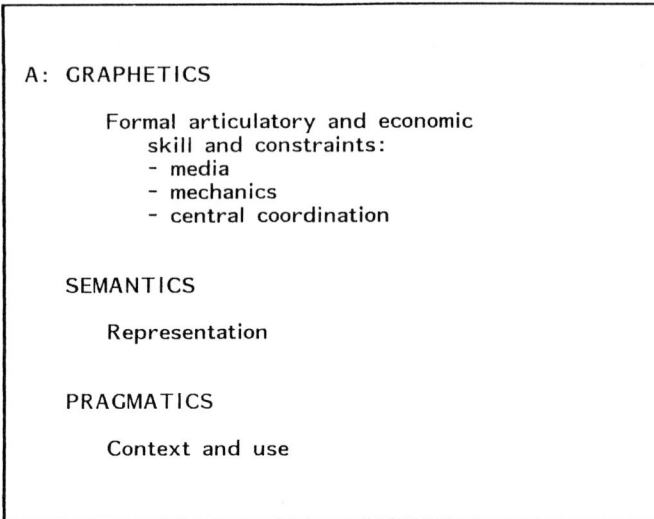

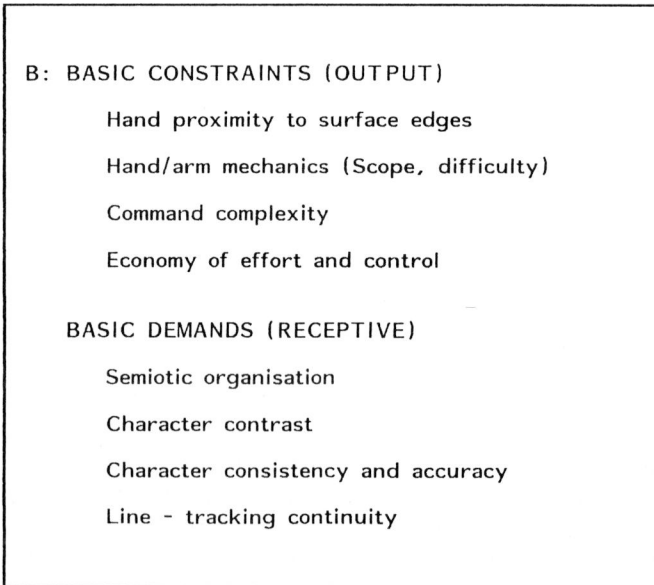

FIGURE 19: (A) Classification of the three broad categories of regularity in writing and drawing. (B) Basic output (writing) and input (reading) constraints affecting script development and use.

A: FEATURES OF ACTION

    Starting position preferences

    Canonical movements

    Maintenance of surface contact

    Anchoring and planning

B: EFFECTS ON SCRIPT

    Starting position for lines of characters

    Direction of lines of characters

    Character form (stroke configuration)

    Within-character stroke order and
    direction in execution

    Size reduction

    Character standardization

    Contraction in character variety

    Character simplification

    Cursivity:
      within character continuity
    - angles → curves
    - closed curves → open
      Across character continuity
    - ligature development

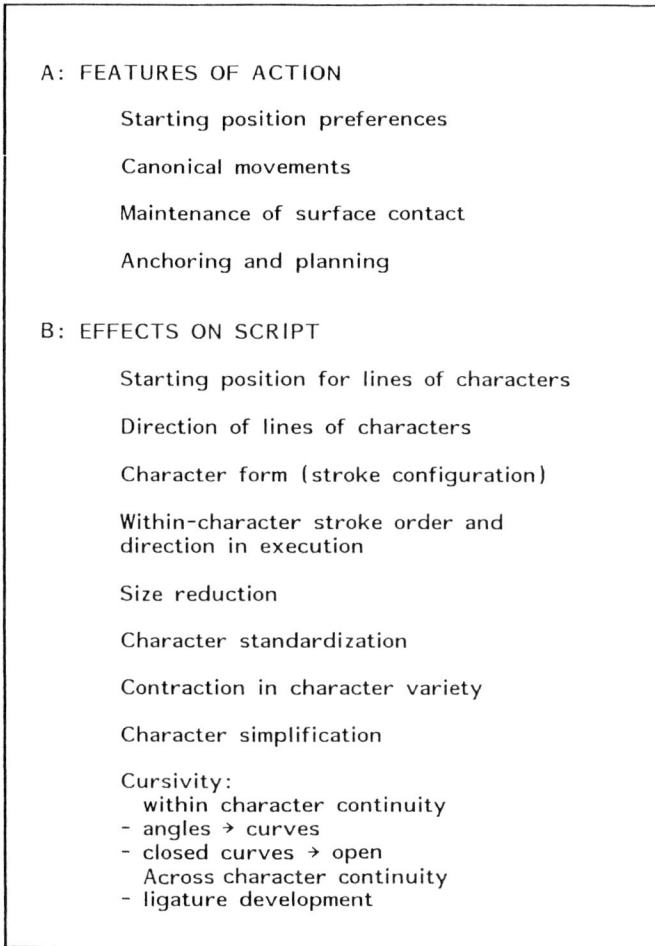

FIGURE 20: Features of action within the graphetic domain (A) that affect the characteristics of scripts (B).

canonical movements. The opposition between these favoured movements and the natural tendency to start working on the right side of the writing surface gave rise to the variety of compromise strategies adopted by major script systems with respect to direction of movement along lines and individual letter construction.

I also referred to the economics of maintaining contact with the writing surface and the impact of this on the development of cursive scripts. The rounding and opening of letters described by Gaur (1987) is clearly related to this principle. There are also the effects of size reduction on letter form, exemplified by the changes to Greek characters described by Jeffery (1961). Finally there are the issues associated with anchoring and planning for anchoring which interact with overall script direction and the compilation of individual characters to determine their actual form.

This is not an exhaustive list of factors even on the production side. As Sirat (1987) and others have pointed out there are important visibility questions. There are problems with successive hand movements spoiling what has already been done.

Although this summary makes passing reference to the receptive aspects of script development, my paper has not really confronted legibility and interpretative issues, which are as significant as production principles. I hope, however, that the examples and themes I have outlined have adequately represented the sort of practical, common-sense logic that has always played some part in the thinking of the major workers in palaeography and epigraphy, often at an intuitive level. I think it is an approach that will continue to strengthen as we develop the sophistication of our analysis and ground it in empirical methods.

II: Dynamics of development: Writing

Dynamics is a general term used to refer to changes with time in the physical state of a situation or object. In this volume, when applied to graphic skills the term is used in two contrasting senses. First, it may denote qualitative or quantitative changes in the form of a child's writing and drawing that could, for example, be associated with changing levels of skill and which may extend over periods of months and years. The second use of the term dynamics in the context of drawing and writing is closer to the physical origin of the term, and relates to the movements of the pen and hand during the process of writing. Recording pen dynamics in the latter sense (sometimes called kinematics or process variables) may allow the researcher to estimate a child's fine motor control for tasks other than just handwriting. This section (which emphasizes handwriting) and the next (whose focus is drawing) are concerned both with long-term developmental trends in the form of children's graphic skills as well as with the control of physical process variables such as pen speed, pressure and rhythm.

The first chapter in this section by Bruinsma and Nieuwenhuis *(A new method for the evaluation of handwritten material)* begins by considering what simple criteria may be used for evaluating changes in children's handwriting. In particular the authors assess the extent to which objective judgements can be made by trainee teachers. An interesting component of their approach is that teachers not only appraised the handwriting of others, but they also made judgements upon their own script, and this leads to recommendations about the potential use of self-appraisal skills in handwriting instruction.

The construction of a handwriting evaluation scale is described by Mojet *(Characteristics of the developing handwriting skill in elementary education)*. In his chapter he describes a factor analysis of the writing performances of 300 primary schoolchildren that resulted in a two-dimensional criterion for assessing handwriting skill based on a combination of the quality of shaping and speed. He then reports measures of a large number of process variables (pen-pressure, pen-speed, etc) from the writing of over 200 children in primary school grades 1 to 6. These measures were also subjected to factor analysis and the results compared with the initial scale. In addition, general trends in the process variables across the grades are documented. Mojet concludes the chapter by setting out profiles for contrasting types of handwriting.

A natural, but logistically demanding, method of studying handwriting development is to follow the progress of particular children over an extended time interval. Sõvik and Arntzen (A developmental study of the relationship between movement patterns in letter combination (words) and writing) describe a study in which a period of three years intervened between initial and final test sessions. A major focus was the relation between the contextual influence of words and certain measures of children's writing performances. The results of the study revealed effects of different writing tasks on children's writing speed and writing accuracy. This highlights an important point for handwriting research and education, that any appraisal of writing performance should take account of the sensitivity of children to the type of task they are asked to perform.

Chapter 2

A new method for the evaluation of handwritten material

Cees Bruinsma & Cock Nieuwenhuis

Handwriting is an important skill in cultural and social life. Children learn handwriting skills at school from their teachers and employ these skills throughout their whole life. It is therefore one of the most important basic skills and more attention should be given to its proper teaching at school. In the past, writing has not received the attention it deserves in the school curriculum considering the important role that it plays in children's cultural development (Vygotsky, 1979). Furthermore, handwriting is a skill which modern technology is unlikely to replace for some time to come (Sassoon, 1984). Assessing progress in the activity of learning to write is an important issue in both the teaching and the learning process. Cognitive, affective and psychomotor aspects play an important role in this evaluation process.

The educational process has three important components: the teacher, the pupil and the task (which includes the lessons, the method and books). Most handwriting researchers (eg, van Beusekom and Versloot, 1982; van Engen, 1986; Hettinga et al, 1988) distinguish between three stages in learning to write: (a) pre-writing; (b) beginning (consolidation); and (c) advanced, (automatic). After completing these stages, pupils should be able to produce slanted, joined-up, fluent, neat and legible handwriting at a reasonable speed, as a well as to evaluate their own handwriting. Every stage consists of orientation, execution and control (van Parreren and Carpay, 1979). In each stage the writing product has to be evaluated.

Development of Graphic Skills
ISBN 0-12-734940-5

1.0 Evaluation of script

The evaluation of both the process of writing and the written product is an important aspect of teaching and this evaluation must be carried out in a systematic and regular way.

To date, the process of writing has been investigated more than the written product (Borysowicz and Blöte, 1984). The process variables can be examined with the help of modern instruments. Most of the experiments can be carried out in the laboratory in such a way as to ensure objectivity on the part of the researchers while retaining the interest of the participants. The handwriting done in the course of the laboratory investigations, however, differs from that done under normal circumstances, as the experimental setting is different from school, where there is a teacher looking on.

In school, the process can be evaluated by observing the three P's (position, pen and paper). To evaluate the results properly, criteria are necessary (van Beusekom and Versloot, 1982; van Engen, 1986; Hettinga et al, 1988); however, it is difficult to choose the correct criteria, and it is not always clear how to apply them.

The neatness and legibility of handwriting can be analysed on the basis of a number of criteria. A distinction can be made between criteria of quality (eg form, size) and those of quantity. When schoolteachers evaluate the results of handwriting, they are often not aware of the criteria they are using. They tend to introduce a pedagogical element into the marks they give. For instance, the mark may be influenced by the degree of concentration and motivation shown by the pupil, and marks can thus be used to reinforce the pupil's motivation. Criteria are an essential part of the judgement process, as an evaluation without criteria gives results that are too dependent on the subjective judgement of the evaluator.

Although evaluating handwriting is part of the daily activity of a teacher, not all methods of teaching writing take evaluation into account. In the available compendia, the number of criteria varies a great deal, and it is not clear how to use them. Not all of the characteristics mentioned can be used to evaluate handwriting, as they are sometimes too difficult to apply or else they are ambiguous. The pupil should also be able to evaluate his/her own handwriting, as one of the goals of education is to make the pupil self-sufficient (Hettinga et al, 1988). In many writing methods, little attention is paid to self-evaluation (Nieuwenhuis, 1988), and yet it has been shown that the more the pupil is concerned with his own work, the more its quality will improve (Camstra, 1981).

In research a great deal of attention has been paid to criteria for evaluating handwriting. It is important to know which criteria to use and how to use them. For instance, whereas legibility, uniformity and fluency contribute to good writing, it is not clear how these criteria can be applied by teachers and pupils. The choice of criteria depends on the context, which may be general (eg, survey and progress) or analytic (eg, remedial: see West and Freeman, 1950).

Handwriting quality seems to be a general concept that cannot readily be described in concrete, quantifiable terms. When is handwriting defined as illegible? And illegible for whom? What norm should be used to establish illegibility? Researchers have grappled with this problem for years and the result has been a wide variety of handwriting scales. Over the years, many checklists have been produced in the literature.

In Table 1 an overview is given of the number of items used in assessment instruments. None of the researchers used fewer than three criteria, while most mention five or more. Instruments 1 to 9 (Table 1) are based on three aspects: writing movement (dynamic, motoric), form-giving (form, size, length, width) and space division (space between letters, words and lines). The scale of de Ajuriaguerra (1964) was developed for the diagnosis and remedial teaching of children with writing problems, and can only be used by trained personnel. Instruments 10 to 17 are more based on school experience. Hamstra-Bletz et al (1987) used seven items to characterize size, form and space. In Canada *The elementary curriculum guide for handwriting* (1965) makes a distinction between teacher evaluation and pupil evaluation of the handwriting product; an analysis with five aspects is proposed, presented on a diagnostic chart for use by teachers and pupils.

TABLE 1: *Overview of the number of items used in various handwriting scales.*

	First author	Date	N(items)
1	Gross	1942	3
2	Gollnitz	1957	3
3	de Ajuriaguerra	1964	25
4	Pijning	1969	25
5	Beetsma	1980	6
6	Pennings	1980	20
7	Borysowicz	1984	25
8	Hamstra-Bletz	1987	7
9	Mojet	1989	13
10	Curriculum guide	1965	5
11	MacLean	1966	6
12	van Beusekom	1982	10
13	van Engen	1986	5
14	Sassoon	1986	4
15	Stott	1985	3
16	Alston	1987	3
17	Hettinga	1988	5

MacLean (1966) suggested six criteria: general appearance, formation of letters, spacing, slant, quality of line, and size and alignment. Mojet (1989) gives an overview of the main factors affecting the quality of handwriting. Slant, size and space are aspects which are found in all checklists. In the teaching-learning process, however, it is not practical to apply exhaustive lists of criteria. A selection of the most important criteria for the teacher and pupils is necessary. To make this selection we return to the three fundamental aspects mentioned above.

For writing, the general appearance is most important, (Mojet, 1989); another important criterion is slant (Sassoon, 1986). The most important criteria for form-giving are size and form (West and Freeman, 1950; Bruckner and Bond, 1955). The most important criterion for space is the space between the words (MacLean, 1966; Sassoon, 1986).

2.0 Subjective evaluation of handwriting

In this chapter a new method for evaluating handwriting is introduced and a set of criteria is suggested. It provides guidelines for teachers and pupils on how to evaluate handwriting and on which to use in the teaching-learning process. We investigated (1) whether the subjects could reliably evaluate various handwriting samples; (2) which evaluation criteria they used most; and (3) whether there was a consensus between them. Moreover, we wanted to know whether the subjects were satisfied with their own handwriting, whether they wanted to change it and whether they were able to change it.

2.1 Subjects

The subjects in this research were 18-year-old students at a teacher training college (Pedagogische Academie Basis — Onderwijs; PABO). In total 64 students, 15 male and 49 female, completed the questionnaires.

2.2 Handwriting samples

In *Part 1*, the subjects had to evaluate 18 handwriting samples obtained from 13-year-old pupils beginning their secondary education. These samples were selected from 50 dictations of 6 sentences obtained in a previous research project (Nieuwenhuis, 1984). They ranged from bad to good. The pupils (*N*=111) in the experiment wrote with their own writing material on their own paper. A dictation passage was used in which all the letters of the alphabet were present, the sentences were short and grammatically and linguistically simple.

In *Part 2*, the subjects had to copy a text and evaluate their own writing.

In *Part 3*, 18 handwriting samples of fellow students were evaluated. Thus there were no age differences between the subjects and the producers of the 18 samples. We selected these 18 samples from a total produced by 22 students at the same institute.

2.3 Methods

In social science research, the measurement of variables is most often done at the ordinal level while the analysis techniques employed require measurement at the interval level. In this study, a method developed in psychophysics by Stevens (1975) to measure variables on a continuous scale was used. The subjects were asked to compare 17 handwriting samples with a standard presented on a card. The subjects took a card with one of the handwriting samples and compared it to the standard one.

They wrote down their judgements on the questionnaire form and rated the sample by magnitude estimation, an ordinal judgement and in words. When the subjects had evaluated one sample they took another card, compared it to the standard, wrote down their evaluation, and so on. In this way the 17 handwriting samples were each compared to the standard. The standard represented the middle of the range of the 18 handwriting samples. To compare the samples for the ordinal judgements, the subjects could choose from the following categories: very much better (+++), much better (++), better (+), same (0), worse (−), much worse (− −) and very much worse (− − −). For the magnitude estimation the number assigned to the standard was 100. If a sample was judged to be three times as nice, it was awarded a score of 300 and if it was a quarter as nice, a score of 25, and so on.

Bruinsma (1987) has shown that there is a nearly perfect linear relationship for aggregated data after logarithmic transformation of the magnitude scores. Although several other studies have shown that the two scores are not exactly the same, because one measures similarity and the other magnitude (Eisler, 1962, 1965; Shinn, 1974), we have followed Bruinsma, since assuming that the category scale scores and the log-transformed magnitude scores measure the same variable allows us to estimate the reliability of the different measures.

2.4 Classification

In the analysis of the words used by the subjects, we used five categories:
1. slant (eg, parallel, equal, smooth),
2. size (eg, height, width),
3. space (distance between letters, words and lines, alignment),
4. form (design and formation) and
5. general appearance.

A system of coding was introduced to fit the students' own words into one of the categories. Two judges were asked to evaluate every fifth questionnaire. In this way the judgements of 13 handwriting samples were analysed. The consensus between the two judges was reasonable (80%).

3.0 Results

3.1 Evaluation by independent judges

For this research we had chosen students, who would be future teachers professionally concerned with their own and other's handwriting. Our analysis showed that the students were able to evaluate handwriting reliably. The median squared correlation between the magnitude estimation and the ordinal judgement of the handwriting samples in Part 1 was .89. For the evaluation of the handwriting samples in Part 3, the median squared correlation between the magnitude estimation and the ordinal judgement was .89. When the subjects filled in the questionnaire they had not received any instruction about the words they should use in the evaluation. Their choice of words included: nice, well done, correct, neat, beautiful (positive) and bad, wrong, awful (negative). The subjects were consistent in their use of words. There was no difference between their use of words in Parts 1 and 3.

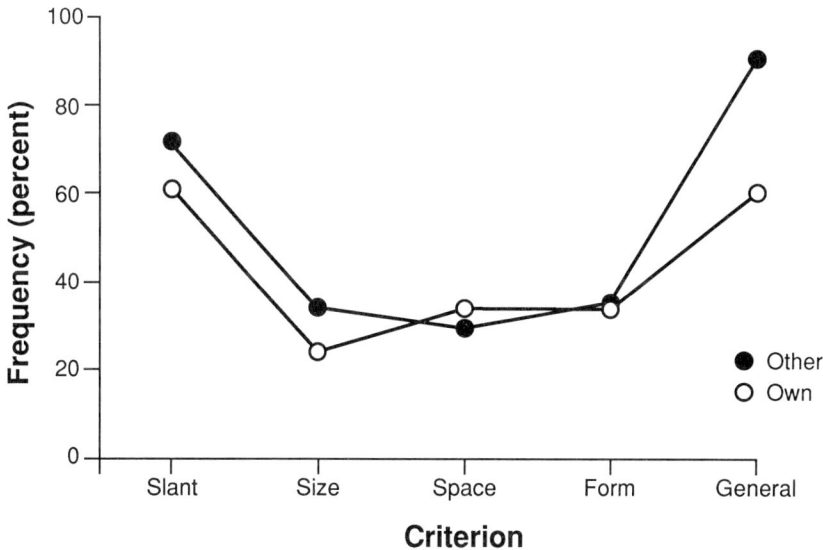

FIGURE 1: The frequency with which the criteria were used when students evaluated handwritings in their own words (N = 64).

The analysis showed that the subjects were able to evaluate handwriting in words. They evaluated the handwriting samples for overall legibility and in detail (slant, size, etc.). The respondents used several expressions for each criterion. For the criterion *slant* they used: backward-leaning, leaning too far forward, not consistently upright, inconsistent in length, etc. For the criterion *size* they used: too small, too large, not consistent in width or length, etc. For the criterion *space* they used: too close, too wide, good spacing, poor spacing, etc. For the criterion *form* they used: bad shape, good shape, clear form, ambiguous form, etc. And for the criterion *general appearance* they used: tidy, untidy, legible, illegible, poor, good, splendid, bad, etc.

Criteria 1 and 5 were mentioned most in the students' own words. In Figure 1 we show the frequencies with which the different categories were used by the 64 respondents. Although the respondents used Criteria 1 and 5 the most, they used the criteria in different combinations. However, there were too few subjects for us to analyse the different evaluation patterns.

3.2 Evaluation of own handwriting

In this research the subjects were also asked to evaluate their own handwriting. They had to copy a text in Part 2. The text was the same as that which had to be evaluated in Parts 1 and 3. The subjects had to evaluate their own handwriting in the same way as they had evaluated other people's. They used several criteria. In Table 2 the frequencies with which these criteria were used are presented.

TABLE 2: Criteria used in the evaluation of handwriting samples.

Criterion	Own	Other's
1. Slant	60%	71%
2. Size	23%	33%
3. Space	33%	29%
4. Form	33%	35%
5. Appearance	60%	90%

In the evaluation of their own handwriting, subjects mentioned Criteria 1 and 5 the most (60%). Criteria 3 and 4 received the same number of mentions (33%) and Criterion 2 was mentioned the least. In the evaluation of other people's handwriting, Criterion 5 was mentioned most (90%). Criteria 2 and 4 received almost the same number of mentions (33% and 35%) and Criterion 3 was mentioned the least (29%). In general, Criteria 1 (slant) and 5 (general appearance) were used the most. This finding could be very useful for practising teachers.

After they had evaluated their own handwriting, the subjects were asked the following questions: (a) Are you satisfied with your own handwriting? (b) Would you like to change it? (c) Are you able to change it? When people are dissatisfied with their handwriting, they might be motivated to try and change it. However, it is possible that they might be dissatisfied with their handwriting and motivated to change it, and yet be unable to see how to do so.

Nearly half of the subjects were dissatisfied with their own writing (43%, while 17% gave no answer). About half (51%) would have liked to change their handwriting (21% gave no answer). Nearly all those who were dissatisfied (42%) saw possibilities for changing their handwriting (42% gave no answer). At the teacher training college the fact that the subjects were dissatisfied with their own handwriting but motivated to improve it was regarded positively. The subjects obviously had a favourable attitude towards working on their handwriting: Educational institutions should offer students the opportunity to improve their handwriting.

4.0 Discussion and conclusion

The evaluation of the handwriting product is an important educational topic, and can be used to improve the quality of handwriting. The ultimate aim of the evaluation process should be to allow self-evaluation. The writer's own responsibility is an important but often neglected aspect of writing lessons. While evaluation is primarily the teacher's task, it is also necessary for pupils to evaluate their own handwriting. Objective criteria are required for the evaluation process. In the literature, various criteria (usually between three and seven) have been proposed. We found five main criteria: slant, size, space, form and general appearance.

In this research the subjects were students in a teacher training college, who would therefore be confronting the problem of evaluating writing products both as pupils and as teachers. They evaluated three kinds of handwriting: the handwriting of 13-year-old pupils, their own, and that of colleagues (18—19 years old). It is particularly important to confront pupils with their own handwriting. The evaluation was expressed in three ways: in the subject's own words, by magnitude estimation, and using an ordinal judgement. Our results showed that the reliability between the magnitude estimation and the ordinal judgements employed in this research was very good. The subjects were thus able to evaluate the handwriting samples reliably. We would recommend that pupils should be taught how to evaluate as early as the pre-writing stage. When pupils are accustomed to evaluate their own handwriting, its quality can be improved.

For the evaluation of their own handwriting, the subjects used a variety of words and expressions, which could be separated into five categories, with slant and general appearance being the most often used. This finding is of particular significance for writing instruction in schools. Even at the pre-writing stage the teacher can instruct pupils in the use of these criteria. Pupils should be taught to use these criteria on their own so as to improve the quality of their handwriting. They must learn to handle and master these criteria at each stage of the learning process, until they can employ several criteria in their self-evaluation. Teachers should be aware of how best to introduce these criteria; for instance, after introducing the two main criteria mentioned above in the pre-writing stage, the teacher should introduce the remaining three criteria (space, form and size) in the second, consolidation stage. We feel more research on the use of evaluation criteria is necessary: knowledge of the patterns of the evaluation process will help to optimize handwriting instruction.

In general, the subjects were very critical in evaluating their own handwriting. In writing instruction at the teacher training college, they had been taught methods and alphabets and presented with standard forms of letters. Nearly half of the subjects were dissatisfied with their own handwriting, and yet for all the students it was legible. This is encouraging, as being very critical of one's own handwriting may be a good trait for a teacher. When teachers are dissatisfied with their own handwriting they are motivated to change it, as they know that their handwriting ought to be an example for their pupils. Teachers at teacher training colleges should be allocated sufficient time to prepare students for this task.

Chapter 3

Characteristics of the developing handwriting skill in elementary education

Joop W. Mojet

Modern equipment has opened up various possibilities for investigating handwriting by providing objective and accurate measurement of several kinds of process variables concerning velocity and pressure phenomena in handwriting. This chapter describes a descriptive and exploratory programme of study which took advantage of such new equipment with the aim of acquiring more knowledge about the process aspects of the handwriting skill during primary education. Expansion of knowledge in this field may be expected to improve our evaluation of developing handwriting skills and to sharpen diagnostic tests for handwriting problems. It should also support our understanding of the differences between dysfunctional and good handwriting.

1.0 Product and process: plan of study

In order to be able to relate process variables to handwriting skill, a provisional criterion of handwriting quality is needed. In this chapter I first describe the construction of a handwriting evaluation scale. The handwriting products of a representative sample of 300 pupils from grades 2 to 6, were evaluated according to this scale and the scores obtained were factor analysed. This yielded a two-dimensional criterion for measuring the handwriting skill, namely the combination of the quality of *shaping* and the *speed* of handwriting.

Development of Graphic Skills
ISBN 0-12-734940-5

In a second experimental study that I describe in this chapter, writing samples from 219 pupils in elementary school grades 1 to 6 were collected on an electronic writing tablet. This computer-controlled tablet registered the X (horizontal) and Y (vertical) coordinates of the tip of the pen and it also allowed recording of writing pressure (Z) during the execution of writing tasks, namely words and rhythmic patterns. These factors make this one of the largest and most comprehensive investigations of the developing handwriting skill in elementary education.

The first set of analyses for this study concerned the variation of a number of derived measures of pen position and pressure as a function of time (process variables) over different writing tasks, namely, words and patterns. Next, handwriting skill was examined in three different ways. First, the relation between the process variables and the duration of handwriting education was treated, under the assumption that the longer the time spent in education the better will be the level of skill. Then differences in the process variables for the four types of handwriting skills (based on the handwriting evaluation scale) were charted. Lastly the relations among the XYZ variables were analysed by means of factor analysis.

In the final section of the chapter I indicate the utility of the present approach to handwriting analysis by a comparison of normal children of our sample with a group of pupils with severe specific learning disabilities from special education.

2.0 The need for a criterion in handwriting

In the literature on handwriting research several authors (eg, Freeman, 1954; West, 1957; Enstrom, 1964; Sõvik, 1975; Phelps et al, 1985), are of the opinion that handwriting skill must be judged on both the quality of the handwriting product and handwriting speed. However, some prefer to look only at quality. For instance Wann (1986, 1987), with reference to Rubin and Henderson (1982), argued that groups of pupils of the same grade level, with good and with bad writing quality did not differ in average handwriting rate. He stressed that bad writers are characterized by the inconsistency of their writing speed. While

I agree with the latter observation, I would none the less suggest that it is relevant to evaluate the writing rate of bad writers in terms of speed. Even though there may be a very low correlation between the quality and the speed of handwriting, it does not necessarily mean that handwriting skill should not be evaluated on the speed aspect. The independence of speed and product quality could lead to a measurement of the handwriting skill, based on at least a two-dimensional evaluation.

In the first study I therefore set out to check the main dimensions of handwriting production, and to create a tool to measure them. For that reason I constructed an evaluation scale, after reviewing twenty of the best known scales, which have been developed in America and Europe since the beginning of this century. The scale contains 14 items. The items are spread over four categories, widely used for the classification of handwriting aspects (Gross, 1942; de Ajuriaguerra et al, 1979).

2.1 Subjects

Three hundred pupils from grade 2 to grade 6 of three Dutch elementary schools took part in this study; 30 girls and 30 boys of each grade level.

2.2 Procedure

Subjects wrote in cursive style a standard text of four short sentences, which they were first allowed to read several times. The writing task took at least two minutes.

2.3 Evaluation scale

The writing samples were evaluated on 14 aspects under four main headings:
(i) Spacing: 1. alignment, 2. distance between words, 3. distance between letters.
(ii) Shaping: 4. slant of downstrokes, 5. letter size, 6. letter proportions (upper-, middle- and lower-zone), 7. calligraphic aspect, uniformity, 8. recognizability of letters out of context.
(iii) Movement: 9. line quality, 10. continuity, 11. strikeovers, 12. writing pressure.
(iv) Speed: 13. number of letters per two minutes, 14. rate evaluated by grade norms.

Each of these 14 items was scored on a 5-point scale (0= very good, 4= very bad) by trained scorers. For most of the items, the principal aspect of evaluation was the (ir)regularity of the writing. The scores of some items were also (negatively) influenced by extremes of performance, such as too wide or too narrow.

2.4 Statistical treatment

To investigate the pattern of correlations for the evaluation items, the scores of the scale were factor analysed. After varimax rotation I identified four factors (see Table 1).

As an extra check on the validity of the items of the evaluation scale, I asked the teachers to rate the quality of the handwriting performances of their pupils on a 5-point scale. Every teacher did this for his own pupils, with his own class as his only reference group. For an overall view I combined the correlation coefficients between the evaluation of each teacher and the scale-items, by using Fisher's z-transformation.

3.0 Results

The results of the factor analysis and the mean correlations with the teachers' ratings are shown in Table 1.

TABLE 1: Factor loadings and correlations with evaluation scale items

Variables	Factor Loadings				Correlations	
	Factors				Education duration	Teacher evaluation
	I	II	III	IV		
Calligraphic aspect	.86				.45	.72
Letter distance	.65				.43	.30
Alignment	.61				.20	.58
Letter size	.70				.29	.43
Recognizability	.61				.01	.52
Speed (number)		.93			.67	.02
Speed (grade norm)		.71			-	-
Line quality			.75		.51	.40
Pressure			.49		.25	.48
Word distance				.56	.18	-
Shaping sum-score					.34	.76

3.1 Handwriting factors from ratings

I now turn to consider each of the four factors in turn.

Factor I. The largest factor loadings on the first factor were: calligraphic aspect .86, regular letter size .70, regular letter distance .65, alignment .61 and recognizability of letters .61. In view of the high loading of the calligraphic aspect, this factor may be interpreted as having to do with accuracy and uniformity of the handwriting. It can be interpreted as control of the *shaping* of handwriting and may be equated with *quality* of the written product.

Factor II. Here the main loadings involved variables relating to the *speed* of handwriting: Speed (S), number of letters per two minutes, which had a loading of .93, and speed, evaluated by grade norms (Sg), with a loading of .71.

Factor III. Line quality had a loading on this factor of .75 and writing pressure had a loading of .49. This factor may therefore be taken as having to do with ease of handwriting or *movement* ability.

Factor IV. The regularity of the distance between words was the only item with an appreciable loading of .56 on this factor which may be interpreted as regularity of spacing. (It is worth noting that Factor I, shaping, received loadings from two items that would generally be viewed as aspects of spacing, namely regular letter distance and alignment.)

Of the above factors, only the first two factors had reasonable explanatory power (eigenvalue > 1.0). It may therefore be concluded that assessment of handwriting skill is adequately carried out on two dimensions and this is the approach taken in the research I describe later. For the dimension of *shaping* or quality of handwriting formation, I used the sum-score of the ratings of the calligraphic aspect, regular letter size, regular letter distance, alignment and recognizability of letters out of context. The dimension of handwriting *speed* I measured by the number of letters written per two minutes. The internal

consistency of the shaping group of items was adequate
(Cronbach's alpha = .82). The test-retest reliabilities of the two
dimensions were also satisfactory; for the combined shaping
score, after a period of two months, it was .79 and for writing
speed it was .85.

3.2 Evaluation and duration of education

The duration of handwriting education correlated with the speed
scores (r=.67) and with the shaping scores (r=.34) (see the bottom
line of Table 1 and Figure 1). There were reliable correlations

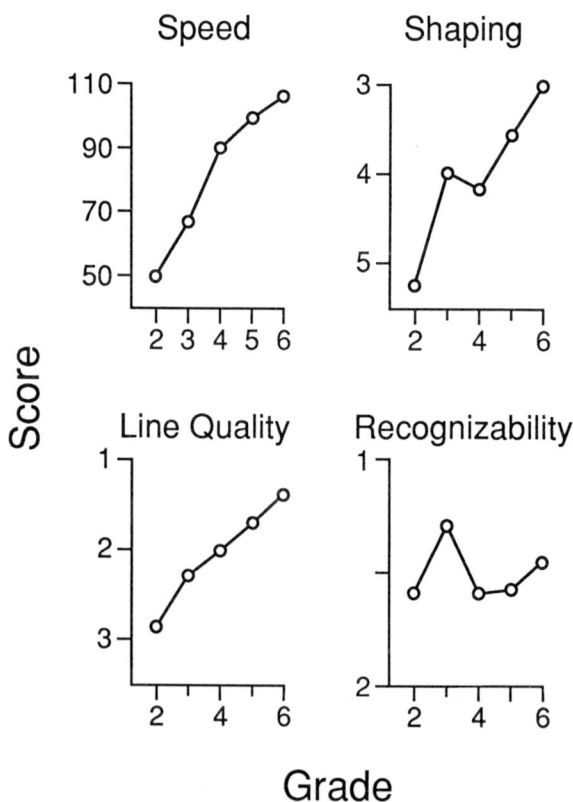

FIGURE 1: *Mean scores per grade of some variables of the evaluation scale.*

between duration of education and the separate shaping items; calligraphic aspect ($r=.45$), letter distance ($r=.43$), letter size ($r=.29$), alignment ($r=.20$). However, the correlation with recognizability of letters ($r=.01$) was not significant. This last fact means that this aspect of writing quality does not increase over the school years (see Figure 1). Despite this latter finding, the degree of loading of this item on factor I and the requirement of readability of the handwriting product suggest that this item nevertheless be retained in the shaping sum-score.

3.3 Evaluation and teachers' ratings

The highest correlations between the evaluation scale and the teachers' overall ratings involved the shaping sum-score ($r= .76$) and the calligraphic aspect ($r=.72$). The recognizability of the letters showed a moderately high correlation ($r=.52$). Handwriting speed did not seem to play any role in the teachers' evaluations. The correlations with the items line quality and pressure were moderately high. These findings suggest that Dutch teachers tend to evaluate only the quality of the shaping of handwriting ie, the quality of the handwriting product. Against the background of the opinion that the evaluation of handwriting skill ought also to be based upon the handwriting speed, their evaluations do not concern the handwriting skill as such. None the less, the correlation coefficients with the shaping scores and the calligraphic aspect suggest that, within this restricted point of view, the teachers make good judgements.

3.4 Indices of handwriting skill

With the above results in mind, the evaluation of the shaping and the speed dimensions may be simplified by use of a 3-point evaluation at grade level. Based on the frequency distributions this produces three intervals containing respectively 30, 40, 30% of each year sample, resulting in a 3 x 3 matrix (see Table 2).

For each grade level a pupil may be allotted an index of handwriting skill varying from 1 to 9. The corner cells (1, 3, 7, 9) in particular can be considered as qualitatively distinct types of handwriting performance: (1 = good form, fast; 3 = good form, slow; 7 = bad form, fast; 9 = bad form, slow). In a later section I will show how this 3 x 3 matrix may constitute a suitable tool for classifying certain differences in handwriting style and handwriting skill.

TABLE 2: *Suggested scheme for assessing handwriting skill*

Form	Speed		
	Fast		Slow
Good	1	2	3
	4	5	6
Bad	7	8	9

4.0 Process variables and handwriting skill

A major goal of the research described in this section was to explore the meaning of a number of objective process variables in relation to the developing handwriting skill. In addition it was hoped to get a better view of several handwriting tasks and of different styles and qualities of handwriting skill.

4.1 Subjects

219 children were drawn from the sample that participated in the research on the Handwriting Evaluation Scale.

TABLE 3: *Distribution of the sample over the grades.*

Grade	1	2	3	4	5	6	Total
Girls	19	17	17	26	16	20	115
Boys	15	17	16	11	24	21	104
Total	34	34	33	37	40	41	219

4.2 Procedure

Each subject wrote five times four repetitive patterns (discontinuous and continuous arcades and garlands (see Figure 2), and two pseudowords **momom** (Enke ,1930) and **molham**.

The writing paper, which had a vertical line spacing of 7 mm, was placed on a 30 x 21 cm capacitive graphic tablet (Philips; resolution .1 mm) connected to a MINC-Digital minicomputer. A ballpoint pen of normal size was used, in which a pressure sensor was fixed. The pen was connected with the computer configuration by thin wires from the end opposite the writing tip. These wires were looped and fixed to the forearm of the subject. The X and Y coordinates of the pen tip and the signal of the force along the axis of the pen (Z) were recorded at 100 Hz.

An example of each task was placed in front of each subject. They had the opportunity to practise until they felt confident of performing it in their own preferred way. No suggestions were given about speed or accuracy of the performance. The pupils were asked to make the patterns in a relaxed easy way, until they got a sign to stop. The length of the patterns was not strictly prescribed in the number of elements that had to be written, so that counting would not hamper the writing movement. During the orientating practising activities the subject was encouraged to perform enough elements (ie, ≥8) when writing a pattern.

	Discontinuous	Continuous
Garlands (left turning)	$\mathcal{UUUUU}$ (3)	$eeeeee$ (2)
Arcades (right turning)	$\mathcal{nnnn}$ (1)	$\mathcal{ooooo}$ (4)

FIGURE 2: *Handwriting patterns (the numbers are the codes used for the patterns).*

4.3 Pre-processing of the writing samples

The handwriting XYZ data were low-pass filtered with an increasing impedance from 6 to 12 Hz. Next the patterns were reduced to the length of 6 elements to get a fixed base for comparison. From the set of sampled X,Y and Z (pressure)-data and corresponding time values a number of XYZ variables were derived as described in the next section. Most of the derived variables involved taking the mean or standard deviation (s.d.). For each derived variable I took the median value over the five replications as the representative value for that person at that task. (Thus the set of values concerning a particular task need not all have come from the same performance).

4.4 Measures of handwriting

Form: For measuring some form characteristics of the handwriting products I distinguished elements within the writing tasks, consisting of one up- and down-stroke (in the case of arcade patterns and words) or one down- and up-stroke (with garlands). The elements were limited by two points, Ymin and Ymax, with relative extreme values on the Y axis. For each element I measured the vertical size, ie, Ymax—Ymin (HEIGHT), the horizontal distance between the two Ymax or Ymin points (HORDIS) and the length of the curve (TRAJEC). For each pattern of six elements and for each test word the means (M) and s.d.s (SD) were calculated on these values. The means were used to give information about the size of the product and the s.d.s to say something about the regularity of the shaping. The s.d. of the Ymin values was taken to indicate the regularity of the alignment (ALIGN).

Speed: The handwriting speed was primarily measured as the production rate, expressed in the duration of the performance of a defined task. If this measure included the time which the pen was off the paper (pauses) it was called total writing time (TOTTIME) and, without the pauses, absolute writing time (ABSTIME). Another measure in the speed domain was the mean pen velocity expressed in cm/sec, labelled M.PENVEL. The mean value of the accelerations and decelerations was called M.AC/DECEL. The s.d. of the writing time per element was used as a measure of the irregularity of the timing of the down and upstrokes (SD.ELTIME).

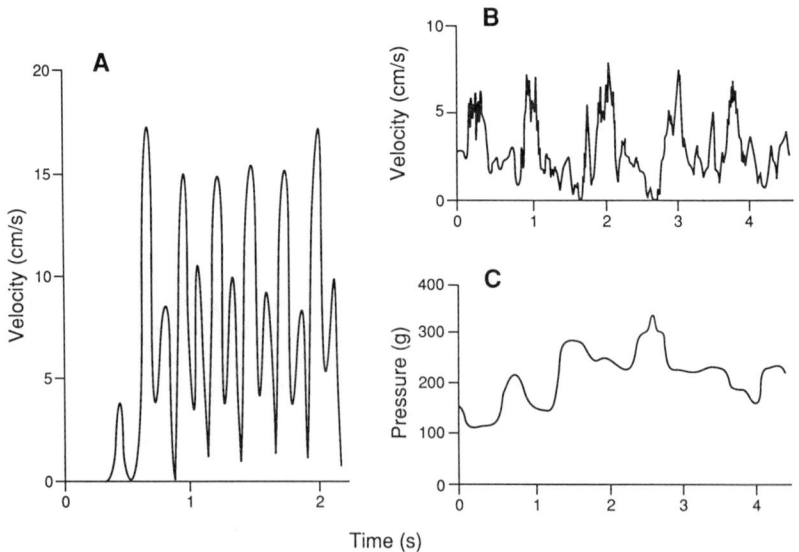

FIGURE 3: *Illustrations of some curves of pen velocity and pressure: (A) Velocity curve of a ballistic performance of* **mm**. *(B) Slow performance with too many velocity peaks. (C) Pressure curve corresponding to (B); note the relation between high pressure and low velocity.*

Movement quality: Proficiently performed writing strokes show one peak per stroke in the velocity curve (see Figure 3A). Such ballistic movements, presumably programmed independently of feedback control, are very economical. One accelerating force is followed by one decelerating force. More peaks mean more separate impulses. In optimal writing movements the number of velocity peaks equals or approximates the number of strokes, in bad performances that number is greatly exceeded (see Figure 3B) (Binet and Courtier, 1883; Freeman, 1921). In

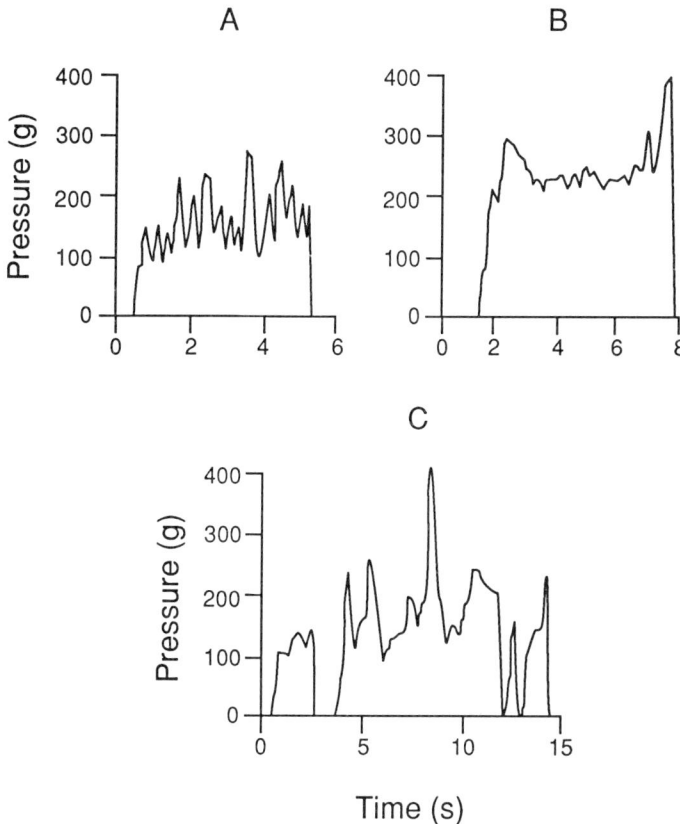

FIGURE 4: Illustrations of pressure curves for **momom**: (A) 12-year-old boy; wide , ie, good, pressure variation (total writing time was 5 sec). (B) 10-year-old boy; relatively high pressure level and restricted amplitude, a combination that means spasmodic writing (total writing time was 6.5 sec). (C) 7-year-old boy; several pauses, zero pressure, and extra peaks (total writing time was 13.7 sec).

this respect I defined for each task the following variables: the number of peaks in the velocity curve (VTOPS), the number of peaks in the velocity curve per second (VPERSEC), the number of shifts in the turning direction indicating a minimum of required impulses and the smoothness of the line (QSHIFT). The minimum possible value of VTOPS for **momom** and **molham** was 25.5.

The continuity of the pen displacements can be disrupted by pauses which appear when the pen tip leaves the writing surface. I distinguished the number of pauses per task (N.PAUS), the mean of pause time (MT.PAUS) and the total duration of pauses per task (TOTPAUS). Cases in which the pen stayed in contact with the paper but the velocity was near 0 (ie, <0.5 cm/sec), were identified as stagnations; STAGN>.2 sec means the total duration per task of all stagnations that exceed .2 sec.

Pressure: As well as the mean and the s.d. of handwriting pressure (M.PRESS, SD.PRESS) I defined some variables concerning the variation of peaks and troughs of the pressure curve, the so-called amplitude. M.AMPLIT was defined as the mean of the differences (> 15 gram) between each successive peak and trough and SD.AMPLIT gave the s.d. of these differences. Irregular extreme peaks in the pressure curve result in a high value of this last variable. Figure 4 displays pressure curves with different amplitudes.

5.0 Results

5.1 Handwriting task differences

The analysis demonstrated that some *XYZ* variables differed significantly depending on the writing task from which they had been derived and showed significant differences between the grades. There was also an interaction effect between the tasks and the grades; this means that the differences between the tasks were not similar for all grades.

A comparison of the four writing patterns by an analysis of variance suggested that the continuous arcade pattern 4 (see Figure 2) appeared to be more difficult than the other three for grades 2 through 6. It was produced significantly larger and more irregular in form and it contrasted negatively on process aspects such as the duration of writing time, irregularity of timing, and numbers of stagnations and of peaks in the velocity curve. Testing these differences between the patterns at grade level showed that they were absent in grade 1.

This latter finding may be explained by the fact that the older pupils of grade 2 and above are less accustomed to make these upside down e's, which are generally practised together with the other patterns only in the first stage of handwriting education in the Netherlands. In writing cursive roman script, **e**, **m**, and **u** are frequently used and so sustain these kinds of movements. (This suggestion is also supported by the fact that the performance of a separate sample of pupils with severe specific learning disabilities did not show the pattern 4 as being different; practising all four patterns had been a part of their treatment, also in the higher grades.) Because of the special status of pattern 4 it has been excluded from further analyses.

The most obvious differences between the pseudowords and the patterns were that the first had a longer mean duration of pauses and greater irregularity of timing of up- or down-strokes. The number of velocity peaks per second within words resembled that found with discontinuous patterns (**mmm**, **uuu**). Of all variables, only the pressure variables were indifferent to the nature of the handwriting tasks.

Differences between words and patterns were also noticeable in the investigations which are reported next. The significant differences between words and patterns led me to treat the data of these two groups of tasks separately. Conclusions drawn from analyses of the writing patterns should not be generalized to the writing of words, without checking.

5.2 Process variables and duration of education

I now turn to look at the relation between the *XYZ*-variables and the duration of handwriting education. As already noted, this coherence can be studied by, first, comparing the means of the successive grades (Table 4) and, second, by correlating the *XYZ*-variables with the number of years of handwriting education for each pupil (Table 5).

TABLE 4: *Means (above) and standard deviations (below) of some XYZ variables for each grade measured on the pseudo-words. Statistically significant (p<.05) differences are indicated by > and <.*

Variable	Grade					
	1	2	3	4	5	6
TOTTIME	11.9	> 8.6	> 7.3	> 6.1	6.0	> 5.4
sec	2.3	1.8	1.7	1.3	1.1	1.3
VTOPS	181	> 135	> 111	> 95	88	81
freq	60.5	36.8	37.1	33.8	28.2	31.4
M. TRAJEC	17.0	> 10.1	> 10.1	> 8.4	8.2	7.9
mm	4.2	2.6	3.4	2.9	1.8	2.3
STAGN. >.1	1.5	> 1.2	> 0.8	> 0.5	0.6	> 0.4
sec	0.9	0.8	0.4	0.32	0.4	0.3
TOT. PAUS	2.1	> 0.1	0.1	0.1	0.3	0.2
sec	1.3	0.3	0.4	0.3	0.5	0.3
SD. ELTIME	0.9	> 0.3	0.2	0.2	0.2	0.2
sec	0.3	0.1	0.2	0.1	0.2	0.2
SD.HEIGHT	0.9	1.1	1.0	0.8	0.8	0.6
mm	0.5	0.5	0.5	0.5	0.3	0.3
SD. HORDIS	3.5	> 2.1	1.9	1.7	1.7	1.5
mm	1.5	0.8	0.7	0.5	0.5	0.6
M.PENVEL	1.2	< 1.4	< 1.6	1.6	1.6	1.7
cm/sec	0.5	0.4	0.5	0.5	0.4	0.5
M.AC/DECEL	0.2	< 0.2	0.2	0.2	0.2	0.2
cm/sec^2	0.0	0.1	0.1	0.1	0.1	0.1
SD.PENVEL	0.8	< 0.9	1.0	> 0.9	0.9	0.9
cm/sec	0.3	0.3	0.4	0.3	0.3	0.3
V.PERSEC	17.0	> 16.1	15.3	15.6	15.2	15.3
freq/sec	2.3	2.3	3.0	2.8	2.7	2.9
M.PRESS	165.5	164.5	> 136.8	137.3	< 165.1	> 131.0
g	64.8	68.4	53.3	46.1	48.9	49.4

5.3 Summary of education/age effects

The following points summarise the main findings relating handwriting variables to age:

TABLE 5: Correlations of some XYZ variables with duration of handwriting education (Note SD.HEIGHT, was calculated on momom only and the second and third entries, −.24, −.35 refer only to grades 2 −4, 2−6 respectively).

Variable	Grade							
	Words				Patterns			
	1−2	1−4	1−4/ 1−6	1−6	1−2	1−4	1−4/ 1−6	1−6
TOTTIME	-.63		-.72		-.65		-.57	
VTOPS	-.43		-.60		-.58		-.48	
M. TRAJEC	-.67		-.56		-.46	-.42		-.34
STAGN. >.1	-.19		-.52		-.37		-.39	
STAGN. >.2			-.34		-.31		-.35	
TOT. PAUS	-.73	-.57		-.43	-.16		-.16	
SD. ELTIME	-.78	-.56		-.43	-.19		-.28	
SD. HEIGHT	.20	-.24		-.35	-.35		-.40	
SD. HORDIS	-.54		-.48		-.20		-.32	
M. PENVEL	.28		29		.37		.33	
M. AC/DECEL	.27		25		.27		.20	
SD. PENVEL	.25	.13			.33		.21	
V. PERSEC	-.20		-.20		-.31		-.22	
M. PRESS		-.21			-.20	-.25		-.11

1. The increase/decrease in the values of *XYZ*-variables was greatest in the first four grades. Later on the developmental changes were less steep.
2. The production velocity (1/TOTTIME) increased with writing experience (r=.72). This phenomenon was also a consequence of the decrease in stagnation time (r=-.52) and in duration of pause time (r=-.57). The production velocity is thus seen to be one of the most important characteristics of the developing handwriting skill.
3. The movement quality rose as the number of velocity peaks per task (VTOPS) decreased (r=-.60).

4. The size of the handwriting product decreased ($r=-.56$) with grade.
5. The regularity of the timing of up- and down-strokes improved ($r=.56$).
6. The regularity of the shaping increased ($r=.35$ to.48).
7. The handwriting pressure showed a moderate decrease over the years ($r=-.20$). There was a notable temporary rise of 30 grams in the mean pressure in grade 5, for both words and patterns (135 to 165 g and 150 to 180 g respectively; Figure 5).
8. It is noteworthy that the correlations of the duration of handwriting education with production speed, movement quality, shaping and pressure declined in the same sequence as those with the analogous items of the evaluation scale (see Table 1)

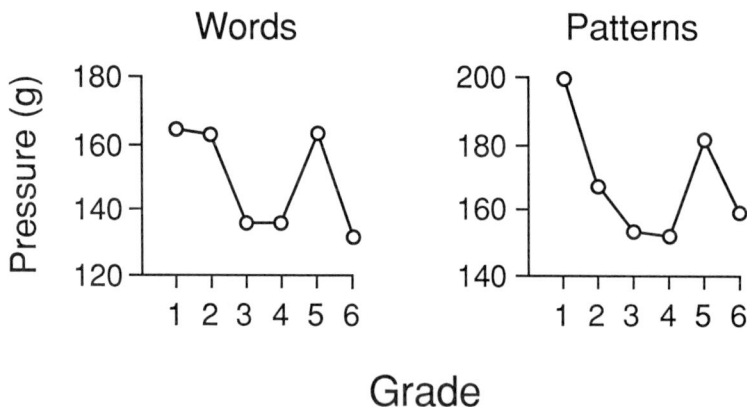

FIGURE 5: *Mean pressure as a function of grade level for words and patterns.*

In Table 4 grades 3 and 5 exhibit somewhat deviating positions. In grade 3 there was a plateau in the product quality of words, but the process quality was still improving. This may be evidence of increasing automatization of handwriting. In grade 5 the mean handwriting pressure showed a significant rise. A similar anomaly occurred with the number and duration of the pauses and the production speed stayed on the level of grade 4. So in grade 5 the quality of the handwriting process declined or at best only stayed at the same level. The quality of the shaping stayed at the same level as the year before.

5.4 Handwriting factors from process measures

In order to investigate the coherence of the *XYZ* variables a factor analysis was performed on grade level as well as on the sample of grades 1 to 6 and grades 2 to 6. There was a remarkable consistency in the factor structures in the different grades and in the sample as a whole.

Starting with the *XYZ* variables as defined above, there was a distinction depending on whether the values were obtained from writing words or patterns. An unexpected finding was that pairs of similarly defined variables that originated from words rather than patterns had higher loadings on different factors. Thus a total of ten factors, five word (w) and five pattern (p) factors, were identified for *production speed* (I), *size* (II), *pausing* (III), *writing pressure* (IV), and *regularity of shaping* (V)

High loadings on *production speed* (Factors Iw, Ip) were observed, not only for variables related to writing duration, but also for those supposed to measure movement quality (number of velocity peaks per task, number of directional shifts and number of short stagnations)

For the patterns, the pen velocity variables (mean, s.d., ac/decel) and the number of velocity peaks per second also had high loadings on *production speed*. For the words, these pen velocity variables had only moderate loadings on factor Iw, but high loadings on *size* (Factor IIw). (In this respect size for words might even have been called the pen velocity factor.)

Pausing (Factors IIIw, IIIp) was determined by the number and duration of the writing pauses. The regularity of timing also showed a clear coherence with this factor. The regularity of timing appeared to be more influenced by pauses than by stagnations.

The stagnations loaded not only on production speed but also, moderately, on *pressure* (Factor IVw, IVp). This is consonant with the finding for pressure and velocity curves, that stagnations often go together with an increase of pressure (see Figure 3B,C). *Pressure* was dominated by three measures of pressure variation (SD.PRESS, M.AMPLIT, SD.AMPLIT). The mean pressure had a somewhat lower loading. In the sixth grade there appeared to be an independent factor of mean pressure. In my opinion it is important to distinguish these two factors.

Regularity of shaping for words (Factor Vw) was primarily determined by the vertical pen displacements (SD.HEIGHT and ALIGNM) acquired from letters in the middle of the word. For patterns, however, the regularity of horizontal displacement (SD.HORDIS) and the length of the trajectories per element (SD.TRAJEC), had high loadings on Factor Vp.

The conclusion from this factor analysis is one that underlines my previous inference, namely, that there is a difference in the import of several *XYZ* variables in relation to the kind of writing tasks from which they were measured. A justified interpretation of these variables is only possible if this relation is appreciated.

6.0 Discussion

Following the extensive discussion of specific changes in both *product* and *process* in children's handwriting, it now seems appropriate to draw the two types of analysis together and consider a practical application of some of the techniques developed.

6.1 Bringing together product and process evaluation

As was stated in the introduction, one way of determining the relations between process variables and handwriting skill is to compare pupils with equal handwriting education but with different proficiency. In an earlier section I developed a matrix-based set of indices for assessing handwriting skill, which was intended for use at any given grade level (Table 2).

It will be recalled that, in this approach, index 1 denotes the most proficient writers of one grade level, who can write fast and with good form, and the opposite is index 9, the slow writers with bad shaping of the handwriting product. Between these extremes there are indices 3 and 7; 3 are the slow writers with good product quality and 7 are the fast writers with bad quality of the handwriting products. I call these four indices types A (= 1), B (= 3), C (= 7) and D (= 9).

By analysis of variance, each variable could be tested across all nine indices. This was first done at the grade level. There were some variations over the grade levels, but in order to get stable outcomes of the analysis of variance the data of grades 2 through 6 were put together. (It may also be considered an advantage to acquire a view on those typical characteristics which transcend the grade levels.)

I now present a short summary of the characteristics of the four types of writing performance, based on differences in the respective variables within grades 2 to 6:

Type A: The fast writer with good form. The handwriting product is relatively small and more regular than average. The horizontal distances between the down-strokes are rather regular, even when writing words. This means some deviation from the model form. I suppose that this happens under the influence of a rhythmical way of writing. The strong regularity of the timing is in accordance with this. This regularity is possible, because there are very few pauses and stagnations in the handwriting. There is a high production speed and a light handwriting pressure. There are few tremor-like symptoms. The pen velocity variations and the mean acceleration and deceleration are low. There are, however, a large number of velocity peaks per second.

Type B: The slow writer with good shaping. The size of the handwriting is average. The regularity of the form of the patterns is good. With the words the vertical regularity is average; the horizontal distances between the down-strokes are very irregular, but this is the consequence of the model-like shaping of letters and the words. The production speed is low and the pen velocity is very low with little variation and few accelerations or decelerations. The timing is very irregular, and this is made worse by many short stagnations (<.2 sec) and many pauses. The number of small tremors in the writing line is very large, as is the number of peaks in the velocity curve per task and per second. Writing pressure is average. I conclude that a good quality of the handwriting product is combined with a dubious process quality. The handwriting lacks ease and rhythm and makes a spasmodic impression. One could speak of excessive control.

Type C: The fast writer with bad shaping. The dimensions of the handwriting product are large, especially the height. The regularity of the height is poorer than average. The production speed is high; there are very few pauses and stagnations, either long or short. This is beneficial to regular timing. The large sizes and the high production speed lead to a high pen velocity. The mean acceleration and deceleration is very high, and the number of velocity peaks per second is very low. This last fact together with the high production speed means that there are also relatively few peaks per task. The handwriting product is of below average shaping quality, which is consistent with unhampered dynamic processes, but with a certain lack of form control.

Type D: The slow writer with bad formation. The handwriting product is large and irregular. The production speed is low. The number of pauses and stagnations is high, especially the longer ones (>.2 sec). The timing is as a consequence very irregular. The variation in velocity and the mean acceleration are high. The number of velocity peaks per second is relatively low and the handwriting pressure is very heavy, with high peaks. Both the handwriting product and process are insufficient. With regard to the process quality the absence of continuity and fluency attracts attention. The heavy and unrhythmic handwriting pressure is a symptom of a problematic motor coordination, which may lead to fatigue. The force regulation seems to be less subtle than that of the other types, especially A and B.

A comparison of both fast types (A and C) versus the slow ones (B and D) highlights not only differences related to speed in the strict sense (production speed, total pause duration), but also the more regular timing on the part of A and C. When the combination of A and B (good form) is compared with C and D (bad form) it may be observed that, besides the expected differences in form regularity and size, good shaping quality goes together with low variation in pen velocity, low mean accelerations and a relatively high number of velocity peaks per second. This is not the case, however, with the number of velocity peaks per task.

The relation between good shaping and high number of velocity peaks per second was contrary to expectation and it also contrasts with the phenomenon that, from grade 1 to grade 2, the value of this variable significantly decreases. This last fact is in agreement with the view that a relatively high number of velocity peaks per task or per second means that the writing stroke is far from being rhythmic or ballistic. When I investigated the relation of the XYZ variables to different writing patterns, it turned out that more rounded pen movements (continuous patterns) went together with a relatively great number of velocity peaks per second. Good control of shaping shows the same relation.

I conclude that the interpretation of the number of velocity peaks per second is somewhat ambiguous. Because of its positive relation with the quality of the shaping I interpret this finding as an expression of the continuous control of movements, in contrast to jerky movements, especially with type D, which seem a consequence of discontinuous control, as distinguished by Hay (1979, 1984).

The pressure variables did not show a strong correlation with the duration of handwriting education. They discriminated very effectively, however, between type D and the other types, ie, type D has the greater mean and variation of handwriting pressure.

6.2 Application to children with learning difficulties

In addition to the normal children from regular primary education, a group of children with severe specific learning disabilities and severe handwriting problems took part in the investigation. Sixty-seven percent of them belonged to type D (index 9), and the others had indices 6 or 8. I wanted to know in what respects the handwriting of these children differed from that of the normal or regular sample of children. In respect of the duration of their handwriting education, the pupils from special education were considered as third to sixth graders.

The comparison of the normal and the special pupils was based upon three differently defined samples taken from the combined grades 3 through 6:
1. All available regular pupils
2. Only the regular pupils with index 6, 8 or 9
3. Only the regular pupils with index 9

In the last two cases, only normal children who wrote poorly were compared with the special education pupils. As expected, the normal pupils generally showed better product quality for both words and patterns. This better shaping quality ($p<.001$ for MHEIGHT and MTRAJEC) went together with a relatively low variation in pen velocity ($p<.001$ for SD.PENVEL; $p<.001$ for M.AC/DECEL) and with a relatively large number of velocity peaks per second ($p<.001$). For words, however, the samples of pupils with index 9 differed significantly in mean size ($p<.05$) but not in form regularity or number and variation in velocity peaks.

Regarding some process variables which were not related to shaping quality, there was a remarkable difference between the two groups of pupils, depending on the kind of writing task. When writing words the regular pupils obtained better values on process variables such as production speed (higher, $p<.001$), number (smaller, $p<.001$) and duration (shorter, $p<.001$) of stagnations. This was the case for all three differently defined samples. When writing patterns, however, the special pupils showed better process quality, (production speed, $p<.01$; number and duration of stagnations, $p<.001$) including mean writing pressure ($p<.05$).

In contrast to the pupils in normal education who exercised with the patterns only in the first months of their handwriting education, the special pupils got practice in writing patterns in the higher grades as well. This might give an explanation of their relatively good process quality when writing patterns, which, however, deteriorated when writing words. I conclude from this finding that the ability to make patterns in a relaxed way, may be a prerequisite for writing letters and words, but it is not a sufficient guarantee for a good performance of the latter.

The irregular and slow execution of the handwriting of words by the special education pupils may be dependent on problems with the force regulation of the motor impulses. Their cognitive motor programming may be hampered by their weak orthographic ability (Mojet, 1989), weak movement planning (van Galen et al, 1986) and the absence of sufficient automatisms (Freeman, 1954), which all together lead to a fragmented execution.

Chapter 4

A developmental study of the relation between the movement patterns in letter combinations (words) and writing

Nils Sõvik & Oddvar Arntzen

Writing is a tool-using skill that is bound to graphic models and related movement patterns. In Europe children usually begin to learn cursive writing in second grade, so that a year later they can combine letters into words. From third grade onwards children can thus carry out writing as a flowing task, even though interruptions will occur within a word, after a word, or after a series of words. However, one expects the legibility as well as the speed of children's manual writing to improve continually until age 15 (Thomassen and Teulings, 1983).

1.0 Elements of handwriting movements

If one observes the writing behaviour of a child who can write fluently, it is apparent that his/her writing is produced by an integrated pattern of coordinated movements subject to visual monitoring and sensory-motor feedback. Skilled movements are complex but precisely coordinated under neural control in accordance with space and time factors. Recent writing research has paid attention to such process variables (Meulenbroek, 1989; Sõvik et al, 1986; Thomassen et al, 1983), and research has confirmed that the movement patterns required for producing various writing units (separate letters or letter combinations) are coherent with the structural aspects of the same units (Meulenbroek and van Galen, 1986; Sõvik, 1975; Sõvik et al, 1989). Such movement patterns, however, are combinations of upward-downward movements (performed

Development of Graphic Skills
ISBN 0-12-734940-5

mainly by the wrist and hand), separate movements (carried out by the fingers) and a general transport movement of the arm that moves the hand to the right during the writing act. In fluent writing the three movement components work simultaneously and must be coordinated (Sõvik, 1975, 1984b).

When taking the combinations of these movement components into account, the writing units could in principle be drawn either clockwise or counter-clockwise, each of which are regular patterns. Thomassen and Teulings (1979) have shown that, in free scribbling tasks, children below school-age produce more clockwise than counter-clockwise movements. This is also true for older children and adults doing fast rotary drawing tasks. These findings are reversed for ordinary writing tasks. Meulenbroek and van Galen (1986) also examined the same phenomena. They found that, with younger schoolchildren, counter-clockwise rotating patterns without acute angles were written at the highest speed and with a relatively high quality. In the same study, the most difficult movement patterns were those where the direction of rotation alternated frequently, resulting in combinations of clockwise and counter-clockwise movements (see Figure 1).

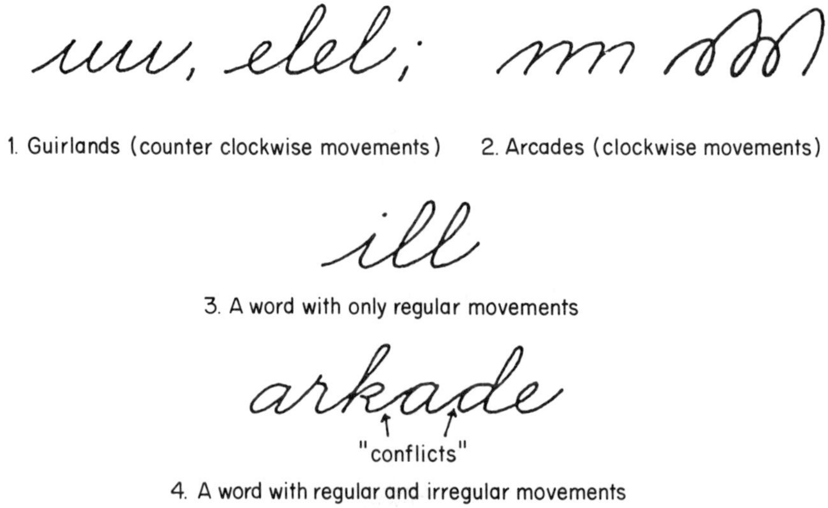

1. Guirlands (counter clockwise movements)   2. Arcades (clockwise movements)

3. A word with only regular movements

"conflicts"

4. A word with regular and irregular movements

FIGURE 1: Illustrations of regular (examples 1,2 and 3) and mixed regular/irregular movement patterns (example 4).

The writing models (letterforms and linking of letters into words) that a child is exposed to at school determine the movement patterns that are learned and developed for later use in fluent writing. Thus the relation between the various movement patterns required for letter combinations and educational criteria of manual writing (accuracy, speed and rhythm) deserve to be investigated. These frequent categories of letter combinations (words), the contextual factors, require analysis and systematic testing with regard to the writing criteria noted above.

Sporadic attempts were made in the 1970s to investigate contextual factors and children's writing performance (Sõvik, 1975) but more systematic studies of the problem were organized and done during the following decade (Meulenbroek and van Galen, 1986; Sõvik et al, 1987a, 1989). A recent study, for example, was done to determine whether the accuracy, speed, and rhythm scores of letters with regularity in movement pattern would surpass the corresponding scores of letters with an irregularity in their pattern (Sõvik et al, 1989). When studying the effects of irregularity in the introduction or ending of a target letter of a word, the velocity seemed to be disrupted more than the accuracy of the letter. Similarly, the predictions about finding a negative effect on writing rhythm from an irregular movement pattern when starting and/or ending a letter were verified to some extent.

Unfortunately, only a few rather specific task variables were used in the previous study. Firstly, only separate letters or pairs of letters were used as task variables; and secondly, not all the letters of the alphabet were tested. Consequently, more comprehensive studies are needed before general conclusions can be drawn concerning the relationship between contextual factors requiring various movement patterns and measures of accuracy, speed and rhythm in children's writing.

2.0 Research hypotheses

The present study was organized to meet this need. In Problem 1, it was expected that a series of words with easy (mainly regular) movement patterns would surpass a comparable series of words with difficult (mainly irregular) movements with regard to children's writing speed. However, it was not expected that different movement patterns would affect the accuracy or rhythm of children's writing performance.

In general, research on handwriting, including studies of the relations between contextual factors and children's writing performance, has provided little empirical information based on a longitudinal approach. Consequently, Problem 2 required having the study repeated when the subjects were three years older in order to examine the stability of the relationships between variables described in conjunction with Problem 1.

Although cross-sectional studies have confirmed the developmental trends of children's writing performance (significant age differences in accuracy and speed scores from 9 to 11 years inclusive), it would be useful to have the findings confirmed by the longitudinal data of the present study (Problem 3) (cf Askov et al, 1970; Sõvik, 1975).

An experiment was done with third-graders (9 years old) and replicated with the same subjects three years later to answer questions raised in Problems 1 to 3.

2.1 Subjects

Twelve third-graders (8 boys, 4 girls) were randomly selected from the public schools in Trondheim as subjects for the experiment. They were then randomly assigned to the two groups, which were matched for sex and age.

2.2 Tasks

The following sentence was divided into three parts of approximately equal length: **Den flinke gra katten gjorde hõye hopp over den gamle biske hunden.** Each part was dictated twice to the subject whose writing was expected to be legible and done at normal (individual) speed. When the subject had completed the sentence he/she had to write the series of separate words chosen as task variables for the experimental group to which he/she belonged. These were the tasks; Group 1: **ane elu elvene ulevle** (easy); Group 2: **gro abg kasser agmbrk** (difficult). It should be noted that movement patterns required writing each of the four letter combinations (words) chosen for Group 1 were considered as easy because the required movements are mainly counter-clockwise whereas the tasks for Group 2 were defined as difficult because they involved mostly alternating clockwise and counter-clockwise movements. The instructions given for writing the two different series of separate words were similar to the ones given for writing the sentence. In each series of test words the second and fourth set of letter combinations were meaningless words.

2.3 Procedure

Writing took place with A4 paper superimposed on a digitizing tablet. A pen with a ballpoint cartridge was connected to a digitizer controlled by a microcomputer. Points were registered whenever a change in the X- or Y-coordinates of the pen position was greater than or equal to 1 mm. Thus, the sampling rate varied from 0 to 125 coordinate pairs/sec, the latter was the maximum sampling rate of the digitizer. The coordinates were processed and stored on disk in the microcomputer. Cursive writing which all subjects had learned at school was used in the execution of the task variables.

The subject did not receive a display of the sentence dictated as the first task in the experiment. The four separate test words that came next, however, had been written by the experimenter with high precision in cursive (height of loop-letter about 10 cm) on a sheet of paper and placed in front of the subject while executing the task (one task at the time). In the experimental situation, the experimenter always dictated the task (word) asking the subject to write it at his/her normal speed. The subject was told not to copy the graphic model, only to use it if he/she forgot the spelling of the task. With time for instruction and recording of data the writing of the sentence and the four separate letter-combinations took about 25 min.

2.3 Measures

Subjects' writing specimens, ie, the paper used on the digitizer when they wrote the test items, were collected and scored on a 7-point scale for accuracy by two persons already trained in this work. The correlation between the raters' scores was 0.86, which is in line with corresponding inter-rater reliability in previous studies (Feldt, 1962; Sŏvik, 1975). The time (speed) used in writing each of the items was scored by the computer. Further measures of the subjects' writing trajectories were as follows:

1. By means of a map reader the sum of the relative lengths of the breaks in the words written in the test (not in the sentence) was found and used as one of the writing rhythm criteria.

2. The maximum absolute velocity (mm/sec) for the writing of each of the four words was measured.

3. Models were developed for each item by an adult who had a high quality of writing rhythm. A 1−7 point scale was then used to rate: (a) the similarity between the trajectories of the model and those of the test-items; (b) how even/uneven the trajectories of the subjects' writing performances were.

4. A rhythm-score of each of the writing performances was then calculated as follows: The score of similarity between model and trajectory (3a) was added to the score of even/uneven trajectory (3b), to give a 2—14 point scale. This was then reduced by: (a) interruptions in the trajectory (0—7 points) and (b) extraordinary high maximum velocity (0—7 points).

3.0 Results

3.1 Equivalence of general writing performance

Before data analyses of the experiment began it was important to check whether Groups 1 and 2 were equal with respect to general writing skills. The average group performances in writing the sentence (described above) were thus compared.

TABLE 1: Mean (with s.d.s in parentheses) of writing performances (accuracy and speed in sentence) in Group 1 (easy tasks), Group 2 (difficult tasks) and total sample at grade levels 3 and 6.

Subjects	N	Grade 3		Grade 6	
		Accuracy	Speed	Accuracy	Speed
Group 1	6	3. 4 (1. 4)	83. 7 (20. 7)	3. 2 (1. 0)	69. 8 (8. 7)
Group 2	6	3. 4 (1. 4)	94. 5 (28. 5)	3. 3 (1. 2)	92. 0 (27. 1)
Total	12	3. 4 (1. 4)	89. 1 (24. 4)	3. 3 (1. 3)	80. 9 (22. 4)

Table 1 contains the mean and standard deviation of accuracy and speed for Groups 1 and 2 in each grade. t-tests were run to investigate whether there were substantial accuracy and speed differences between the two groups. As for accuracy, the average score was exactly the same in grade 3 and the difference between the two groups was very small three years later. Although a difference between the two groups was found for writing speed in favour of Group 1 (easy tasks) for both grades, the differences were not statistically significant. It may thus be assumed that Groups 1 and 2 were equal with regard to functional writing skill when the experiment started in third grade. Similarly, the two groups seemed to be equal as regards functional writing when the experiment was replicated three years later. It should be noted, however, that neither the average accuracy score nor the speed score (sentence) for Total sample improved significantly from grades 3 to 6.

3.2 Differences as a function of task

Analyses of variance on writing accuracy, speed, and rhythm for the test-words revealed no significant differences between the groups in accuracy. In contrast, however, a reliable difference between subjects' performances in grades 3 and 6 in favour of sixth grade was found [$F(2,11)=6.24$, $p<0.03$], with no interaction between task and development. The left portion of Figure 2 presents the developmental trends in accuracy for both groups over the period in question.

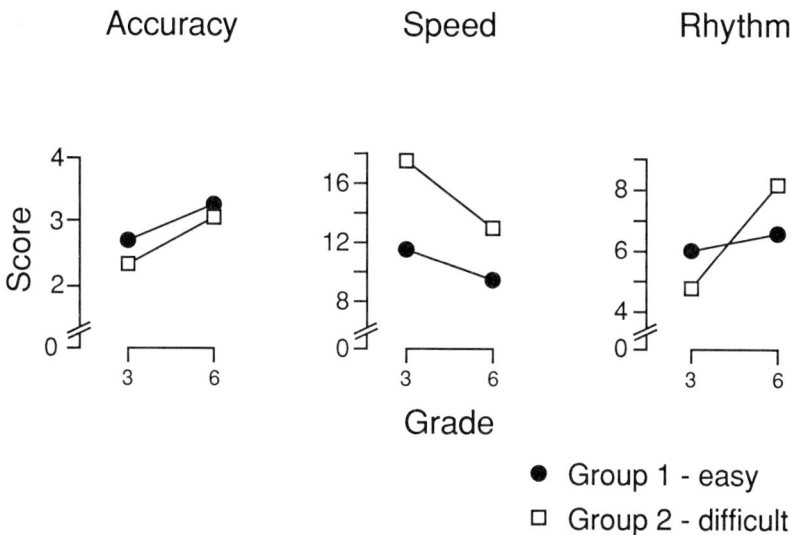

FIGURE 2: Average accuracy, speed and rhythm scores in grades 3 and 6 as a function of easy or difficult task material assigned to the two subject groups.

The results of the analysis of variance using average writing speed as dependent measure indicated a significant difference between the group performances in favour of Group 1 (easy tasks; $F(2,11)=4.83$, $p<0.05$). Even though the trends of progress over the three years in the subjects' writing speed were in accord with our expectations, these differences did not reach an acceptable level of statistical significance ($p<0.11$). The interaction between task and development was not significant. The writing speed performances for Groups 1 and 2 are illustrated in the middle of Figure 2.

Finally, the analysis of variance for writing rhythm gave no significant difference between Groups 1 and 2, but a reliable result in favour of the grade 6 performances was disclosed when progress from grade 3 to 6 was tested [$F(2,11)=10.90$, $p<0.01$]. The right side of Figure 2 indicates the developmental trends of subjects' writing rhythm over the three years. These show that Group 2 (difficult-tasks) progressed considerably more from grades 3 to 6 than did Group 1 (easy tasks). There was also an interaction between task and development [$F(2,11)=5.07$, $p<0.05$].

3.3 Correlation analysis

Table 2 presents correlations between the various dependent measures calculated for the various tasks used in this experiment and the replication after three years.

It was important to check the relation between variables 1 and 3, (ratings of accuracy in writing a sentence and test-words) at third grade, which equalled 0.88. The correlation between the parallel variables at sixth grade (variables 6 and 8) was 0.52. In other words, a significant relation between the accuracy of sentence and test-words in the experiment was found at both grades. Variables 2 and 4 were measures of the time spent writing the sentence and the test-words at third grade. The comparable measures in grade 6 were variables 7 and 9. The correlation for writing time was significant at sixth grade ($r=0.65$), but a positive, insignificant result at third grade ($r=0.36$).

The intercorrelations between accuracy, time, and rhythm of

subjects' writing experimental task variables in grade 3 were as follows: There was a substantial correlation between variables 3 and 5 (accuracy and rhythm), whereas low negative correlations occurred between variables 3 and 4 (time), and variables 4 and 5. According to Problem 2, the stability of the relationships between accuracy, time, and rhythm in the subjects' writing could be investigated by studying the corresponding relationships (variables 8−10) in grade 6. In general, the intercorrelations were the same at both grades. Although the correlation coefficient between variables 8 and 10 (accuracy and rhythm) was not statistically significant, it was moderately high ($r=0.43$).

Some of the correlational data in Table 2 relate to the developmental trends of children's writing performances (Problem 3). By comparing pair-wise variables with equal designation for the two grades one can examine the consistency

TABLE 2: *Pearson product-moment correlations among dependent measures of subject's writing performances (accuracy, speed, rhythm) in functional writing (sentence) and experimental task variables (words) at grade levels 3 and 6. High scores are consistent with good performance except for variables 2,4,7 and 9 (N=12).*

Measure	Grade 3					Grade 6				
	1	2	3	4	5	6	7	8	9	10
Grade 3										
1 Acc(s)	1.00	.08	.88	.14	.69	.59	−.36	.29	−.73	.35
2 Tm(s)		1.00	.18	.36	.22	−.14	.42	.08	.13	.42
3 Acc(w)			1.00	−.14	.79	.49	−.27	.49	−.73	.43
4 Tm(w)				1.00	−.07	−.03	.55	−.33	.33	−.08
5 Rh(w)					1.00	.44	−.42	.75	−.54	.62
Grade 6										
6 Acc(s)						1.00	−.18	.52	−.32	.35
7 Tm(s)							1.00	−.24	.65	−.16
8 Acc(w)								1.00	−.17	.43
9 Tm(w)									1.00	−.29
10 Rh(w)										1.00

in the various writing parameters considered. Hence, it is noteworthy that accuracy in sentence (variables 1 and 6) presented a significant correlation ($r=0.59$), and the time spent on writing the sentence (variables 2 and 7) also produced a moderately high correlation, ($r=0.42$).

4.0 Discussion

Because handwriting is an instrumental behaviour, it is usually defined operationally. Hence, parameters of the writing act and the legibility of this behaviour can be analysed, described, or rated. In previous research on writing, accuracy (legibility) was therefore considered the main criterion on this activity (Askov et al, 1970; Herrick, 1963; Sõvik, 1975, 1981). To date, however, no completely objective method has been developed for measuring accuracy, although the reliability of the rating system, like the one used in the present study, has been tested and found satisfactory (Feldt, 1962; Sõvik, 1975). In recent writing research, scientists have also paid more attention to process variables, but they have chosen somewhat different process variables as criteria for their studies (Kao et al, 1986; Thomassen et al, 1983). In the present study, writing speed (time) and writing rhythm were used as criteria for subjects' writing performance besides writing accuracy. With a computer being used to measure the writing time, the problem of objectivity and reliability (for the measuring procedure) should be unquestionable. The characteristics of the writing rhythm can be studied by various curves using adequate computer programs (Thomassen and Teulings, 1979). We believe that the absolute velocity curve is advantageous as a basic display for assessing writing rhythm. Although the procedure has been applied in previous studies (Sõvik et al, 1987a, 1987b), and should be valid and fairly objective, no reliability check has yet been done on the method. This information should be kept in mind when this criterion on children's writing performance is reported.

4.1 Task effects

According to Problem 1, a difference between the average group performance was predicted for writing speed but not for writing accuracy. The predictions were confirmed by our data and the results are in line with the findings of a previous study in which similar but more specific task variables were applied (Sõvik et al, 1989). No such specific letter-by-letter analyses were carried out in the present study but in general each of the four task variables was defined to represent easy or difficult movement patterns. Our previous study, however, presented data which indicated that not all introductory or ending movements defined as regular movements would be in keeping with our present expectations, even though the general trend was clear. This information should be considered when interpreting related data in the present study. However, information on the positive effects of continuous writing (motion) patterns, without acute angles, on speed performance supports related research by Meulenbroek and van Galen (1986) that counter-clockwise rotating writing patterns are recommended for writing speed, and also partly for writing quality. This point should be taken into account when planning the curriculum for writing instruction in schools.

No predictions were made with regard to group differences in rhythm for two reasons: The reliability of our writing rhythm measure had not been tested, and the results of previous related studies concerning this parameter were rather ambiguous. The means of writing rhythm for Groups 1 and 2 indicated no significant difference between easy and difficult movement patterns with regard to this factor.

4.2 Age effects

Problem 2 was raised to examine the stability of the relationships between variables as specified in conjunction with Problem 1. No significant interactions were found between the group and development factors in the analyses with accuracy and speed as dependent measures. The results can be taken as evidence of stability in the relationship between movement patterns and accuracy/speed measures of manual writing. It has already been reported that no significant difference was found at third grade for writing rhythm between Groups 1 and 2. Corresponding data in grade 6 subjects' performances were consistent with this result. Although no prediction was made with regard to the relationship between movement patterns in cursive writing and writing rhythm, the recent findings seem to indicate stability over the three-year period, namely that various movement patterns used in fluent writing do not affect children's writing rhythm. It should also be kept in mind, however, that a significant interaction was detected between the movement patterns factor and the development factor as far as rhythm was concerned. Similarly, consistency was found in our data with regard to accuracy and speed from third to sixth grade. It follows that the relationships between children's hand motion required for easy vs difficult patterns and writing accuracy, time and rhythm revealed in grade 3 in principle are the same in grade 6, and probably also later. This should be tested in the future.

Previous research has shown that children's psychomotor functions related to their writing performances will develop continuously from age 7 to 11 inclusive (Jones and Seashore, 1944; Sõvik, 1975). It follows that predictions of finding a parallel development in children's psychomotor skills, eg handwriting, have been verified in cross-sectional studies (Sõvik, 1975, 1980). The present study checked such developmental data in a longitudinal study and tested whether writing accuracy and speed would increase substantially from grade 3 to 6 inclusive.

Significant differences were found between grades 3 and 6 on writing accuracy, which agreed with our expectations. The correlation between accuracy in grades 3 and 6 supported a developmental trend in children's writing accuracy from age 9 to 12 inclusive. Some evidence of a developmental trend in writing speed was found, but this was not statistically significant. It may be concluded, however, that this result agrees, in principle, with previous related research performed in different countries. The findings clearly show that older children generally write faster than younger children (Athenes, 1984; Sõvik, 1975; Wann, 1986).

When writing rhythm was taken into consideration, there appeared to be a substantial progress from third to sixth grade. Whereas no interactions were found for the measures of accuracy and speed, a significant interaction was revealed regarding rhythm. Although subjects in Group 1 (easy task) increased their average score of writing rhythm from grades 3 to 6 to some extent, the progress in rhythm for subjects in Group 2 (difficult task) was much greater during the same period. The finding should indicate that the development in cursive writing rhythm from grades 3 to 6 has been somewhat different for the two groups. It is reasonable to believe that environmental factors, eg handwriting instruction and training at school, might have caused this divergent progress for the two groups in writing rhythm.

Accuracy (legibility), speed and rhythm were all used as the criteria for measuring children's progress in writing in the present study. The main reason why these three criteria were chosen was that they (legibility and speed in particular) have been emphasized in former research on handwriting (Suen, 1983; Sövik, 1975, 1981).

To reach more general conclusions concerning the relationships between movement patterns and writing performance a longitudinal study including a greater number of dependent variables should be organized and performed. The study should also include older children and adults. Similarly, a longitudinal study that concentrates on analyses of the relations between the various deviations (errors) in children's writing performance (accuracy scores) and models used in writing instruction could be of great interest to researchers and educationalists alike.

III: Dynamics of development: Drawing

In this section the focus broadens from handwriting to take in the closely allied skill of drawing. Wong and Kao *(The development of drawing principles in Chinese)* consider potential cultural influences on children's acquisition of graphic skills. Their work extends the concept of a general grammar of drawing principles, originally established from the drawings of US children, and also alerts the Western reader to the remarkably precise and sensitive control that Chinese children must acquire in their skill development. They compare and contrast the constraints imposed by Western and Chinese scripts and the confusions that may occur for children in cross-cultural environments. They also examine the extent to which drawing tasks that violate the general principles a child has acquired may result in slower writing and poorer control.

The chapter by Vinter and Mounoud *(Isochrony and accuracy of drawing movements in children: Effects of age and context)* moves completely into the realm of drawing. It takes as its starting point the observation that skilled adults tend to preserve constancy in the timing of movements of quite different extent (the isochrony principle). Thus, for example, a circle of large diameter is drawn in about the same time as one of small diameter. To achieve this, the speed of movement of the pen must be adjusted. Vinter and Mounoud provide a detailed analysis of how isochrony develops in children and how it is affected by the cognitive requirements of the drawing task.

Chapter 5

The development of drawing principles in Chinese

Tsz Hang Wong & Henry S.R. Kao

In the context of children's education, the term *drawing* has a wide usage. It may refer to children's pictures of humans, their copies of simple geometric shapes, written letters, printed numbers and their construction of maps. These drawings are typically assigned to three separate areas: art, writing and geography (Goodnow, 1977).

1.0 General principles of drawing

Goodnow and Friedman (1972) analysed children's drawings of people from the approach of stroke sequences, and found that they make use of principles that specified where to start and how to proceed. These drawing principles were named *left-right sequence, paired sequence, top-to-bottom order* and *from core to accessories*. The first three principles were strong in older children but not in preschool children. These young children tended to draw from right to left, bottom to top and in radical sequence rather than paired sequence. These principles were used to explain a number of interesting phenomena in children's drawings. For example, X-ray drawings, where the body is visible through the clothes, are due to the drawing tendency of beginning from the *core* and going to the *accessories*. Goodnow and Levine (1973) and Goodnow (1977) also found that there were some similar principles in US children's copies of geometric figures. These were: starting at the *topmost point*; at the *leftmost point*; or with the *vertical line*; starting at the top and coming down *left oblique* when the figure had an apex; drawing all *horizontal lines from left to right*; drawing all vertical lines from *top to bottom*, and *threading* (joined lines).

Examination of these principles revealed developmental trends in children's drawings and were used to explain commonly observed phenomena when children copy figures such as errors in shape, errors in orientation and the behaviour of page-turning.

It is interesting to consider the possibility of cultural differences in childrens' drawing. Goodnow et al (1973) found that Israeli children also displayed principles similar to the US children when they copied geometric figures except for four aspects: The Israeli children much preferred to start from right to left; when the figure had an apex they would draw down the right oblique first; and they would start with horizontal lines and draw with discontinuous lines rather than threading. Moreover, Goodnow et al (1973) found that the US children tended to draw circles in a counter-clockwise direction but their Israeli counterparts drew in the opposite direction. Goodnow and colleagues (1972, 1973, 1977) concluded that children's drawing behaviour displays a general pattern that cuts across a variety of contexts. This pattern is the so-called *grammar of action* or the drawing principles which are affected by the scripts that children have learned. The differences in drawing principles among children are attributed to the different orthography and stroke sequences of the scripts they have learned.

Previous studies have mainly employed Western children as their subjects. Consequently, there is little information about the drawing principles of Chinese children. Chinese is a completely different script compared to Western alphabetic scripts and it is more complex. A Chinese character is not composed of letters as is an English word, but has its own features, and people learn the Chinese script word by word. Unlike the English script, the Chinese script stresses starting with horizontal lines rather than vertical lines and writing discrete strokes rather than continuous paths. Both Chinese and English scripts show a tendency for vertical lines to be written from top to bottom; horizontal lines from left to right; and drawing down the left oblique from an apex. Chinese characters, however, do possess more vertical lines and horizontal lines (Figure 1). Chinese children, therefore, may display some drawing principles which are different from those of Western children. As a result, the

(A)：

人口手足火山石日月木天地刀尺布米衣田牛花羊花牙舌耳眼瓜果魚肉風雨狗貓馬兔車船門

(B)：

剪指甲放假了龍船木馬遊戲唱歌滑梯拍手大風新年花貓讀書玩具母雞冬妹同學果肉口天門笑
衣夏天弟姐田山洗草小坐游魚人爸花姊生日手地火狗海水哥媽羊牛玩球刷牙寫字先生晚早

(C)：

讀書要用功地清潔常做運動蜜蜂牛奶雞蛋前後左右農夫小鳥飛起早睡火車姊表弟工人好學放
假了媽做成績過馬路洗手外婆青蛙漱口兒童澡家務作春機上課新年快樂生日會講故事朋友來
遊戲太陽貓捉鼠秋天狗守門牛耕田量大掃除公園聖誕節白兔玩具多郵差月亮下雨起林魚哭鳥

(D)：

人了七八九十又力上大小也子下才工千口久己山心火方毛止午日夫友片以王水太牛今什我見
你吧伯快走地住比五天六手不中月故後便風送怎食飛前科洋娃突屋香活神星美客要些事長
知東底兩青門物拉拋迎長抱肯朋泡忽邱叔杯房易牀候害訓祝捉迷旁夏畜哭被特旅乘哪倒茶病容
海陣捉破四去生可白功他打出本叫瓜冬只面要是秋紀亮看孩勇很空受岸怪妹爸和的來到花
兒雨居呵怕兔河肥玩夜放泳呀林姐念物呢具店狗拍肯爬早共有同好老找別伸車弄坐沖每貝
沒位吹地朵年先回在羊吃西她多池衣忙向成用正台外半天失石仙平行舌肉色自再全米安升尾
作助把冷那步弟身姨紅柄昨咬抓求困買着鄉黑就雲陽進游猴愛媽裏會園葉落節圓搖壺跟鼠
跳哥家個起班校師們紙眞笑拿草氣站時隻高書帶原訓祝恭問做教採梨涼晚唱啊都清理偸魚張
得務掉救敢動許鳥這常請鄰課躺遮樣廠樂熱鬧場散賀鴨醒遲糕幫還聲盞鮮續說歌領麼趕碌學
舉樹頭貓嗎開黃遊話新顯體都題雜讓聽爲讀排堂習細停現夠商蛋連從接羞貪通淺彩假果探望
婆國情掛眼荷野惡副圖演漸蜜遠對輕貌漂數饒隊畫發溫換帽趁幾量最等然間替裙跑越期街握
富傘極蛙趣興圖憐餘談稻穀蝴蝶撲摩輪綠覺難寶蜂碰過爺農賊路慌腳楚電塘舅照鈴亂晴遍獅
意禮蟬樫斷鵝雙蟲鈴道躲想暖頭機橋蕉講謝點嚇雖警邊離麗響露驚顧瞧臉髒灘能像滿窩睡
網

FIGURE 1: The Chinese words that children normally learn in nursery school (A), first-year kindergarten (B), final-year kindergarten (C), and first grade of primary school (D).

main purpose of Experiment I presented here is to find out the differences between the drawing principles of Chinese children and their Western counterparts.

Experiment II goes beyond the identification of differences in drawing principles to explore the underlying processes by determining the reasons for errors. Goodnow and Levine (1973) found that there are more errors when children copy stimuli with patterns which violate the children's usual drawing principles than when they copy stimuli with patterns which adhere to their drawing principles. However, previous studies have not told us the reasons. It is essential to discover why children make mistakes in order to help children develop proper responses. Stelmach and Teulings (1983) found that reaction time was slower but writing time was unaffected when subjects copied stimuli which were unexpected (expectancy was defined by the probability of presentation). It was suggested that the identity of the stimulus to be written is programmed or reprogrammed in advance, and for an unexpected stimulus, there is inappropriate preparation that must then be reprogrammed. This reprogramming accounts for the extra time needed before writing. In other words, the reaction time necessary for a principle-violated stimulus may be slower than that of a principle-adhered stimulus because the patterns of the former do not adhere to the usual drawing tendency and the subjects prepare inappropriately. If this hypothesis is right, errors in copying a principle-violated stimulus may be due to non-reprogramming or faulty reprogramming.

Kao et al (1983) suggested a complexity-dependency hypothesis that states that writing pressure is related to task complexity and increases in the free-hand mode of handwriting. In Kao et al's research complexity was defined by the number of turning movements. For the complex stimulus, it has been supposed that the progression direction and the starting direction of each stroke are constantly changing so that the writing paths of some strokes may be inconsistent with others and violate their usual drawing principles. In the present study, stimulus patterns that violated the children's usual drawing principles were used and so might be assumed to be complex and might therefore be written with heavier pressure. If this hypothesis is right, more errors in principle-violated figures might be due to the absence of the extra force which is exerted to counter the usual drawing tendency. In Experiment II, the reaction time, writing time and writing pressure were studied under two contrasting conditions in order to test the concept above.

2.0 Search for drawing principles in Chinese

In Experiment I, Chinese subjects were asked to draw geometric shapes based on those used previously by Goodnow and Levine (1973). The stroke sequences of the subjects' drawings were compared with those of their US counterparts, the data of the US subjects being taken from the previous work.

2.1 Subjects

Five groups of Chinese subjects in Hong Kong were employed. All of them were Chinese-English bilinguals, right-handed, normal-sighted and middle class in background. The five age groups were:
Group 1: Just started nursery school.
Group 2: About to finish the first year of kindergarten.
Group 3: About to finish the last year of kindergarten.
Group 4: About to finish first grade.
Group 5: College students.

These groupings are similar to those in Goodnow and Levine's research (1973) so they can be compared. Half of the children in Group 1, Group 2, and Group 3 were from a school in Sam Shui Po and the others were from a school in Kwun Tong. The children in Group 4 were drawn from Tai Koo Primary School. The subjects in Group 5 were from the University of Hong Kong. The number of subjects in each group was respectively, 21, 20, 20, 20, 20. Male and female were evenly distributed within each group. The mean age in each group was respectively, 3 yrs and 6 months, 4 yrs and 7 months, 5 yrs and 11 months, 7 yrs, 22 yrs and 5 months.

2.2 Procedure

Fifteen geometric designs were taken from Goodnow and Levine's research (1973). Figure 2 illustrates these designs. All lines were 56 to 63 mm long except design 10, which has a 37 mm horizontal crossbar. The top angles for triangles, inverted Vs and diamonds were 60 degrees.

Designs were drawn on 200 mm square opaque paper and assembled in a booklet. The order of presentation for every subject is displayed in Figure 2.

Stimulus designs were presented one at a time, each subject being given as much time as they wished on each design. Subjects were asked to copy the stimulus on the 200 mm square paper. An experimenter sat next to the subject and recorded the direction and sequence of all strokes on a shielded page. The model and the copy were vertically aligned on the table.

2.3 Data analysis

Copies were first coded as correct or incorrect. Drawing paths on correct copies were then analysed for the observance of rules. Correctness was liberally defined. When the copies did not have any of the features below, they were defined as correct:

a. incompleteness (eg, abandoned diamonds)
b. distortions to the extent that no one could recognize the original (eg, a circle was drawn for a square)
c. major changes in the position of parts of the original (eg, the cross bar moved from the centre to the end point of the vertical line)
d. large changes in orientation (eg, left-right or up-down rotation).

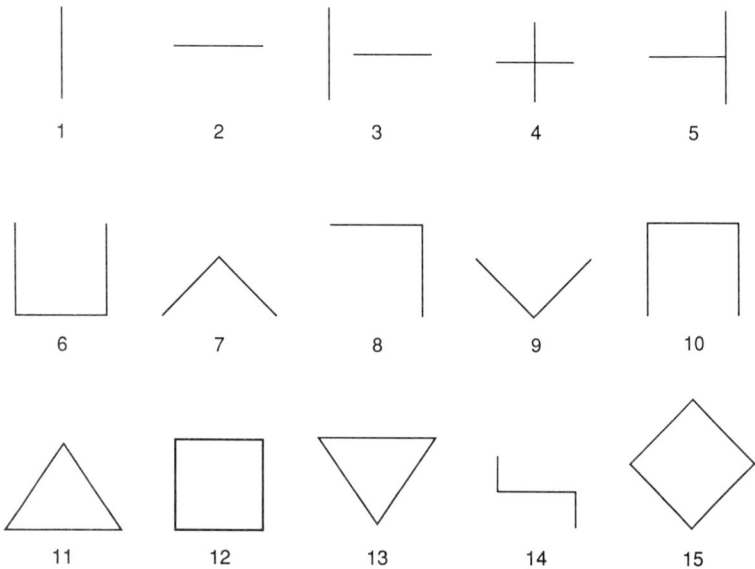

FIGURE 2: Designs used in Experiment I, numbered in their order of presentation.

According to Goodnow and Levine's suggestion (1973), three criteria were used to judge which stroke sequence would be given the status of a principle. This status was given if the stroke sequence: (1) was found in not fewer than three stimuli; (2) brought out differences among age groups and among stimulus; (3) was in the form of a binary choice as far as possible.

In this study, the mean percentages of subjects that used various stroke sequences across all designs were calculated for each group. If the stroke sequence met Goodnow and Levine's (1973) three criteria, these stroke sequences were then considered principles.

The differences between the percentages of the appearance of the drawing principles for the Chinese subjects and the US subjects were then calculated and tested for significance.

3.0 Cultural differences in drawing principles

The percentages of children observing each drawing principle in each group are shown in Figures 3 through 6. The curves with filled circles illustrate the development of the drawing principles in the Chinese subjects and the curves with empty squares illustrate the development of the drawing principles in the US subjects in Goodnow and Levine's (1973) study.

The difference in the strength of each principle between the Chinese subjects and the US subjects was tested by z-scores. The differences in the two drawing principles, starting with the vertical line and coming down the left side from the top of the apex, are significant at the .05 level. In addition, the differences in the two drawing principles, drawing all verticals from top to bottom and all horizontals from left to right, are significant at the .01 level. The strength of all these drawing principles is stronger in the Chinese subjects except for the principle of starting with vertical line.

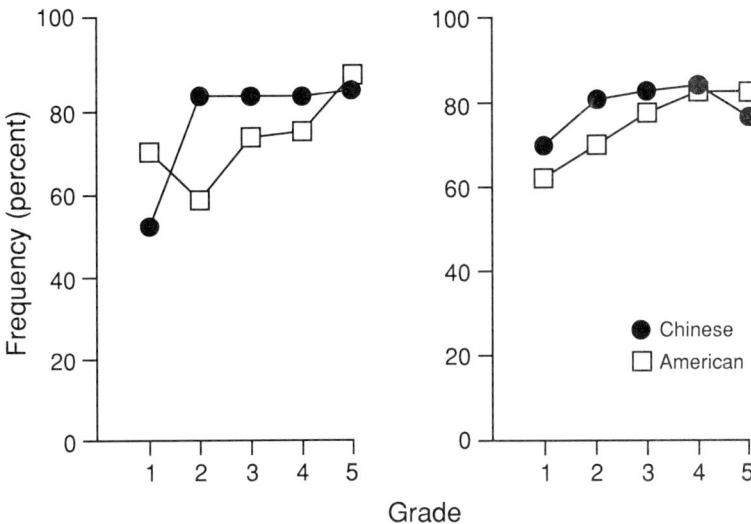

FIGURE 3: The percentage of children observing the principles of starting at the leftmost point (left) and starting at the topmost point (right).

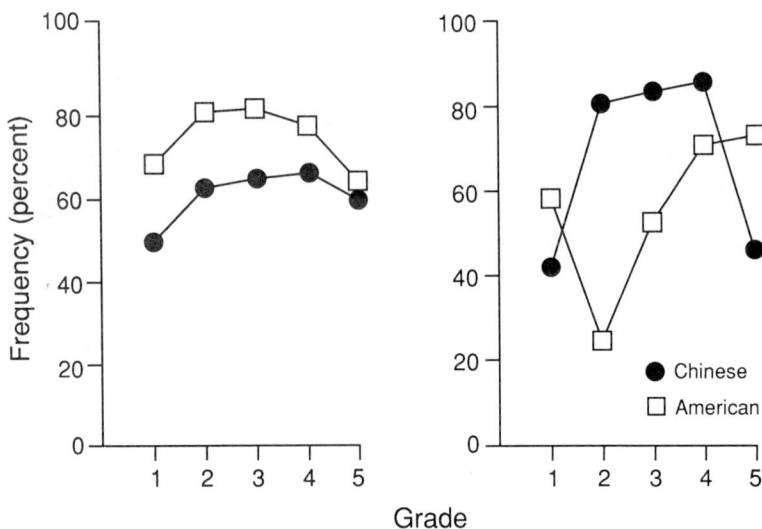

FIGURE 4: The percentage of children observing the principles of starting with a vertical line (left) and starting from the apex and down to left (right).

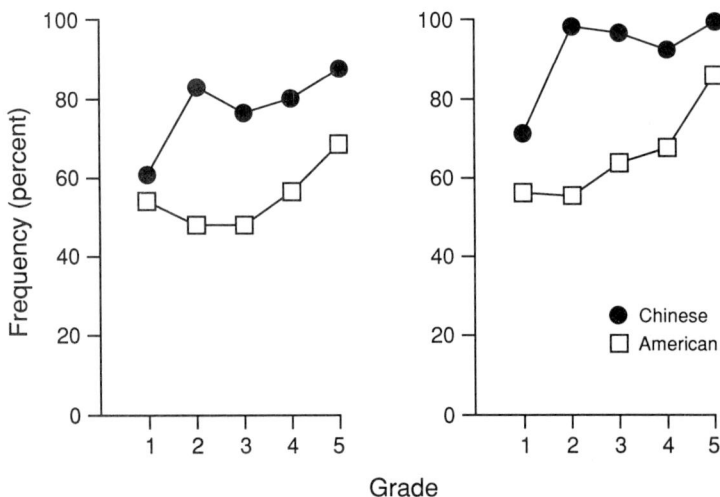

FIGURE 5: The percentage of children observing the principles of drawing all horizontals from left to right (left) and drawing all verticals from top to bottom (right).

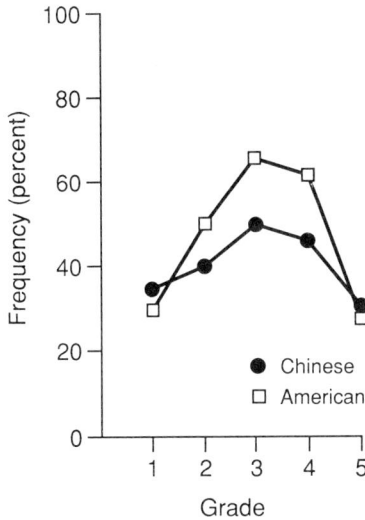

FIGURE 6: The percentage of children observing the drawing principle of threading.

From the results mentioned above, it was found that the developmental trends of the two starting principles, starting at the topmost point and starting at the leftmost point, were not similar between the Chinese and the Americans. The Chinese observed such principles earlier than the Americans. However, the strength of such principles was not significantly different between them.

The principle of starting with the vertical line developed in each age group similarly for both the Chinese and the US subjects. However, the strength of observing this principle was significantly different. Chinese tended to adhere to this principle less.

For the principle of starting at the top and coming down to the left oblique when the figure had an apex, the developmental trend and the strength of this principle were significantly different between the Chinese subjects and the US subjects. The developmental trend of the Chinese was an inverted-U shape but that of the US subjects was an upright-V shape, and the Chinese tended to prefer to draw by starting at the top and coming down to the left oblique.

For the two principles, drawing all verticals from top to bottom and drawing all horizontals from left to right, the developmental trends and the strength of these two principles between the Chinese subjects and the US subjects were significantly different from each other. The developmental trend of the Chinese was a cubic function, but that of the US subjects was quadratic. Moreover, the strength of observing such principles in the Chinese was much greater than in the US subjects. Finally, the developmental trend and the strength of the threading principle were very similar in both the Chinese and the Americans.

4.0 Chinese-American script differences

There are about seven thousand popular Chinese characters. In order to have a comprehensive concept of the orthography and stroke sequence of the Chinese characters, 762 Chinese characters have been sampled and analysed. These characters were recommended by the Educational Department of Hong Kong and some publishing companies. It was said that these words are popular and representative of the population and they are taught to the children before they have completed first grades. In Hong Kong, children spend much time learning Chinese script at the beginning of their schooling (see Figure 1).

Of these 762 Chinese words, 551 (72%) are formally taught to be written starting at the topmost point while 310 (40%) are taught to start at the leftmost point. Hence, this latter principle might be expected to be weaker than the former one. Because these two principles may be in conflict with each other in some words, the principle of starting at the topmost point is always stronger. However, the strength of the principle of starting at the leftmost point is very strong in the words that use both this principle and the principle of starting at the topmost point. As a result, Chinese children learn to write many Chinese words starting at the topmost point and leftmost point when their schooling begins, which is in strong contrast with US children who just learn to write 52 letters including capitals and small letters.

Given the intensive practice of the Chinese children, it is not surprising to find that the developmental trends of these two principles, starting at the topmost point and starting at the leftmost point, emerge earlier in the Chinese children than US children.

Of the 762 Chinese words, 691 have vertical lines and 153 of these (22% of 691) are formally taught to be written with a vertical line at the start. This percentage is small because written Chinese words always start with horizontal lines rather than vertical lines, in contrast to English script. Goodnow (1977) showed that English letters typically start with a vertical stroke, so it is not surprising that the strength of the principle, starting with a vertical line, is significantly weaker in Chinese than in Americans although the developmental trends are similar to each other.

There are more Chinese characters with the apex structure than there are English letters with this structure. The stroke sequences of all these Chinese words are from the top of the apex and down to the left oblique. Yet, in the English script, only the capital letter A has this structure and stroke sequence. So the fact that the strength of the principle, starting at the top and coming down to the left oblique, is stronger in Chinese than in Americans may be attributed to this cultural or script difference.

Among the 762 Chinese words, 98% have horizontal lines and most of them are taught to be written with the horizontal lines going from left to right. Of the 762 Chinese words 90% have vertical lines, and 97% of these words are taught to be written with the vertical line going from top to bottom. Although writing horizontal lines from left to right and writing vertical lines from top to bottom are principles that are also found in English script, only a small number of the 52 English letters have horizontal lines or vertical lines or both of them. It may be supposed that the strength of these two principles of progression, drawing all horizontal lines from left to right and drawing all vertical lines from top to bottom, is stronger in Chinese than in the

Americans largely because of the greater exposure to these kinds of stroke sequences in the Chinese script.

Although the difference between the strength of the threading principle between Chinese and Amercians is not significant, a stronger tendency to draw in a continuous path is found in Amercians. This may be due to the cursive writing practised by the Amercians but not by Chinese.

The findings of this study are consistent with previous studies that showed that drawing principles are affected by the scripts a person learns (Ilg and Ames, 1964; Goodnow et al, 1973). However, previous studies employed subjects that had only learned one script. These previous studies have not told us about how drawing principles are affected when someone learns two different scripts simultaneously with some stroke sequences of these two scripts dissonant from each other. In the present study, students in Hong Kong were employed. They had learnt both the Chinese script and English script simultaneously in school. It has been mentioned that although some stroke sequences in the Chinese script are similar to those in the English script, some of them are different and could be conflicting.

From the results of this study, it is proposed that these two different scripts affect the drawing principles employed by the Chinese through an averaging process. It is easier to clarify this idea by discussing the drawing principle of starting with a vertical line. Starting with a vertical line is stressed more in English script than in Chinese. If an additive process determined the strength of this drawing principle, it would be stronger for the Chinese (who are exposed to both scripts) than for the Americans (who are only exposed to English script). If, on the other hand, an averaging process applies, the drawing principle would be weaker for the Chinese than for the Americans. For example, suppose a numerical weight for the principle of starting with a vertical line learned from the English script is 4 units and from the Chinese script is 2 units. Americans just learn the English script, which stresses this principle so that they are given 4 units of weight for this drawing principle. However, Chinese in Hong Kong learn both the

Chinese script and English script. If the additive model is right, Chinese will have 6 units of weight for this drawing principle, so that the drawing principle of starting with a vertical line is stronger in Chinese than Americans. If the averaging model is right, Chinese will have 3 units of weight for this drawing principle, so that this drawing principle will be weaker in the Chinese than in the Americans. The results of the present study support the latter model. However, this is just a tentative model, which needs to be studied further. A control group of subjects who only know the Chinese script should be added.

In addition to the principles discussed above, this study also revealed other principles. The first principle is starting from a vertical line and progressing left, which is also reported by Goodnow and Levine (1973). The second principle is starting with a vertical line and then progressing left and downwards. This principle is found in designs 10, 12, and 14. The third principle is starting at the apex and coming down to the left oblique and then the right oblique. This principle is found in designs 7, 11 and 15. The fourth principle is drawing straight lines horizontally or vertically. These principles are also common in the Chinese script.

These findings have implications for child education. It has been found that some writing principles of Chinese script are incompatible with those of English script. For example, Chinese script tends to start with horizontal lines but the English script is taught to start with vertical lines. However, children in Hong Kong are encouraged to learn both Chinese and English scripts in schools. Therefore, children may feel confused when they learn both scripts. As a result, teachers should help children to distinguish between these two scripts and always remind them how to write the characters correctly when they write either Chinese or English.

5.0 Reaction time, writing time and writing pressure

In Experiment I, certain drawing principles were established in Chinese subjects. Moreover, it was observed that when children drew certain figures, for example, designs 5, 6, 9, 13, 15, etc., they performed diligently with hesitation. After analysing the figures, it was doubted that the reaction time and writing pressure were different when they drew the figures which violated their usual drawing principles. The purpose of Experiment II was aimed at comparing the reaction time, writing time and writing pressure in the drawing of figures that either violate or adhere to the principles.

5.1 Subjects

Four groups of Chinese children were employed:
Group 1: Those who just started nursery school
Group 2: Those who were going to finish the first year of kindergarten
Group3: Those who were going to finish the last year of kindergarten
Group 4: Those who were going to finish the first grade.

Half of the subjects in Groups 1, 2 and 3 were drawn from a school in Aberdeen and the others drawn from another school in Wanchai. The children in Group 4 came from three primary schools. Each group consisted of 10 subjects and an even distribution of the sexes. The means of the age in each group were, respectively, 3 yrs and 8 months, 4 yrs and 9 months, 5 yrs and 11 months, 7 yrs and 1 month. All subjects were right-handed, normal-sighted and of a middle class background.

5.2 Procedure

Ten geometric designs were used. Figure 7 illustrates these designs. Using the numbering of Figure 10; five pairs of counterparts were formed using designs 1 with 6; 2 with 7; 3 with 8; 4 with 9; and 5 with10. The first one of each pair of counterparts (1−5) was designed to violate the usual drawing principles adhered to in its counterpart (6−10). The pattern of design 1 violated the drawing principle of starting with vertical line and then progressing to the left and down. The patterns of design 2 and 3 violated the principle of starting at the apex and coming down to the left oblique and then the right oblique. The pattern of design 4 violated the principle of starting with a vertical line and progressing to the left. The pattern of design 5 violated the principle of drawing straight lines horizontally or vertically.

All the designs were drawn on photo-slides; the stimuli were presented in random order and controlled by the computer. The size of the stimuli displayed on the projection screen was 3.5 cm x 3.5 cm. Each stimulus was presented 5 times, so that the total number of trials was 50 for each child.

Before running the experiment, 20 children were asked to copy these geometric designs as the pilot study. Their drawing paths and errors were recorded. It was found that subjects made more errors in drawing designs 1−5 than in designs 6−10. These results were consistent with Goodnow and Levine's finding (1973) that more errors were made in the drawing of principle-violated figures. Thus, the first five designs of these 10 geometric figures were validated to be principle-violated and the last five designs to be principle-adhered.

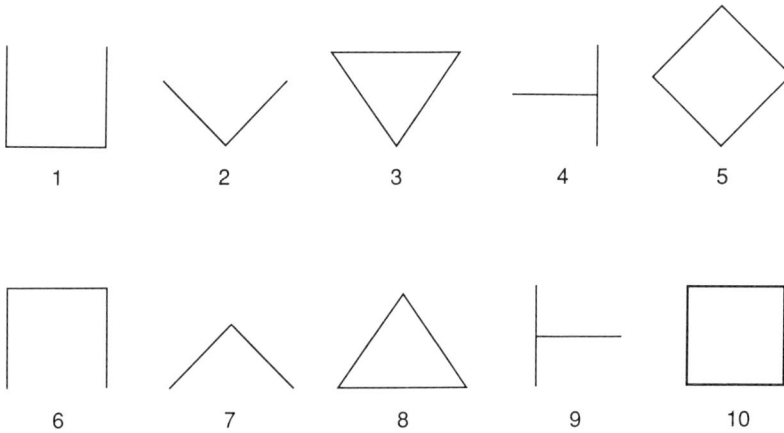

FIGURE 7: Designs used in Experiment II, numbered in their order of presentation.

The subject was seated comfortably with his two arms resting on the top of the writing platform (Kao et al, 1983), placed directly in front of the projection screen where the stimulus was displayed. He/she was asked to use his right hand to draw with a pen. Before drawing, a paper sheet with a 4 cm square frame and centre dot was placed on the aluminium plate of the pressure transducer. The subject was then asked to position the pen tip just over the dot without making contact with the paper and, at the same time, to pay attention to the screen. When the subject was ready, a 2 second fixation cross was displayed on the projection screen. Immediately after the fixation point, a stimulus was presented. The subject needed to respond after he/she had recognized the stimulus by drawing the figure at a normal writing speed on the paper within the square frame. Shortly after the subject had completed the drawing task, a new sheet of paper was supplied by the experimenter. A new trial was initiated again after 15 seconds.

5.3 Data collection and analysis

Reaction time, writing time and writing pressure were measured for each trial. Reaction time (RT) was the duration between the start of stimulus presentation and pen contact with the pressure transducer and writing time (WT) was the total duration of pen contact with the pressure transducer. Writing pressure (WP) for each trial was computed by dividing the sum of all observed pressure values within that trial by the number of data points sampled at 10 msec intervals throughout the task duration. Only correct responses were considered and analysed in a factorial design. The SPSS package was used to perform a Manova analysis in order to see how the independent variables, age and stimulus, affected RT, WT and WP.

6.0 Results

Tables 1, 2 and 3, illustrate the main results for RT, WT and WP respectively.

TABLE 1: Mean reaction time in sec for each age group and stimulus.

Stimulus	Group				Mean
	1	2	3	4	
Principle-adhered	3.08	2.28	2.32	1.81	2.39
Principle-violated	3.84	2.70	2.49	1.88	2.74
Mean	3.46	2.49	2.40	1.84	

The analysis of the RT data presented in Table 1 showed that significant differences in RT were found with the different age groups and stimuli ($p<.01$, and $p<.05$ for their interaction). RT decreased as the age of subjects increased. RT was also longer when the children tried to copy the principle-violated designs. The interaction effect was tested by Tukey's analysis, and revealed that the greatest difference between the RT caused by the stimulus was found in Group 1, the youngest group. It was shown that the children in Group 1 responded more slowly than the other groups when they were asked to draw the principle-violated designs.

The analysis of the WT data presented in Table 2 showed that a significant difference in WT was found across the different age groups ($p<.01$). Roughly speaking, the WT decreased as the age of subjects increased, but this relation is not perfect. No significant effect was found for the stimuli

TABLE 2: Mean writing time in seconds for each age group and stimulus.

Stimulus	Group				Mean
	1	2	3	4	
Principle-adhered	6.35	4.53	4.34	3.63	4.73
Principle-violated	7.33	4.22	4.49	3.80	4.98
Mean	6.84	4.38	4.42	3.72	

The analysis of the WP data presented in Table 3 showed that a significant difference was found between the different stimuli ($p<.05$). The WP was heavier when the children copied the principle-violated designs. However, no other significant effect was found.

TABLE 3: Mean writing pressure in gram for each age group and stimulus.

Stimulus	Group				Mean
	1	2	3	4	
Principle-adhered	151	182	176	144	164
Principle-violated	143	199	192	160	174
Mean	147	190	184	152	

7.0 Discussion

The previous results are consistent with Stelmach and Teulings' (1983) finding that RT is slower but WT is unaffected when the subject copies a stimulus with an unexpected pattern. They suggested that the identity of the stimulus to be written is programmed (and, occasionally, reprogrammed) in advance. These results are also consistent with the complexity-dependency hypothesis of Kao et al (1983), which suggests that the more complex the free-hand writing task is, the heavier is WP. Therefore, the principle-violated stimuli can be regarded as unexpected and complex, resulting in a longer RT and heavier WP. Previous research has only studied adult subjects. The findings of our experiments extend these generalizations to show that the results also apply to children.

More errors are found in drawing the principle-violated stimuli and it is suggested that the greater number of errors may be due to the failure of reprogramming the usual drawing principles, before children can draw a given stimulus. Besides that, it may be due to the absence of the extra effort to counter the usual drawing tendency when children execute the task. The former factor is cognitive and the latter one is motor.

In the present study it was found that RT decreased significantly as age increases. This is consistent with the results of other RT studies of children's drawing behaviour (eg, Hulstijn and Mulder, 1986). The finding may be explained from three approaches. Firstly, Luria (1932) suggested that RT is slower in young children because general excitation produced by the stimulus spreads not only to the motor system, but also to other parts of the brain, causing a somewhat diffuse response which interferes with the appropriate response. As children grow older, this diffusion, or general excitation, becomes less likely. He suggested that a functional barrier built up in older children results in a more efficient response to a given stimulus. Secondly, Elliot (1964) suggested that the role of attention as a regulator of RT is essential. He believed that young children are less likely to be paying close attention to the stimulus, and thus are less ready to respond, as contrasted to older children. Finally, Surwillo (1974) suggested that neurological maturation, marked by differences in information processing, produces faster RTs in older children.

The results of the present study also showed that WT is longer in younger children, but it did not decrease in a strictly monotonic fashion. The WT of the children in Group 3 was slightly slower than that of the children in Group 2. The relation between the writing time and the age found in this research is consistent with several previous studies (eg, Meulenbroek and van Galen, 1986) but inconsistent with some other studies (eg, Hulstijn and Mulder, 1986) in which it was found that WT decreased as age increased. Learning to write is a complex process in which the development of cognitive functions and the motor system plays an important role (Thomassen and Teulings, 1983). Recently it has been suggested that the acquisition of the handwriting skill might occur in discontinuous stages (Wann, 1986). Therefore, perhaps a consistent relationship between the writing time and age was not found in the present study because the age interval among the different age groups was too small to contrast the developmental changes. If the interval among the different age groups had been large enough, this consistent relationship might have been obtained. It is a fact that previous studies which have shown this monotonic relation between the writing time and the age have employed different age groups with large age intervals among them, for example, age groups of six-year-olds, ten year olds and adults have been employed (Hulstijn and Mulder, 1986). However, the studies which have not shown this consistent relationship have employed different age groups with small age intervals among them, for example, 1st grade, 2nd grade and 3rd grade students were employed (Meulenbroek and van Galen, 1986). Similarly, the present experiment employed groups of small age intervals, and the consistent relationship was not obtained. It may be that writing time decreases as age increases over a broader age range.

Finally, these findings have some implications for child education. The hesitation in drawing figures or writing script found in children may mean that they indulge in a form of problem-solving, in which case we should not hurry them or disturb them. Furthermore, the fact that children draw or write some characters heavily and others lightly may not mean that the children do not try their best. Perhaps it is the way they respond to different stimuli.

This study found that certain drawing principles of the Chinese are similar to those of the US children, but some of them are different. These differences are attributed to the different scripts that have been learned. Furthermore, the results show that reaction time is longer, writing pressure is heavier but writing time remains unchanged when subjects copy figures which violate these general drawing principles. This is consistent with earlier suggestions by Stelmach and Teulings (1983) on response programming, and Kao et al's (1983) complexity-dependency hypothesis for writing pressure. Given the consistency of these results, it could be concluded that the greater number of errors in drawing the principle-violated stimuli is due to the failure of reprogramming the usual drawing principles and the absence of the extra force to counter the usual drawing tendency.

Chapter 6

Isochrony and accuracy of drawing movements in children: Effects of age and context

Annie Vinter & Pierre Mounoud

The graphic execution of a geometric figure, whether it is simple or complex, involves coordinated participation of perceptual-cognitive mechanisms, devoted to the analysis of the figure to be produced, and perceptual-motor mechanisms, devoted to the planning and adjustment of the movement's parameters as a function of the characteristics of the intended figure. Thus, this motor behaviour — the drawing of a figure — appears appropriate for studying the relationships between perceptual, cognitive and motor aspects of behaviour.

A plethora of perspectives and methodologies can be used to study graphomotor activity. Consider for instance the drawing of a circle. One can be interested in different aspects such as the planning of this activity (eg, asking the subject to draw a unique, discrete circle of a given size) or, by contrast, the maintenance of an already current drawing activity (eg, continuously and repeatedly drawing a circle). This dimension, planning versus maintenance of a current activity, is related to the dimension contrasting the study of goal-aimed movement and the study of movement for itself (ie, at least partially released from constraints linked to the plan of action). Furthermore, whether discrete or continuous, a graphic skill can be performed under contexts that differ in the degree of constraint.

The present chapter reports an exploration of relations between perceptual, cognitive and motor aspects of a graphic skill, performed in a discrete mode and realized within different contexts. Our interest is related to the effects of context on the

Development of Graphic Skills
ISBN 0-12-734940-5

subject's ability to produce sizes and size ratios of a given value (spatial aspects), and on the subject's ability to regulate the movement's velocity as a function of its amplitude (ie the trace length in the case of drawing). The so-called *Isochrony Principle* (Viviani and Terzuolo, 1980, 1983) and its potential sensitivity to context effects constitutes the central focus of this chapter. Furthermore, a developmental perspective is proposed.

1.0 The isochrony principle

A general compensatory mechanism has been demonstrated for the timing of movements and seems to characterize motor acts as different as drawing or handwriting (Viviani and Terzuolo, 1980, 1982, 1983; Viviani and McCollum, 1983), manual pointing (Fitts, 1954), stroking (Michel, 1971) or kicking activity in infants (Thelen and Fisher, 1983). This mechanism, called the Isochrony Principle, has a long history in literature (Binet and Courtier, 1893; Freeman, 1914), and states that the velocity of a movement is proportionally tied to its linear extension (or trajectory's length), so that the execution time is maintained approximately constant. It has been suggested that this principle links velocity to the amplitude of a movement plan. In the case of curvilinear trajectories, however, perfect compensation between velocity and amplitude is never observed, which has been expressed by different laws, such as the One-Third-Power-Law (Viviani and Cenzato, 1985; Lacquaniti et al, 1983, 1984; Sciaky et al, 1987; Schneider, 1987; see also; Wann, 1989; Wann et al, 1988).

Isochrony is observed early in human development, and in very different motor tasks: cutting geometrical figures with scissors (Corbetta, 1989), manual pointing (Hay, 1981), visuo-manual tracking (Viviani and Zanone, 1988). Current developmental data are rather consistent with regard to the hypothesis of an invariant time structure of movement in motor skills (Wann, 1986; Wann and Jones, 1986; Pellizer and Hauert, 1989), and invariance in duration across variations in amplitude of movement (isochrony) may be expected to be present from a very young age. But the nature of the development of this characteristic is at present an open question.

Most experiments in visuo-manual tracking (Zanone, 1987; Pew and Rupp, 1971; Dunham et al, 1985) or experiments based on the coincidence-anticipation paradigm (Bard et al, 1981; Dunham and Reid, 1987) mention a general and gradual improvement in performance with age. In handwriting tasks, a *monotonic* increase in mean writing speed is usually described (Ayres, 1912; Sõvik, 1975; Ziviani, 1984; Rigal, 1976). A similar developmental trend is also shown in drawing tasks with geometric figures (Broderick and Laszlo, 1984, 1987, 1988).

Some measures of motor skill, however, contrast with this picture of motor development as conforming to monotonically increasing performance. A comprehensive set of studies of childrens' pointing by Hay (1978, 1979, 1981, 1984) suggested a *non-monotonic*, U-shaped developmental pattern for some movement's parameters (accuracy for instance) with an initial decline followed by later improvement in performance. Dividing pointing movements of children into three classes, according to kinematic criteria proposed by Brooks et al (1973), Hay (1979) observed a non-monotonic progression, starting with a predominance of fast *ballistic* movements at 5 years, followed by the emergence of *discontinuous ramp* movements (low and constant velocity, long durations), and *step* movements at 7 years, and leading to the appearance of *continuous*, medium speed and single step movements at 9 years. Further support for a significant developmental change at age 7 was derived from analyses of the corrections made by the children in their movements while wearing deviating prisms (Hay, 1981).

Similar discontinuities in motor control development can be found in studies examining lifting movements for objects of different weights (Hauert, 1980; Gachoud et al, 1983), visuo-manual tracking performances (Mounoud et al, 1983, 1985), pointing movements at lateralized targets (Pellizer and Hauert, 1989) as well as in the acquisition of handwriting skill (Wann, 1986, 1987; Meulenbroek and van Galen, 1986, 1988). A general conclusion based on these studies might be that the age at which the decline in performance occurs, as attested by different measures, differs as a function of the complexity of the motor skill.

2.0 Context and age effects in drawing movements

The present chapter describes an analysis of potential context effects on the child's drawing parameters when geometric figures (circles) of different perimeters were to be produced. Consistent developmental milestones have been established for drawing geometric figures, and circles are the first figures children can draw. Many children succeed in these activities by 3 years of age (Arnheim, 1956; Piaget and Inhelder, 1969; Blöte et al, 1987). However, in our studies the drawing situations were more complex. Different sizes of figures were required and biomechanical conditions for drawing changed as a function of the required circle perimeter (eg, a finger movement, wrist movement, arm movement).

Two independent experiments were conducted, and three different experimental contexts were selected: 1) drawing circles of different perimeters in a random order of execution with regard to the size (first experiment: *random* context); 2) drawing circles of different perimeters, presented as a series of circles in an increasing order of size (second experiment, part A: *seriation* context); 3) drawing circles of different perimeters and spatially assembled in such a way that they represented a bear (second experiment, part B: *bear* context).

We chose to study the age range from 5 to 9 years. This was particularly relevant for the seriation context, because within this range, the cognitive ability which underlies the mastering of the seriation operation undergoes well-documented development (Piaget and Inhelder, 1941). Different stages have been described, and success at the closest seriation task of Piaget and Inhelder (seriation of sticks of different lengths) with regard to our own drawing task was achieved at around 8–9 years.

Within this perspective, we suggest that the random context is predominantly *perceptually* loaded, in that it is the least constrained of our experimental tasks and perceptual processes involved in this task can be carried out in a relatively free context. By contrast, the seriation context is *logically* loaded in that the task is logically structured on the basis of the seriation operation. Finally, the bear context could be considered as mainly *spatially* (and cognitively) loaded. In copying the bear, the main problem the child encounters is mastering the spatial relationships the different sub-elements of the figure have with each other. Both perceptual and cognitive determinants are important. As an interdependency between cognitive and motor development has been documented (Hauert, 1980; Gachoud et al 1983; Mounoud, 1986), the differential load of cognitive determinants in our drawing tasks might be manifested by different age effects on movement parameters.

Different working hypotheses may be suggested for context and age effects on drawing movements. In general, we hypothesized non-monotonic development of the relationship between velocity and trace length, but postulated that isochrony might also be affected by the different contexts of drawing. Isochrony we expected should be higher in the random task than in the other ones, as each figure was presented alone, without any systematic size relations with regard to the previous and successive figures. Relations between velocity and amplitude might thus be expected to be facilitated because of the lack of extraneous interference in the estimation of perimeter. Furthermore, we expected accuracy to be worse in the bear task than in the others, because of the effects of overlap between components of different sizes. Finally, we expected the invariance of the size increment over the series of circles (the perimeter progression) to be respected only at around 8 to 9 years in the seriation task, (ie, when children are able to cognitively master the corresponding operation). By contrast, in the random task, we expected this index would be either consistently good over age, or would improve with age, depending on the development of the ability to reproduce sizes in drawing.

2.1 Subjects

Two separate groups of right-handed children were studied for the two experiments. Subjects were drawn from public schools in Geneva. Summary statistics on sex and age range as a function of task are presented in Table 1.

Drawings of 19 other children (9 girls, 10 boys, age range: 5 to 8 years) were eliminated because of too much distorted curvature in the circles produced or particularly inaccurate size reproductions due to the subjects

TABLE 1: Subject sample for each task in terms of sex and age range (years) for each age bracket.

Age group	Task: Seriation and Bear		Random	
	N, Sex	Age range	N, Sex	Age range
5	10f, 12m	4.7—5.3	7f, 4m	4.6—5.3
6	11f, 13m	5.7—6.4	4f, 5m	5.7—6.3
7	10f, 11m	6.7—7.3	6f, 3m	6.7—7.2
8	12f, 20m	7.6—8.3	3f, 7m	7.7—8.4
9	10f, 10m	8.7—9.4	6f, 6m	8.7—9.3
Total	119		51	

choosing to locate the drawing in a space without enough room for the components. We paid particular attention to the problem of inadequate spacing because various studies have revealed that size reproduction in children's drawings may be a function of the space they left free after they had executed a first figure (Silk and Thomas, 1988; Thomas and Tsalini, 1988).

In addition to the children listed in Table 1, a sample of 20 right-handed adults (10 women, 10 men) was added for the seriation task only. The average age was 28 years, ranging from 21 to 42 years. These adults were unaware of the aims of the study and were drawn from the Faculty of Psychology in Geneva.

2.2 Apparatus

A special kind of Edison pen was used in these experiments. This pen, when moving, perforates a sheet of thermic paper at an adjustable frequency. Frequency was selected according to the child's spontaneous rhythm of tracing and ranged from 25 to 50 Hz. This apparatus might be considered rather archaic, but it is very easy to use with children as young as 4 years old. The models given to the subjects are reproduced in Figures 1 (A: seriation task, B: bear task) and 2 (random task).

The circles were drawn in china-ink on an A3 format white sheet of paper. Circles were presented in an increasing order of size and aligned with regard to their bases in the seriation task. In the random task, 5 different models were used and randomly assigned to the subjects in order to avoid eventual systematic effects of neighbouring in the child's perception of the sizes. Respective perimeters of the circles were of 6, 12, 18, 24 and 30 cm in the seriation and random tasks (perimeter progression of 6 cm), and of 3, 6, 12, 24 and 30 cm in the bear task (perimeter progression varying, 3, 6 and 12 cm).

2.3 Procedure

Both experiments (seriation and bear tasks, random task) were based on the same factorial experimental design with two between-subject factors (age, sex), and two within-subject factors (trial, circle size).

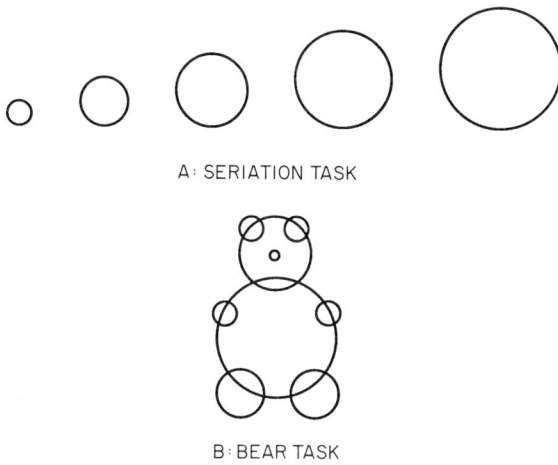

FIGURE1: Model of the seriation task and the bear task.

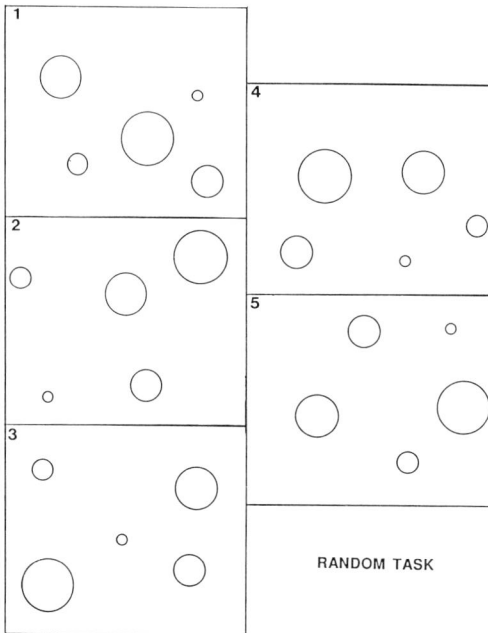

FIGURE 2: Models of the random task (5 different designs).

Each subject was asked to draw the figures on a white sheet of paper of the same format as the model. No starting rule (Kirk, 1985) was imposed (where to initiate the execution of the figure, up or down for instance) and the direction of the drawing movement (clockwise or anticlockwise) was free. Both were noted by the experimenter. The circles, however had to be performed in one single movement, without stopping, under a spontaneous and natural rhythm of drawing. If subjects stopped drawing in the course of the execution of a figure, they were asked to draw it again. Instructions given to the subjects focused attention on the expected accuracy of the size of the circles' reproduction, as well as the regularity of the curvature of the figure. Before starting the experiment, a practice period of several trials was needed to ensure a good understanding of the instructions by the child and to train the subject to produce regular shapes. Instructions were repeated by the experimenter several times during the experiment, in particular with respect to the requested accuracy of the reproduction size.

In the seriation task, the children had the model (Figure 1) in front of them continously, and were asked to reproduce the series of circles in an increasing order of size. Three trials were required, each being performed on a separate sheet. The procedure was identical for the adult sample. Then, the bear model (Figure 1) was introduced to the children, who had to copy it, starting with the circle of their choice. No progression rule (Kirk, 1985) was given with regard to the order of execution of the circles, and the experimenter had to note the sequence choosen by the subject. Two trials were required for the bear task.

In the random task, the child was shown one of the models (see Figure 2) and was asked to attentively observe the range of sizes of the figures he would have to copy. Then, the experimenter indicated the first circle to be drawn, masking the other ones during the copying. Once the figure was complete, the second circle was shown, again masking the non-target ones on both the model and the subject's sheet. This procedure was repeated until the five elements of the series were drawn. No active comparison between the different sizes of either the figures drawn, or the model figures was allowed during the task. Thus, each circle was copied in isolation. Three trials were requested and ten different orders of execution of the series of circles were used, randomly assigned to subjects and trials. Then, a control-seriation identical to that reproduced in Figure 1 was also required, to estimate any discrepancies between the two samples of subjects selected for each experiment.

2.4 Measures

The X and Y coordinates of the points made by the discharges of the Edison pen were digitized by means of a Calcomp 9000 digitizer table (spatial resolution of 0.1 mm). Measures recorded were the trace length (P), time taken (T) and average velocity (P/T) for each circle. (We should point out that the Edison pen presents a major limit for the study of graphomotor activity because of its low sample rate. A consequence of this limit is that it is not possible to compute derivatives such as tangential velocity, acceleration, etc. What is called velocity corresponds to an average speed of execution obtained by directly dividing P by T.) The measures obtained for the circles of identical sizes in the bear task (see Figure 1B) were averaged, when it was established that this procedure did not introduce any bias in the data. Thus, 15 circles for each child were obtained in the seriation and random task (plus 5 circles in the control-seriation task), and 10 in the bear task.

Two analyses were carried out, one concerning isochrony (understood here as a simple principle assessing constancy of execution time), the other being related to the accuracy of reproduction of size.

2.5 Quantifying the accuracy of drawing

The spatial gain index (the ratio of the length of each produced trace to the corresponding length of the trace in the model) was computed. Then, relations between the sizes of the different circles produced within each series were analysed by computing the mean trace length progression (normalized with regard to the model trace length progression), and its coefficient of variation. This progression index corresponds to the mean of the ratios between observed serial trace increment (difference in trace length between two consecutive circles when they are ordered according to size) and model serial increment (the value of which was always 6 in the seriation and random tasks, but which varied in the bear task; 3, 6 or 12).

2.6 Determining the degree of isochrony

A simple expression for isochrony is

$$T = k P^\alpha \tag{1}$$

where the power index α should tend toward 0 for complete isochrony (constancy of time). Considering that $V = P/T$ in our study, Equation (1) can also be expressed as

$$V = k'P^\beta \tag{2}$$

with perfect isochrony implying that the exponent should be 1. A logarithmic regression of the $V-P$ relation allows a precise estimation of the parameters by expressing equation (2) as

$$\log V = k' + \beta \log P \tag{3}$$

The slope β of this logarithmic regression, as well as the coefficient of correlation between the two variables, were individually estimated for each child.

3.0 Results

2355 cases were collected for the seriation task, including the adults' performances and the control-seriation data (38 outliers were then eliminated). The bear task includes 1132 cases (30 missing values, 28 outliers ejected), and the random task includes 801 cases (9 outliers eliminated). Outliers were eliminated on the basis of an inspection of the entire data distribution, without any knowledge of the experimental task and/or age group which they belonged to. Analyses of variance (SPSSX) were carried out for the different dependent variables to examine age and context effects. We report in Table 2 only the significant effects, which are explained in the results section.

TABLE 2: Results of analyses of variance

Analysis	Effect	Statistic	p-level
Isochrony;	Context	$F(2,253) = 40.77$	.001
slope index	Age	$F(4,253) = 4.08$	.003
	Linear trend	$t = -3.08$	.002
	Quadratic trend	$t = 2.55$	.011
Accuracy;	Context by age	$F(8,744) = 2.35$	.017
gain	Context	$F(2,744) = 12.92$	.001
	Age	$F(4,744) = 8.26$	.001
	Linear trend	$t = 4.23$	.001
	Quadratic trend	$t = 3.90$	.001
Accuracy;	Context by age	$F(8,744) = 3.13$	.002
mean trace	Context	$F(2,744) = 60.08$	.001
progression	Age	$F(4,744) = 10.63$	.001
	Quadratic trend	$t = 6.25$	.001
Accuracy;	Context	$F(2,744) = 4.47$	.012
coeff. of variation	Age	$F(4,744) = 22.03$	.001
	Quadratic trend	$t = 4.12$	.001

Before discussing the results, we should point out that no effect for sex on the dependent variables was found. Nevertheless, if the entire set of data was examined, girls appeared to draw faster than boys, whatever the age and task. Data on sex differences for speed are controversial in the literature. Usually, no sex effect is reported for speed of handwriting or drawing (Harris and Rarick, 1959; Smith and Reed, 1959; Meulenbroek and van Galen, 1986; Sciaky et al, 1988), although some studies have revealed faster speeds for girls than for boys (Groff, 1961; Sõvik, 1975; Ziviani, 1984).

3.1 Analysis of size accuracy

The analysis comprised two parts: First, the accuracy of size reproduction was examined; second, the trace length increment

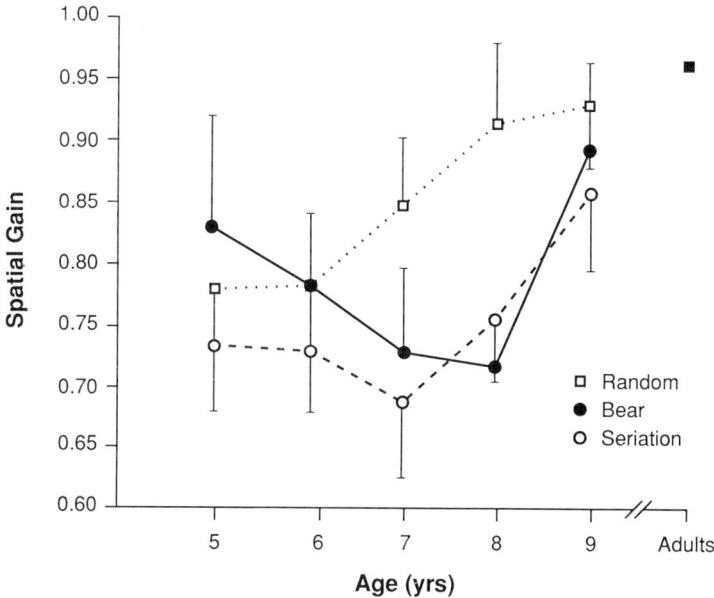

FIGURE 3: Analysis of accuracy: spatial gain (mean and 95% limit of confidence) as a function of age.

over the series was analysed. Figure 3 displays the results for the spatial gain as a function of age and task.

Because the gain index was less than 1, the produced sizes always underestimated those of the models. As expected, the adult value was the highest one, and close to 1 (.96). Figures were significantly more accurate in the random task than in the other ones, which is in line with our hypothesis. The worst performances were recorded in the seriation task, whereas we had expected them to be observed in the bear task. A significant age-by-task interaction should be pointed out: differences between tasks mainly characterized the 7- and 8-year-old children, while they were essentially negligible at 5, 6 and 9 years. A general improvement of accuracy with age was observed, although the quadratic (U-shaped) trend was significant in the seriation and bear tasks; The geometrical gain decreased between 5 and 7 or 8 years, and increased again between 7 or 8 and 9 years.

Mean normalized perimeter progression was computed. This value is equal to 1 when the observed mean progression is identical to that of the model. The coefficient of variation provides information on the regularity of the progression indice over the series. Figure 4 presents the results as a function of age and context (upper: mean trace progression; lower: coefficient of variation).

The perimeter progression varied significantly as a function of context. The highest values occurred in the random task, and the lowest in the seriation task. Although these differences were systematic, they appeared more important with age, as indicated by the significant age-by-context interaction. Again, a clear U-shaped relation was observed (see upper part of Figure 4). Progressions decreased between 5 and 7 or 8 years, and increased again between 7 and 9 years. Similar results were mentioned by Thomas and Tsalini (1988) with size scaling effects in the drawing of a man. In the random and bear tasks, the results were, moreover, better at 9 years than at 5 years.

In agreement with our hypothesis, children succeeded in accurately reproducing sizes in the random task by adequately copying the performed perimeter from the model. Indices such as the spatial gain and the mean perimeter progression were indeed consistently the highest in the random task. But, contrary to our expectation, the bear task seemed to be an intermediate task, which usually led to accurate results close to those obtained in the random task, while the biggest deviation with respect to the model sizes (underestimation) was found in seriation.

Of course, in the random and bear tasks, the good fit between the progression index and the model shown in Figure 4 resulted from the rather accurate size reproduction (see Figure 3). We thus may suspect that the inaccurate performance of children in the seriation task with regard to the value of the mean progression index was partly due to their tendency to keep constant the perimeter increment over the series. If true, a

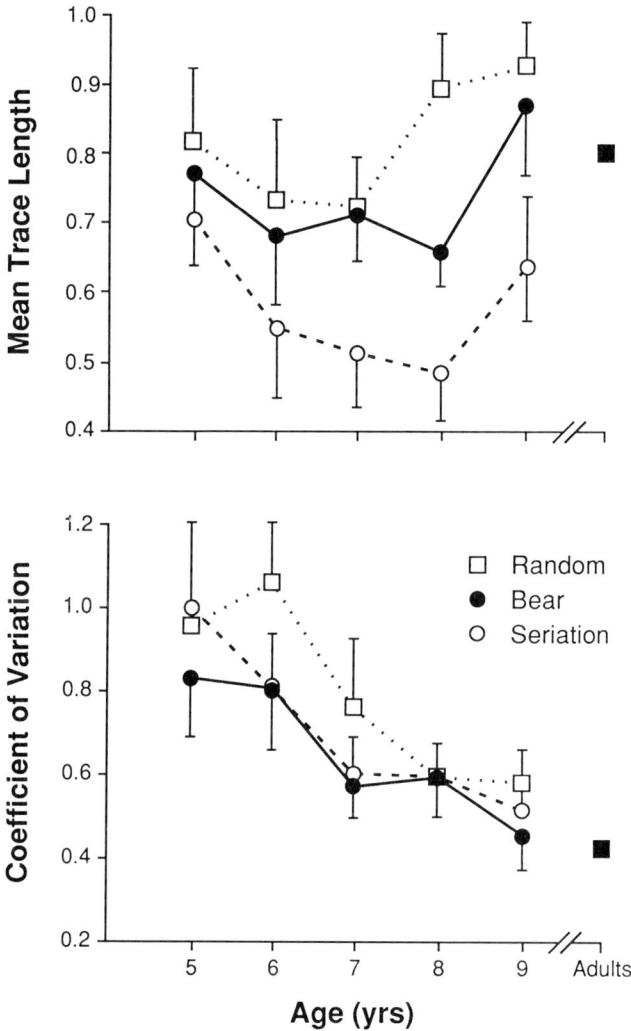

FIGURE 4: Analysis of accuracy: mean trace length progression (upper) and its coefficient of variation (lower) as a function of task and age (mean and the 95% limit of confidence).

dispersion index of the mean progression should reflect the special status of the seriation task with respect to the other conditions. The lower part of Figure 4 displays the coefficients of variation of the perimeter progressions as a function of age and context.

The context effect was significant; a greater variability of the perimeter increment was observed in the random task than in the seriation condition. This gives some support to the idea that, in seriation, the lower values of the different parameters qualifying performance with respect to accuracy resulted from the child's goal to keep constant the trace length increment. Nevertheless, if this hypothesis turns to be correct, then the absence of differences between the seriation and bear tasks is rather unclear. But an order effect may account for this absence of differences (recall that the children drew the bears after they had performed the seriation task three times).

The lower part of Figure 4 also reveals that, whatever the task, the coefficients of variation decreased significantly as a function of age. The dispersion of the perimeter progression was maximal at 5 years, indicating a great irregularity in the perimeter increment over the series, although there was accuracy in the mean. This is not the case at 9 years, at which age the mean index appeared to be at least as accurate as at 5 years (Figure 4 upper), but was associated with regular and stable serial perimeter increments (Figure 4 lower). These results suggest that the seriation task induced a global planning of the perimeter to be performed, possibly based on comparisons between successive pairs of figures, whereas more local planning was elicited by the random and, possibly, the bear tasks. The specific problem encountered by children in the seriation task was to coordinate the two requirements of a regular increment with accurate size reproduction.

3.2 Analysis of isochrony

Because no significant differences in average speed or trace length as a function of age were found between the control-seriation task (performed after the random task) and the main seriation task, the two samples were combined except for analyses in which the trial factor was considered a within-subjects factor.

As expected, a strong covariation between velocity and trace length was observed whatever the experimental task.

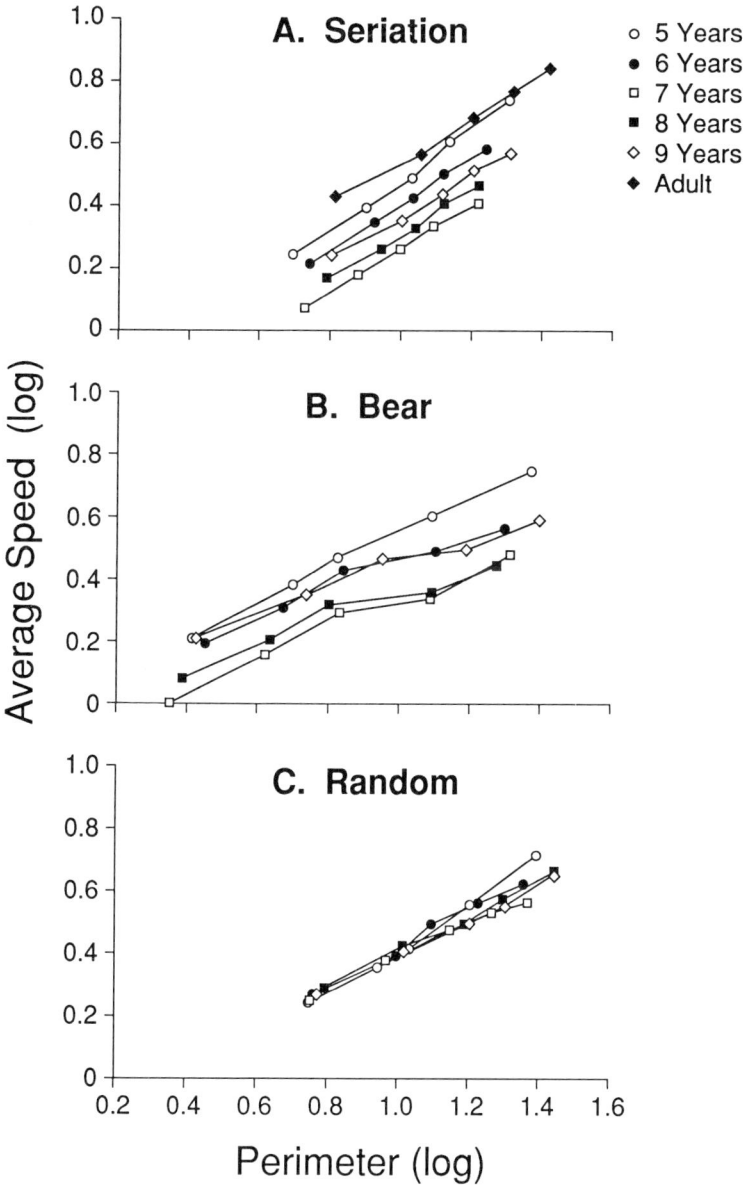

FIGURE 5: Plots of observed velocities and observed perimeters (both axes in log units) as a function of task and age. Note that the model size range is different for the bear task.

Correlations computed on the entire set of data equalled .66 for
the seriation task, .67 for the bear condition, and .68 for the
random task. The observed perimeters and velocities
(logarithmic values) as a function of age and task (seriation;
bear; random) are plotted in Figure 5. This clearly demonstrates
that the age effect was more important in the seriation and bear
tasks than in the random task. Results obtained for the different
ages were completely differentiated in the seriation task, while
overlapping was common in the random task. More specifically,
Figure 5C shows that, in the random task, there was perfect
overlap in relation to the smallest range of sizes (from 0.7 to 1.1
in log). Age differences emerged only with respect to the highest
range of sizes, which may suggest that it is more appropriate to
analyse age effects in the isochrony principle by using large
rather than small figure sizes. The main effect in terms of age
was the decrease of average speed between 5 and 7 years,
followed by a regular increase between 7 and 9 years. Average
velocity in adults was higher than in 9-year-old children, which
suggests a further increase of speed after age 9. This result, the
clear decline of speed at 7 years, is in agreement with Hay's
results.

TABLE 3:   Coefficient of correlation between V and P and percentage of
variance accounted for by regression

Age (years)	r values			r^2x100		
	Seriation	Bear	Random	Seriation	Bear	Random
5	.89	.87	.84	80	75	70
6	.87	.81	.81	76	66	66
7	.87	.79	.81	76	63	65
8	.82	.76	.84	67	58	71
9	.87	.83	.90	76	68	81
Adults	.92	-	-	85	-	-

The parameters of the log-regression between velocity and
perimeter were computed individually for each subject. Figure 6
displays the mean values of the slope, and Table 3 lists the
coefficients of correlation, as well the percentage of the variance

explained by each regression ($r^2 \times 100$). The latter may be considered as a measure of the statistical reliability of the slope estimates.

Whatever the age, the correlations were rather high (from .77 to .90), which suggests some general global influence linking velocity and perimeter. The r^2 values show that at least 58% of the variation of velocity was explained by the variation of perimeter (or vice versa), and 85% at maximum for our data. There was no significant effect to be reported with the correlations. Turning to the slope of the function relating velocity and perimeter, it will be recalled that a slope value of 1 is expected for a complete isochrony. Mean slope values ranged from .41 to .80 in children and they strongly distinguished between the different experimental tasks. They were significantly higher in the seriation task than in the two other tasks, and higher in the random task than in the bear task.

Dynamic compensation between speed and trace length was thus strongly affected by the context within which the drawings

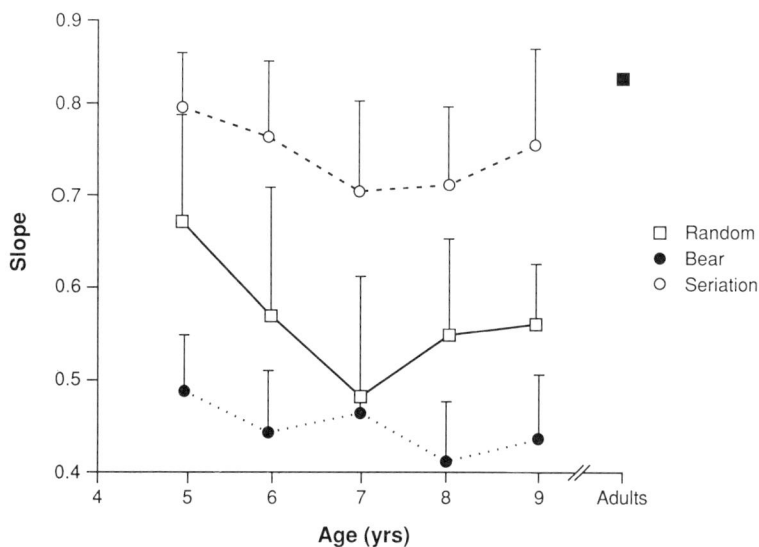

FIGURE 6: Analysis of isochrony: slope of the velocity-perimeter regression (mean and the 95% confidence interval) as a function of task and age.

were performed, and the results appear rather counter-intuitive: the velocity-trace length covariation was optimal, ie, tended towards complete isochrony (slope = 1), when a strong constraint was imposed on the regularity of the trace length increment, as in the case of the seriation task. It might have been more intuitive to expect a good covariation in the random task, where the velocity-trace length compensation was free of any supplementary constraint. Furthermore, speed-perimeter regulations were considerably disorganized in a classical drawing task, such as that of a bear drawing. We will further elaborate on this context effect within a more critical perspective.

A significant age effect for the slope values was also evident where the distribution tended toward a U-shaped function (the quadratic trend was significant). Slopes decreased between 5 and 7—8 years, and increased again between 7—8 and 9 years. Interestingly, isochrony seemed to be higher at 5 years than at 9 years whatever the task, such that data from the adult sample did not differ from those obtained at 5 years. These results related to age support our hypothesis of a non-monotonic evolution of isochrony, and are in line with other developmental data related to skill acquisition.

4.0 Discussion

The greater isochrony of movements in the seriation rather than the random task was quite unexpected. Different hypotheses may account for this result. One is based on a methodological and economic argument. The order in which the circles were drawn in our tasks was, by necessity, different; the smallest one for the seriation, any size for the random task, and systematically one of the two biggest (head or trunk) for the bear task. We observed that drawing increasingly larger circles (seriation) was the most favorable condition for observing isochrony, whereas drawing increasingly smaller figures (the bear task) was the least favorable. When a series of circles is to be drawn, it is possible that the first figure would be drawn with maximally controlled movement, involving a lower velocity than would be spontaneously selected for tracing a figure of that given size. Underestimating the velocity for a small size (seriation) might be a favorable condition for isochrony, because velocities will necessarily increase afterwards both because of the increasing size and a weaker control of movement. By contrast, underestimating the velocity for a big size (bear) might have the reverse effect on isochrony. From this line of reasoning, the random task would constitute the more appropriate context for measuring isochrony, and the context effect we reported here would mainly be due to an anchoring effect on the first executed figure.

Asking the subject to draw a series in decreasing order of size would be an important test of this hypothesis and was done in a pilot study (Mounoud et al, 1985). However, the results reported there do not lend support to our present methodological argument. Isochrony was also high in that drawing context, and a developmental trend similar to the one we observed in the present study was reported. Thus, a more substantial hypothesis may be suggested. We may argue that the seriation context constrains the subject to globally planning movement over the entire series. The subject's goal is seen not as the execution of a particular movement size, but as the execution of a particular size increment which does not change through the series. A corresponding velocity increment would be associated with the selected amplitude increment, and would remain approximately unchanged over the series. A good covariation between perimeter and velocity would result from such global planning. The seriation task would be a facilitating context for isochrony but the random task would be neutral. The bear task might appear to be a non-facilitatory task because of the predominance of local size differences.

Our results show that if isochrony characterizes movement from an early age, it undergoes non-monotonic development. This was clear in both the random and the seriation task, where a decrease between 5 and 7 years and then an increase in performance was observed. Isochrony surely constitutes a very basic property of human motor organization; however, it cannot be conceived of as an automatic compensatory mechanism. The kind of development that it undergoes during childhood shows that determinants of a higher order intervene in this process. The explanations offered currently to account for this discontinuity in motor skill acquisition are all interesting, but, in our opinion, none may be sufficient.

Hay (1981) suggested that the decline in performance at around age 7 was mainly due to the use of visual and kinaesthetic feedback processes to calibrate movement. Consistent behavioural evidence lends support to this hypothesis (see, for instance, Corbetta, 1989, for a similar finding in a bimanual coordination task), but it is also known that infants go through a similar developmental progression for reaching movements. They strongly rely on visual feedback processes between 4 and 5 months of age, and again between 7 and 10 months (Bushnell, 1985; von Hofsten, 1980; Mounoud, 1983; Lasky, 1977; McDonnell and Abraham, 1981; Vinter, 1990). If the use of visual feedback to calibrate movement inevitably involves a decline in performance, and thus is non-monotonic in development, what must be explained is why such phases are recurrent in development. Therefore the question remains: why does movement need to be visually calibrated several times during development? And why do the non-monotonic periods always occur after a phase of competence in which movement is correctly pre-programmed?

Wann (1986) stated that a non-monotonic trend in handwriting acquisition may be due to the fact that at a certain time in the acquisition process, writing pressure (on the pen) may be responsible for the dysfluency of stroke production. Writing pressure would be higher at a certain time of development because, in learning to write, the child has to perform smaller and more continuous strokes, involving the more distal parts of hand and finger muscles. This factor may be important, but it is strictly linked to writing skill. However, a non-monotonic trend seems to characterize many motor skill acquisition processes, with rather conclusive evidence for a critical period at around 7 years.

Meulenbroek and van Galen (1988) suggested that the decline in performance observed in handwriting with respect to some parameters (number of velocity inversions) may occur because children at this age try to produce more accurate shapes of the graphemes. We did not observe more accurate size reproduction at 7 years, but nevertheless reported greater regularity for the spatial aspects of drawing movements at this age than earlier. The implicit hypothesis of Meulenbroek and van Galen is that decline at one level benefits progress at another level. A non-monotonic trend would emerge as long as higher control is put on some aspects of movement without the capacity to integrate or coordinate these specific aspects with the other. From this perspective, a fundamental determinant of discontinuity might be searched in the manner that behaviour (or movement) is segmented. The segmentation problem is certainly one of the important questions in developmental psychology (see Mounoud, 1986; Vinter, 1988), but it still remains unclear why behaviour should undergo a segmentation process several times in development.

Mounoud (1981) stated that different coding systems appear during development at defined ages (the conceptual coding system appearing at around age 2), implying a repetitive process of knowledge construction. Motor skills would not escape this recurrent re-building process. Therefore, during childhood, conceptual factors transform characteristics of the perceptual-motor coordinations that already exist or that are established during this time. Thus, behaviour is always under the control of at least two organizations that depend on the coding system upon which they are based. Although appealing, this model does have an important shortcoming in regard to the discontinuity problem, because it does not take into consideration the role that the level of complexity of motor skills can play in the appearance of these non-monotonic periods.

How can we account for our results with this latter perspective? The performance of the 5-year-old children, which seems optimal with regard to isochrony, may be controlled by the previous perceptuo-motor behavioural organization, and not yet be affected by the re-building process that characterizes developing conceptual organization. When children become sensitive to the logical structure of a seriation task, with respect to the property of length, (which requires a primitive understanding of transitivity and occurs at around 6 years according to Piaget and Inhelder, 1941), a temporary disorganization between temporal and spatial aspects of movement may result. Seven-year-old children would be completely focused on the necessity of producing a regular trace length increment, adopting in consequence a stronger control of movement, with a strategy of constant velocity. Visual feedback is strictly needed at that time. Then, between 8 and 9 years, movement can be released from this control, and children can focus on accuracy and learn to coordinate absolute with relative size reproduction. At that point, movement can again manifest one of its natural and spontaneous characteristics (isochrony).

In conclusion, beyond the developmental aspect, our study suggests that context plays an important role in the assessment of drawing skill, although this role may interact with age. Detailed task analysis appears indispensable for such an assessment, and may constitute a fruitful direction of research for the understanding of motor skill acquisition.

IV: Individual differences: The development of style

In studying differences in handwriting as a function of factors such as task or age, an investigator is likely to minimiZe any differences in handwriting that may exist between children within any one of the groups in the experimental design. This might be a matter of choosing measures that are insensitive to differences between individuals or the investigator may employ selection procedures designed to maximiZe the homogeneity of each group in the experiment. None the less, individual differences are the basis for distinctive styles of handwriting that, for example, allows us to recogniZe the handwriting of particular individuals. Such differences are the focus of this section.

One very potent influence on handwriting style is whether an individual writes with the left or the right hand and the first chapter in this section tackles a topic of much debate in the area of left-handed writing; namely, the purportedly inferior handwriting posture of the left-hander. Athenes and Guiard *(Is the inverted handwriting posture really so bad for left-handers?)* argue that some common assumptions concerning left-handed posture may be unfounded. In particular they suggest that the inverted posture is a reasonable solution to the constraints imposed on a left-handed writer learning a script system designed for right-handers.

Sassoon *(The effect of teachers' personal handwriting on their reproduction of school handwriting models)* develops an argument that may be seen as a challenge to those concerned with the teaching of handwriting. She suggests that the personal script of each teacher tends to distort the letterforms of the officially adopted model in the curriculum so that children evidence features in their handwriting that are an amalgam of the two. It may thus be questioned whether there has been sufficient recognition of this fact in the development of model letterforms for handwriting instruction.

An activity in which much capital is made of individual differences in handwriting is graphology, in which pronouncements about an individual's personality are made on the basis of a detailed examination of handwriting features. The question of whether handwriting style does afford a reliable index of personality is still an area of scientific debate. However, clearly, individual style does emerge from the uniformity of the taught school model. Wing, Watts and Sharma *(Developmental dynamics of handwriting: Appraising the relation between handwriting and personality)* provide a statistically based demonstration that personality may play a role in the emergent individuality of letterforms in schoolchildren.

Chapter 7

Is the inverted handwriting posture really so bad for left-handers?

Sylvie Athenes & Yves Guiard

Writing with the left hand is now accepted in school. Nevertheless, there are no recommendations founded on scientific knowledge about the best posture to adopt. By and large, educators advise against two major features observable in left-handed writing. The first is the extreme slanting of the page in a clockwise direction, which leads to vertical writing. The second feature concerns the hook shape depicted by the limb holding the writing implement, characteristic of the so-called inverted handwriting posture (see Figure 1, bottom drawing). The arguments put forward against these practices, however, remain rather vague (Ajuriaguerra et al, 1961; Clark, 1957; Zazzo, 1962). In practice, most of the time, the teacher lets the child choose what she thinks is best for herself, merely intervening to avoid postures that look too distorted.

Clearly, the reference for what is considered normal has been the posture adopted by right-handers; the most normal-looking posture for the left-hander, as seen by right-handers, is that mirroring their own (see Figure 1, top drawing). This is a puzzling fact since many educators would agree that "writing with the left hand is not the same as writing with the right hand with only a change of hand" (Clark, 1957, p.85). Why then are left-handers not taught to adopt a posture that would address the specific requirements of left-handed writing ?

1.0 Movements in left-handed writing

Contrary to other everyday tasks such as knitting or sewing, handwriting cannot be achieved through the simple trick of mirroring movements of right-handers. Such a strategy, obviously, would lead to mirror writing. The left-handed child has to learn to copy the product of the task without copying the movements producing it. In all likelihood, it is not enough to simply restore the correct aspect of the letters while nevertheless mirroring the posture of right-handers. In fact, one is left with several perceptual and mechanical problems. It is generally admitted, however, that these inconveniences are minor and hardly avoidable. We would like to suggest that these problems might not be that minor and that they drive the left-handers to seek postural solutions to the writing problem other than those judged appropriate by educators.

NON-INVERTED HAND POSTURE

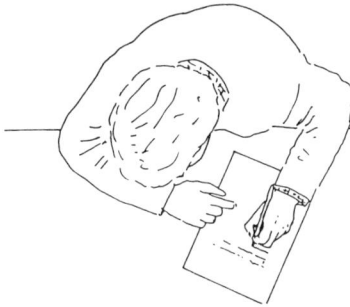

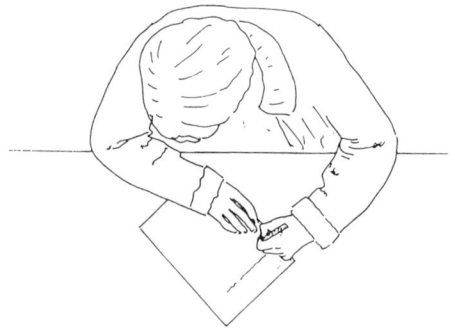

INVERTED HAND POSTURE

FIGURE 1: *The two most frequently observed handwriting postures in left-handers.*

One notable problem encountered by left-handed writers is the lack of visual feedback during the writing. The left hand holding the pen tends to hide what has just been written, thereby inducing very specific spelling mistakes such as duplication or omission of letters (Ure, 1969). In order to avoid this problem, it is possible to slant the page markedly to the right (clockwise), although this leads to the vertical writing often frowned upon.

Another problem is attached to the position of the right, non-writing hand, which typically rests on the right side of the sheet of paper. As a consequence the pen is then pushed towards the point where the page is held down (rather than drawn away). Should the paper be thin, it will tend to crumple or crease.

As first suggested by Guiard and Millerat (1984), the inverted handwriting posture might well be an attempt to get around these difficulties. The writing hand, being placed above the line in progress, does not prevent the visual feedback. It also enables the right hand to rest on the left side of the sheet of paper. This perspective is a new one since all the studies pertaining to the inverted handwriting posture have been carried out in order to find correlations with neuropsychological parameters such as cerebral laterality (Gregory and Paul, 1980), reading ability (Bryson and McDonald, 1984) and visuomotor organization (Smith and Moscovitch, 1979). In view of a rather unconvincing link with pathology and neuropsychological factors, we are left with a behaviour which might be an adaptative solution to the writing problems encountered by left-handers.

The purpose of our study was, therefore, to explore the left-handed handwriting posture from a more ecological perspective. Handwriting is primarily a tool and as such, it has to follow certain rules: it is of the utmost importance that one can read what one has just written and, in most cases (for example in taking notes) one has to be fast. This last characteristic *writing speed* is the criterion we chose to estimate the adequacy of the different postures under study to the task of writing.

2.0 Adult writing posture

We first summarize a study of handwriting posture in left- and right-handed adults. Then, in a later section, we consider the evolution of the left-handed writing posture in schoolchildren.

2.1 Subjects

All the subjects were adults, aged 19 to 51. We tested a group of right-handers ($N=16$) and a group of left-handers ($N=32$). Left-handed subjects were further divided into two groups with respect to their handwriting posture (i.e. inverted versus non-inverted as defined below).

2.2 Procedure

Subjects wrote a standard sentence 12 times. They were photographed from above.

2.3 Measures

Left-handed posture was classified according to the criterion of Guiard and Millerat (1984), who characterized the handwriting posture quantitatively in terms of the slant of the writing forearm relative to the page. We measured the angle between the forearm and the vertical edges of the sheet of paper. We call this angle the relative slant of the forearm. A value of 0 deg for this slant means that the forearm is oriented vertically to the page; a value of 90 deg means that the forearm is perpendicular to the edge of reference, that is, horizontal to the page (see Figure 2).

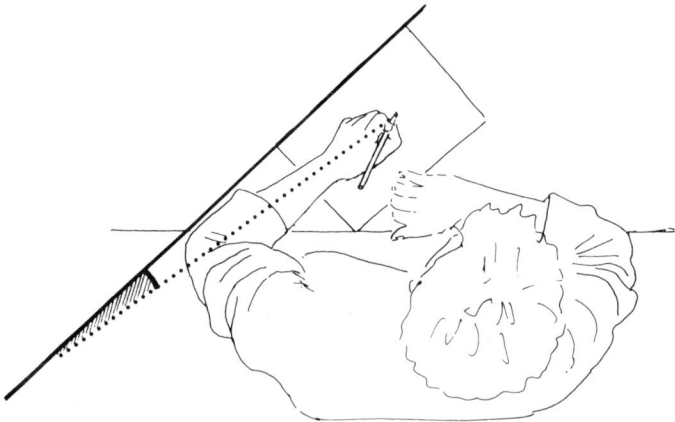

FIGURE 2: Forearm slant relative to the vertical edges of the sheet of paper; in this illustration, the relative slant (angle R) is 9 deg.

Writing speed was defined in terms of the time needed to complete a standard sentence. This time was, in fact, the mean of twelve consecutive trials of the same sentence. For each group; left-handed inverters, left-handed non-inverters and right-handers, we calculated the correlation between the time needed to write the standard sentence and the relative slant of the forearm.

3.0 Results

Figure 3 shows the distribution of the relative slant of the forearm for left-handers. This distribution is clearly bimodal, with one mode around 0 deg corresponding to the non-inverted handwriting posture and the other mode around 90 deg corresponding to the inverted handwriting posture.

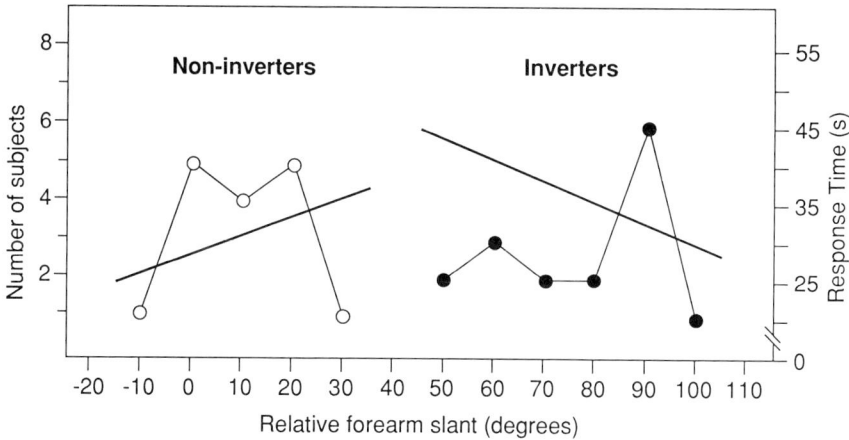

FIGURE 3: Correlation between the relative forearm slant and writing speed for inverting and non-inverting left-handers.

Among right-handers, we did not find a significant correlation ($r=.14$; $p>.10$): the speed of writing did not seem to depend upon their handwriting posture, as defined by the relative forearm slant on the page. For left-handers on the contrary, we observed a significant positive correlation for non-inverters ($r=.59$; $p<.05$) and a significant negative correlation for inverters ($r=-.58$; $p<.05$). This means that non-inverters tended to write faster when their forearm was resting more vertically on the page, whereas inverters tended to write faster when their forearm was resting more horizontally on the page (Figure 3).

While writing speed does not depend on handwriting position for right-handers, it apparently does for left-handers. As far as writing speed is concerned, the best results are observed where the values of the relative slant are either minimum or maximum. In other words, whether the writer is an inverter or a non-inverter seems to be less important than his/her being definitely one or the other. Slower writers are found in the middle of the spectrum where the relative slant of the writing forearm is oriented diagonally in the page.

4.0 Evolution of left-handed postures

Clearly, in view of the results obtained with adults, further questions can be asked about the origin of the observed bimodal distribution and its correlation with writing speed: Do these two very characteristic handwriting postures diverge gradually from a single posture or are children inverters or non-inverters from the beginning? If the latter, what about children whose handwriting posture falls between the extremes?

Previous studies (Coren and Porac, 1979; Peters and Pedersen, 1978; Bryson and McDonald, 1984) have attempted to describe the distribution of inverted handwriting postures among a population of left-handed schoolchildren. However, most of these studies were unsatisfactory. Firstly, the children were dichotomized into inverters and non-inverters, without confirming whether the distribution was in fact bimodal. Secondly, the results rested on subjective assessment, where the subject or an observer assessed the posture according to a model. In the Coren and Porac (1979) study, the subjects themselves assessed their posture according to a model. In the Peters and Pedersen (1978) study, the teacher estimated the handwriting posture of the pupils also on the basis of a drawn model. In the Bryson and McDonald (1984) study, neither the pupils, nor the teacher had to judge the posture, but the experimenters categorized the handwriting posture according to two criteria that would be very hard to quantify: the position of the writing hand and the orientation of the pen towards the top versus the bottom of the page.

To describe the development of handwriting postures, we have chosen the criterion we had previously used with adults, the relative slant of the forearm. Knowing that the older the children the larger the incidence of inverters (Peters and Pedersen, 1978), it seemed reasonable to anticipate that the shape of the distribution would change with the age of the children.

We decided to use right-handers as a control group for the following reason. We know that the handwriting posture of right-handed adults is quite stereotyped, whereas left-handers show a remarkable between-subject variability. Furthermore, we assumed that the stereotyped handwriting posture of right-handers reflects the fact that it is well-suited for its purpose, whereas the variability of left-handers reflects the lack of precise instructions as to an adequate posture, resulting in a search by the individual for a solution. Therefore, it was interesting to compare the evolution (if any) of the variability of the two groups (right-handers and left-handers) as they learn to write.

4.1 Subjects

For this study, 273 children belonging to 7 primary schools were selected according to the following procedure: all the left-handed children of each school were recruited for the experiment, and for each left-hander the teachers were asked to identify a right-hander (matched on age, sex and school performance).

4.2 Procedure

Each child was required to write a standard sentence and a photograph was taken as the tip of the pen reached a target spot on the page (middle of the upper half of the page).

4.3 Measures

In addition to assessing the relative slant of the forearm already described in our study on adults, we determined the slant of the page on the table relative to a vertical defined by the table edge. (A previous study by Guiard and Millerat (1984) had shown that inverters slant the page towards the left whereas non-inverters slant the page towards the right.) Thirdly, we measured the absolute slant of the forearm on the table relative to the table edge. These three variables allowed us to describe the posture without having to use the subjective estimates of an observer.

5.0 Results

Figures 4 and 5 depict the three measures of slant observed in
non-inverters and inverters. Knowing the distribution of the
relative slant of the writing forearm on the page in adults and
having some expectations about its evolution in children, we felt
that observing the slant of the page and the absolute slant of the
forearm would help us understand the mechanism behind this
change. Indeed, either rotating the page on the table, or
changing the absolute slant of the forearm, would result in
changes in the relative forearm slant.

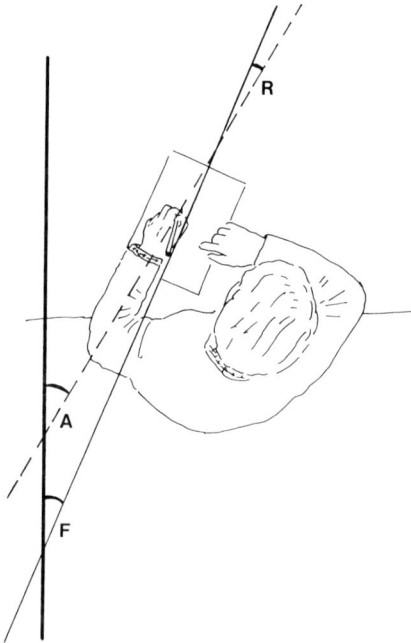

FIGURE 4: Slant of the sheet of paper on the table, absolute and relative
forearm slants for non-inverters (A (absolute forearm slant) = 31 deg; F
(slant of the sheet of paper) = 24 deg; R (relative forearm slant) = 31 deg−24
deg= 7 deg

5.1 Changes in right-handed posture

For right-handers, we observed no significant differences in
posture between boys and girls, so we pooled their results. There

was no significant evolution of the absolute forearm slant between the first class and the last class in primary school; $F(4,125)=1.56$, $p>.05$. In contrast, we observed a significant increase of the slant of the page on the table from about 0 deg to about 10 deg; $F(4,124)=4.55$, $p<.01$. This implied a significant decrease of the relative slant of the forearm on the page from about 30 deg to about 20 deg; $F(4,125)=5.59$, $p<.001$.

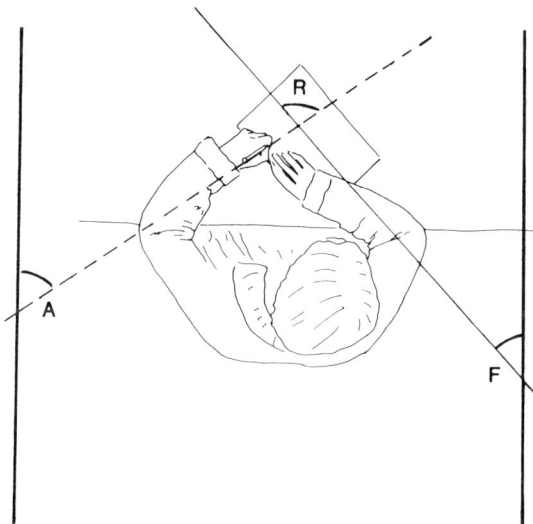

FIGURE 5: Slant of the sheet of paper on the table, absolute and relative forearm slants for inverters (A (absolute forearm slant) = 55 deg; F (slant of the sheet of paper) = −42 deg; R(relative forearm slant) = 55 deg−(−42 deg = 97 deg).

Male and female right-handers, who presented a similar evolution of their handwriting position, are pooled in Figure 6. The position of their writing forearm on the table is very stable from the very first class onwards. In contrast, the page is set very straight on the table when the right-handed children first learn to write, then towards the end of primary school right-handers rotate the page in the anti-clockwise direction, giving it the slant to the left that we observed in the adults. As a consequence, the forearm becomes parallel to the vertical edge of the page, resulting in the 0 deg relative slant we also observed in adults.

5.2 Changes in left-handed posture

Because our results for left-handers show a significant difference between boys and girls we shall present their results separately.

Right-handers

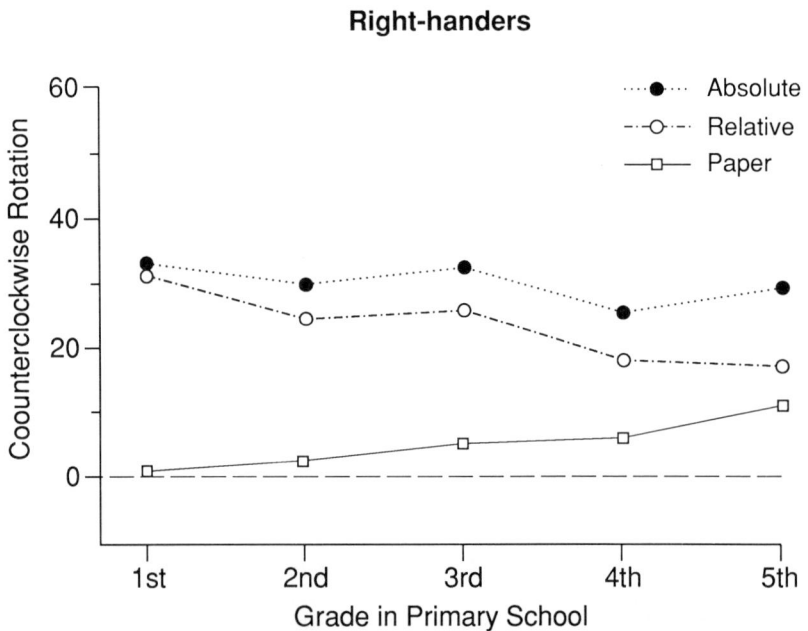

FIGURE 6: Absolute forearm slant, relative forearm slant and slant of the sheet of paper for right-handers. in primary school grades.

Left-handed girls showed no significant evolution of the absolute forearm slant, a finding reminiscent of what we observed with right-handed children. Nevertheless, the slant was larger for left-handed girls (mean = 41.2 deg) than for right-handers (mean = 31.1 deg). The statistical analysis showed no significant change, either for the slant of the page, or for the relative slant of the forearm. However, the distribution of the relative slant of the forearm in each class suggests that it tends towards a dichotomy in the last classes. In other words, it is only towards the end of the primary school that the left-handed girls seem to move towards the handwriting posture of the adults.

Figure 7 shows the results for left-handed girls. In the first class, left-handed girls have a standardized handwriting posture with the page straight on the table, and about 45 deg clockwise rotation of the forearm on the table. In the last class, two postures seem to be emerging, due primarily to the slant of the page on the table (the absolute slant of the forearm on the table being only marginally variable). The page is either slanted towards the right and therefore the relative forearm slant moves towards the vertical axis of the page (0 deg), or the page is slightly slanted towards the left (5 deg) and the relative forearm slant moves towards the horizontal axis of the page (90 deg).

Among left-handed boys (see Figure 8), we found no statistically

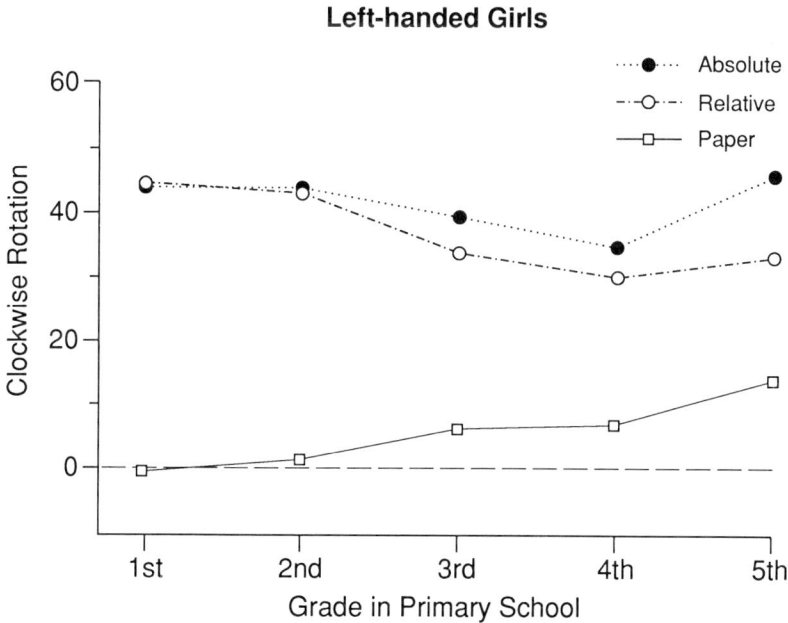

FIGURE 7: Absolute forearm slant, relative forearm slant and slant of the sheet of paper with respect to primary school grade for left-handed girls.

significant changes of handwriting posture during primary school. Unlike left-handed girls, the distribution of the relative forearm slant and the distribution of the page slant did not tend towards a dichotomy: from the first to the last class, the page was kept approximately vertical on the table, with the relative forearm slant (51.2 deg on average) being therefore virtually identical to the absolute forearm slant (52.5 deg on the average). In other words, the forearm of left-handed boys was kept in a diagonal orientation relative to the page throughout the primary school.

Left-handed Boys

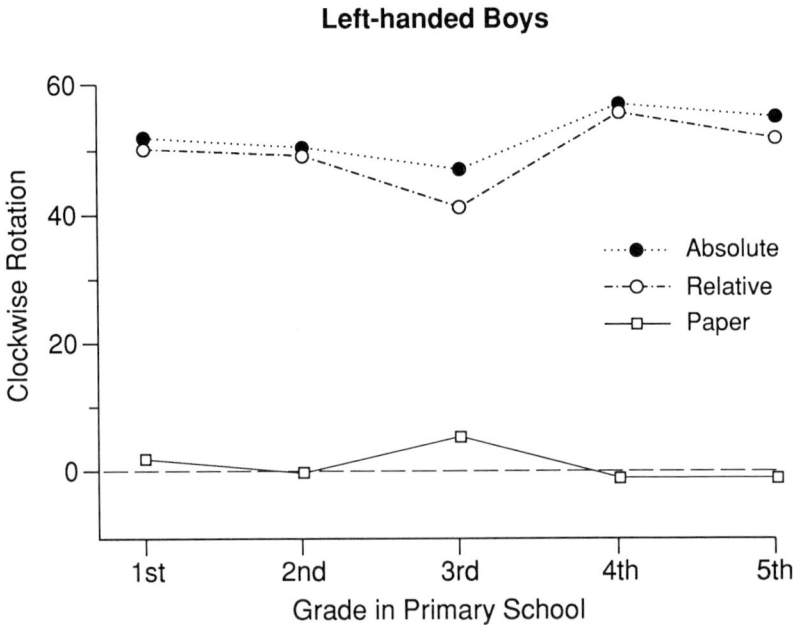

FIGURE 8: *Absolute forearm slant, relative forearm slant and slant of the sheet of paper with respect to primary school grade for left-handed boys.*

6.0 Conclusions

In summary, in the left-handers the relative forearm slant is centred around 45 deg, which is the intermediate value between the two postures characteristically observed among the adults (0 deg for non-inverters and 90 deg for inverters). However, the data collected with left-handed girls suggested the emergence of an inverter/non-inverter dichotomy in the last class. Therefore, we would like to conclude that, for the left-handers, the transition between the standard starting posture observed in primary school children and the two postures observed in adults takes place after primary school for boys, whereas for girls it is already emerging during the last class of the primary school.

Interestingly, the absolute slant of the forearm has a different value according to the group under observation (mean for the right-handers = 30.9 deg; mean for the left-handed girls = 41.2 deg; mean for the left-handed boys = 52.5 deg). This variable is also the only variable which does not change significantly with age and learning of handwriting; the evolution observed for the relative forearm slant is solely due to the rotation of the page which tends towards the slant present in the adults.

We have not observed in children the typical handwriting postures of the adults. It seems therefore that the relevant change must take place after primary school. The posture adopted by the children is intermediate between the two postures observed in adults. This intermediate posture was still to be seen in a small number of the adults we tested and those were scoring poorly for writing speed. Thus, it seems that choosing either the inverted or the non-inverted handwriting posture is less crucial than the very act of choosing a definite posture.

In conclusion, we would like to note that our results did not reveal any sort of impairment linked to the adoption of the inverted handwriting posture. In fact, the handwriting performance of inverters was just as good as that of non-inverters, thus justifying the freedom given to the child to choose one or the other of the two postures.

Chapter 8

The effect of teachers' personal handwriting on their reproduction of school handwriting models

Rosemary Sassoon

In Great Britain there is no nationally prescribed handwriting model. Schools are free to choose whatever letterform model and method of teaching handwriting they wish. When teachers change jobs they may have to learn to demonstrate a completely different handwriting model, both on the blackboard and on paper. This chapter describes two studies concerned with teachers' representation of their school handwriting model. It also compares certain details of these representations with the same details as they appear in the teachers' personal handwriting.

In the last decade there have been a number of studies of handwriting models used in British schools. Rubin and Henderson (1982) carried out a questionnaire survey to ascertain which models are most frequently used in schools in certain localities. Brown (1985), in a study of schools in Birmingham, reported that teachers supplement published workbooks with material of their own. She also noted the variety of the writing of children within groups being taught the same system. Sassoon (1988) documented this latter aspect in greater detail, looking at the effects of different models and teaching methods on how children learn to write. This work showed that, although schools may claim to be using a certain handwriting model or scheme, the teachers' reproduction of the model varied considerably, sometimes in essential elements of models. In some cases the whole purpose of the model was negated.

Development of Graphic Skills
ISBN 0-12-734940-5

Personal handwriting is seldom consistent in all elements. A scheme for classifying selected sets of handwritten letters was outlined in Eldridge et al (1983). This classification presented a measure for summarizing the variation within personal handwriting as well as between two writers. Wing et al (1983) analysed the variation in letterforms depending on their position in the word, so these studies already detail certain variations in adult cursive handwriting. In this chapter, directed toward educational issues, I take relevant variation and inconsistency to be more concerned with (separate) letters occurring in copybook models, with teachers' representations of such models, with their personal handwriting and with their young pupil's handwriting.

In theory it might be possible to chart all instances of inconsistency between all these scripts occurring in any element and, for example, to measure exactly variations in letter slant, ascender or descender height, or angle of each upstroke. However, the present chapter describes two field studies that were not designed to use any sophisticated measuring equipment. It is part of a body of work that seeks to find simple techniques of analysing letters that may enable teachers and other practitioners in the field of handwriting to use previously written examples for survey and research purposes, and to come to an understanding of the complexity and variability of the written trace.   The analysis of letterforms in this study is confined to the level necessary to illuminate specific points about those elements where teachers deviate when reproducing a handwriting model and where these deviations might be connected with their personal handwriting.

1.0 Study 1: Teachers' handwriting

Study 1 was part of a larger investigation that looked in detail at the teaching of handwriting in six schools in the south east of England, reported in Sassoon (1988). The details of the handwriting models used in each school were known (see Figure 1 for an example). It was therefore possible to make comparisons between elements of the teachers' personal letters and the way they reproduced the school model in relation to the same elements of the supposedly taught model. It was also

possible to look at specific deviations from the model on the part
of some of the teachers and how these deviations affected some of
their pupils.

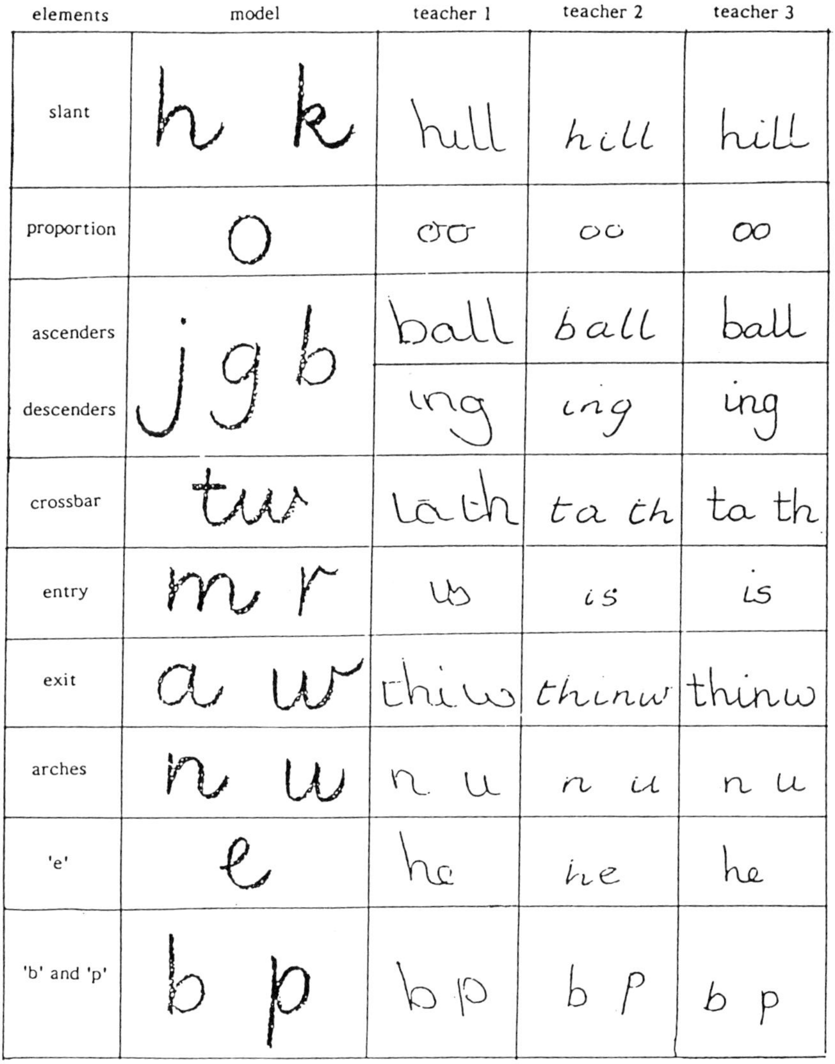

elements	model		teacher 1	teacher 2	teacher 3
slant	h	k	hull	h i ll	hill
proportion	o		oo	oo	oo
ascenders		b	ball	b all	ball
descenders	j g		ing	ing	ing
crossbar	tur		lach	ta ch	ta th
entry	m r		us	i s	is
exit	a w		chius	thinw	thinw
arches	n u		n u	n u	n u
'e'	e		he	he	he
'b' and 'p'	b p		b p	b P	b p

*FIGURE 1: One of the models, a modification of Marion Richardson's letters,
separated into elements that would allow comparison between teachers'
personal handwriting and their reproduction of the school model.*

1.1 Method

Six schools were chosen because they had used, over a period of years, a particular model or method. In each school three teachers were tested; the teacher responsible for the handwriting policy of the school (who in 3 out of the 6 schools was the head teacher), and the two teachers directly responsible for the classes of 7- and 9-year-old pupils who also took part in this investigation. Each teacher was interviewed separately. They were asked to write out the same sentences as their pupils, first in their personal handwriting and then in the model they would use in the classroom.

This allowed two comparisons to be made:
1 Between each school's model and the teacher's representation of it.
2 Between the representation of the model and each teacher's personal handwriting.

The purpose of these comparisons was to see whether a personal deviation, linked to the personal handwriting, can affect how a teacher represents the school model. In this abbreviated description, only one element, the slant of the teachers' handwriting, is reported. For complete details the reader should refer to Sassoon (1988).

2.0 Results

Overall it was found that the slant of the teachers' reproduction of the model was in every case the same as that of their personal handwriting. Of the 18 possible teachers, one was omitted as she had just joined her school and was still teaching upright print script instead of the forward slanting italic model. In the school where the emphasis was more on method than model (based on Sassoon, 1983) the slant of the taught letters corresponded with the teachers' personal handwriting, one forward, one upright and one variable. The formal models in the other five schools all had a slight forward slant. Of the personal handwriting and the reproduction of the model by the fourteen remaining teachers: seven slanted forward and seven did not. Of these, five teachers had an upright handwriting and two showed a backward slant.

3.0 Study 2: Rating similarity of handwriting samples

In the second study, examples of teachers' personal handwriting and their reproduction of school models were obtained during in-service courses on the teaching of handwriting held in various centres throughout Great Britain. When comparing two sets of examples of handwriting it is first necessary to decide which of the many elements of strokes or letters to take into consideration. Elements of adults' personal handwriting are likely to be more difficult to analyse than separate letters. It was decided to concentrate initially on only three aspects: (i) slant, (ii) proportion of the height of the letter base (*x-height*) to the height of the ascender, (iii) letter width.

At the time of data collection — 1985 — most schools taught print script during the first few years of school. Whether a formal model is in use or not, print script letters are accepted as letters with straight terminals. The proportion of the letters may vary slightly, being round, or sometimes oval, depending on the designer of the handwriting model. Although usually upright, print script models occasionally have a forward slant.

3.1 Method

To obtain the examples teachers were asked, with no explanation, to "take down" three sentences. These were the same sentences used for both children and teachers in the six primary schools where first study took place. The next instruction that the teachers were given was: "Now write the same sentences in the model that you teach the children in your class at school". In this way over 200 examples were obtained.

Of the original examples, some had to be discarded because they were incomplete. Others were omitted because they were in cursive or semi-cursive writing which, without exact information about the model in use, would have made any detailed comparison difficult. With these losses 110 examples of representations of print script models were left.

3.2 Scoring

The examples were first carefully marked by the author, taking a considerable time to make some of the decisions, finding that the comparison between the widths of letters to be the most difficult to make. Two independent markers, who were not specialists in letterforms, were also enlisted: (i) AT, a retired secondary school teacher, (ii) MM, a housewife with two school-age children.

The markers were asked to make quick visual judgements. They were required to judge whether each of the three elements was similar or dissimilar in each pair of samples. Three suggestions were offered to assist the markers in their judgements: (i) That a ruler and set square could be used in any cases where they were uncertain about the slant of letters. (ii) That where there was doubt about the proportion of base to

ascender height, ruled pencil lines could be made along the lines of
writing to assist in the judgement. (iii) Where there was doubt about the
proportions of letters then the judgement should be concentrated on the
letters **n** and **o**. Both markers reported that the task took them about one
hour to complete.

4.0 Results

4.1 Similarities and dissimilarities in slant and proportion

In 68 cases out of 110 (62%), the three markers agreed that all
three elements were similar in the teachers' personal writing
and in the versions of the school model used by the teachers. The
author found 290 elements of similarity overall and 40 elements
of dissimilarity. AT found 279 elements of similarity and 51
elements of dissimilarity. MM found 312 elements of similarity
and 18 of dissimilarity. Table 1 shows the divergence in the three
markers' scores.

*TABLE 1: Ratings by three independent markers of
similarities (S) and dissimilarities (D) in teachers' personal
handwriting and their representation of print script*

Marker	Slant		Ascender		Width	
	S	D	S	D	S	D
RS	78	32	107	3	106	4
AT	78	32	103	7	98	12
MM	98	12	107	3	107	3

The 68 cases in which all elements in the teachers' personal
writing were judged by all three markers to be similar to their
representation of their models provided the starting point for the
next analysis.

No definite conclusions could be reached by comparing the
proportions of the teachers' writing and that of a print script
model because proportions are free to vary in print script
models. However, models are more specific in the matter of
slant. Some are upright, some have a slight forward slant, but

none slant backwards. It was decided to exclude all examples where the slant of the writing was upright or forward as there was no way of knowing whether those teachers might have used an upright or a forward slanting model. This left 28 examples from the original sample of 110, all of these examples slanted backwards in both the teachers' personal handwriting and their representation of print script (see Figure 2). All three markers had been unanimous in their judgement of the similarity of these two points. There are no models in general use in Great Britain that slope backwards. A backward sloping reproduction of a model must therefore be a personal deviation. Where this coincides with a backward slant in the teachers' personal handwriting this is strong evidence that the reproduction of a model can be influenced by the slant of the writer's personal hand.

4.2 Further points of similarity

The similarity in the point of entry of some teachers' personal handwriting and their reproduction of print script may be observed in Figure 3. Some print script models demonstrate a top right entry into the letter **o**, some a central entry, but none recommend a top left entry. Five examples are illustrated to

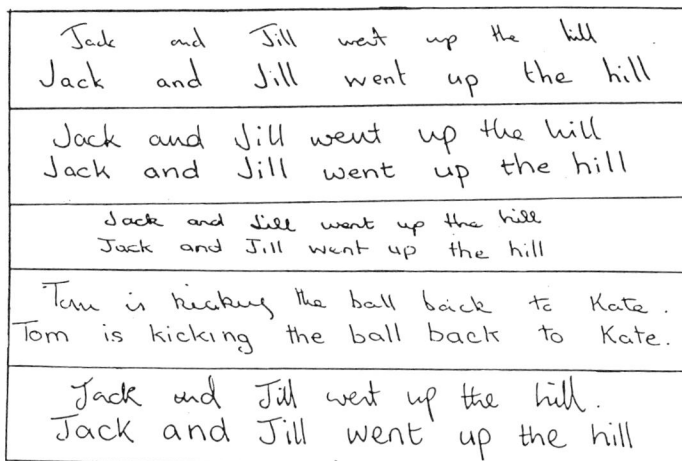

FIGURE 2: Five examples out of the 28 where the backward slant of the teachers' personal handwriting was repeated in their print script

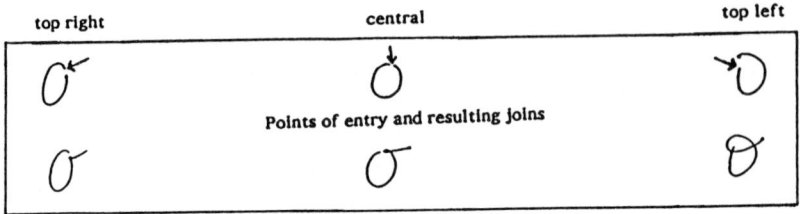

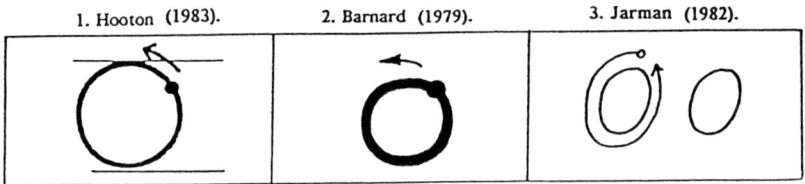

FIGURE 3: (Top) Points of entry and resulting joins. The point of entry to the *o* is usually indicated at the top right for children. Point of entry can be indicated centrally at the top, but not to the top left of the letter as this could result in the letter having an incorrect movement. (Middle) 1) Hooton; 2) Barnard; 3) Jarman. Three examples of how copybooks indicate the point of entry to the *o*. (Bottom) The five most obvious examples of teachers replicating their own point of entry when demonstrating print script.

demonstrate how teachers used their own top left point of entry to the letter **o** when reproducing the school model. The examples that are illustrated are the most obvious. Several others showed the same deviation to a lesser extent.

Two other comparisons were made. The first of these concerned the formation of the letter **b**. This showed that out of the 26 teachers with an undercurve **b** in their personal handwriting, only one (and this could have been explained by the school model) failed to change the formation of their personal undercurve **b** to the print script form. The second additional comparison was based on the fact that eight teachers volunteered the information that they used a certain popular commercial handwriting scheme. This allowed some comparisons to be made against the published model. Even with this small and unsolicited sample it was possible to note personal deviations from the well known model that tied up with elements in the teachers' personal handwriting. These deviations included the terminal and also the crossbar of the letter **t**, the formation of the letter **k**, (see Figure 4), the length of ascending and descending strokes, and the slant of letters.

5.0 Discussion

This study brings out a number points deserving further investigation. The first point to note is that the findings reported

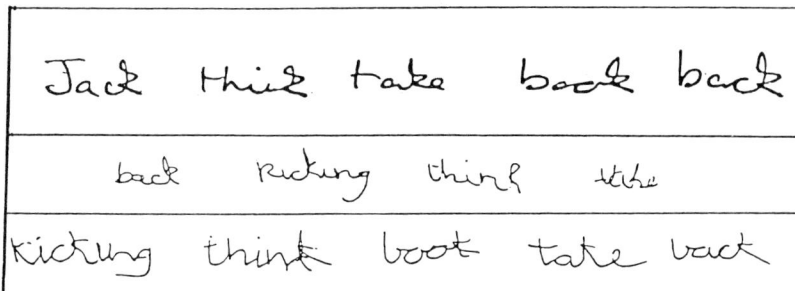

FIGURE 4: *The unusual formation of* **k** *in a teacher's handwriting (top) also seen in the handwriting of two of her pupils (below).*

in this paper have been largely confined to the slant of letters. This element may be relatively easy to measure, but may not be the most important factor in influencing the way children learn to write. It might be asked what other deviations occur in teachers' reproduction of models, that, copied by pupils, cause lasting problems in the latter's handwriting?

Another question that might profit from serious research is how do individuals view their own handwriting, and how do they perceive or judge the writing of others? In this study, there was considerable variability in the judgements of letter slant by those who were not specialists in letterforms. It would be interesting to understand factors contributing to such judgments.

Where teachers find it difficult to reproduce a model, it might be asked whether their deviations arise only from habits in their own writing or, additionally, whether they are unable to perceive the different elements of a model? Why, for instance, do many teachers exaggerate some elements such as the triangularity of italic letters as well as misjudging the proportions of letters and the slant which are the important features of certain well-known models? These deviations are reported in detail in Sassoon (1988), but that investigation did not extend to looking, other than anecdotally, at any possible causes other than those posed by personal handwriting habits.

There are implications for educational planning in the findings reported in the present work. The difficulties that teachers have in reproducing models might suggest that there should be less reliance on a strict model, and more on a method. Such a method would be based on an understanding of what is essential for the acquisition of an efficient handwriting. Initially this would stress such matters as the point of entry and direction of stroke that would ensure the correct movement of basic letters. As long as they are consistent within a pupils' handwriting, such matters as slant and proportion of letters might be better left to individual choice.

In many countries, however, it is still considered that the model is the most important part of a handwriting policy. Certain states and countries alter their model periodically in search of the ideal that will provide pupils with good handwriting. Considerable emphasis is put on the adherence to the slant, proportion and other details of such models in the classroom. The children have to work at reproducing close replicas of the model letters at the expense of automating a natural hand.

Another point that merits consideration is the plight of children in a mobile society. They often have to move to other localities and may be forced to change certain aspects of their handwriting to conform with a new school, state or even national policy. Once they have automated a certain slant or proportion of letter, or certain personal details, it is likely (and individual cases are frequently brought to my attention) that they will encounter similar difficulties to that of their teachers, when faced by a new model. Perhaps, in the future, a focus on method rather than model might circumvent this difficulty.

Chapter 9

Developmental dynamics of handwriting: Appraising the relation between handwriting and personality

Alan M. Wing, Fraser Watts & Vidyut Sharma

1.0 No further graphological research needed?

Statements based on psychological research are sometimes held to be a mere rephrasing of common knowledge. The conclusion we draw in this chapter, that handwriting reflects personality, might seem to fall into this category. Thus, at the anecdotal level, many of us are inclined to blame illegibility in handwriting on personality defects, such as sloppiness or laziness in the writer's attitude. And we might be surprised to find these "failings" in someone with neat, well-formed writing. Furthermore, graphologists are often asked to provide a characterization of personality on the basis of a handwriting sample. More significantly, there is objective research that shows that graphologists are statistically better than chance in matching handwriting samples to personality questionnaire responses (Jansen, 1973).

However, not all the evidence supports a link between handwriting and personality. In the Jansen study the performance level of the graphologists was not a lot better than chance. Moreover, Jensen reported that the matching of handwriting samples to personality was no worse when carried out by people with no graphological training. Doubt is also cast by correlational studies that fail to reveal statistically reliable associations between handwriting and personality. For example, Furnham and Gunter (1987) asked 64 adults to copy a text in their own handwriting and to complete a personality questionnnaire. They then computed correlations between

Development of Graphic Skills
ISBN 0-12-734940-5

ratings of certain features in the writing (such as size, slant, letter connectedness, etc) with measures from the personality test. In the resulting table of correlations (involving four personality measures and thirteen writing indices), only five entries (10%) were reliably different from zero. The authors suggest that the "few significant correlations once again question the validity of handwriting analysis". The authors close with the line that "no further research needs to be done in the field".

1.1 Variation in letter joining

But is this last comment really justified? If handwriting is unrelated to personality it would seem difficult to account for individuality in handwriting styles. In most primary schools, handwriting is taught by children copying a model presented by the teacher. In the UK such letterform models often conform to a looped cursive style (Sassoon, 1988). Some of these letterform models are not well adapted to efficient handwriting where speed as well as legibility is important. Sassoon et al (1989) provide evidence that as children grow older, increasing departures from the taught model are evident and these departures serve to favour faster writing.

Sassoon et al (1989) examined the nature of the join between **th**. In UK schools, children are generally taught to link the

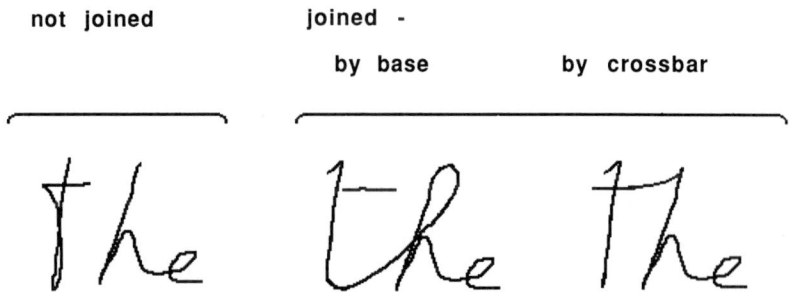

FIGURE 1: *Three forms of joining* **th**: *the form commonly taught in UK schools is shown in the middle.*

characters by taking the pen without lifting, from the base of the **t** to the top of the **h** ascender or staff (see Figure 1). The crossbar has then to be added in later. What Sassoon et al observed in practice is that, as children grow older, they increasingly use the crossbar as the linking device (with or without a penlift after completing the **t** staff). They suggested that this departure from the taught version of the join is an adaptation to the needs of writing quickly but legibly. However, not everybody ends up writing this way. Indeed, in a study of adult writing, Eldridge et al (1984) reported that the variety of joins in the population makes this one of the more powerful features in enabling the forensic document examiner to decide whether two samples of handwriting are of common authorship.

So, in the case of writing **th**, what determines the type of join used? Or, more generally, what factors determine whether a child will depart from the original taught form of a letter? One such factor might well be personality. The development of an individual style of handwriting could be viewed as an indication of a child's readiness to go against the teacher's recommendation. In that case, changes in children's handwriting might be expected to depend on personality variables relating, for example, to independence of thought. A child's educational attainment might also play a part in the development of handwriting style. Children who are academically more able may adapt their writing more because they are doing more written work than those who are less bright. So intelligence may also play a role.

2.0 Personality and children's handwriting

To look at these issues we have examined the handwriting of a group of schoolchildren on two occasions, twelve months apart. We were interested to see whether handwriting features (or changes in these features) would relate to personality factors and/or intelligence. However, there are very many ways of characterizing handwriting. Since the present study was perceived as being exploratory in nature, we decided to limit our examination to two handwriting features drawn from previous work and illustrative of contrasting qualitative and quantitative approaches to handwriting analysis. The **th** join, as studied by

Sassoon et al (1989), was taken as the *qualitative* index. As an
example of the *quantitative* characterization of handwriting we
took measurements of the vertical extent of the letter **d**.

Our choice of **d** height to illustrate quantitative analysis was
based on two considerations. First, in teaching handwriting, a
certain base height, or more strictly, relative base height is
encouraged. In terms of ratio, which is defined as staff height
divided by base height (see Figure 2), the prescribed value would
be 2.0. But, Wing and Nimmo-Smith (1987) observed that adult
writers tend to employ a relatively smaller base, resulting in an
average ratio of 2.4. Moreover, in their study they demonstrated
that **d** ratio is a good indicator of authorship. Therefore, it may
be that departures from the norm (or changes with age) in the
vertical dimension of this letter will be linked with individual
differences in personality and/or intelligence attributes.

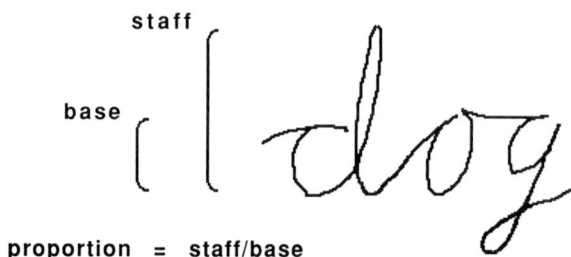

*FIGURE 2: Two measures of the vertical extent of **d**: base, ascender (or staff).
Their ratio, termed proportion, is a size-independent index of letter shape.*

2.1 Subjects

Forty-nine children (31 female) from a school in Hertfordshire in their
fourth year of secondary school with average age 179.7 (SD 3.5) months at
first testing participated in the study with parental permission. Group
testing took place on two occasions, 12 months apart. The first test session
included sampling of handwriting as well as the administration of items
from personality and intelligence tests as listed in Table 1 and described
in a following section. It lasted approximately 40 minutes. The second
session was completed within 20 minutes and was primarily to obtain a
further set of handwriting samples.

*TABLE 1: Brief definitions of personality factors and
intelligence sub-tests used in the study.*

Test / Trait   *High-scoring if:*

Jesness Behavior Checklist

Unobtrusiveness (1)	not quarrelsome or meddlesome
Responsibility (3)	adequate work habits, good care of equipment
Considerateness (4)	polite, tactful, kind towards others
Independence (5)	make decisions without undue reliance on others
Rapport (6)	harmonious relations with eg teachers
Enthusiasm (7)	cheerful, active, involved with others
Sociabilty (8)	capable of getting along well with others in groups
Conformity (9)	compliant with accepted social conventions
Calmness (10)	self-confident, composed, high self-esteem
Social Control (13)	absence of loud, attention-demanding behaviour

Eysenck Junior Personality Inventory

Extroversion	sociable, impulsive
Neuroticism	emotionally labile

RavenVocabulary Scale

Vocabulary	good on definitions (high verbal IQ)

Wechsler Adult Intelligence Scale

Digit Symbol	rapid use of a digit to symbol code (high spatial IQ)

2.2 Procedure

After a brief warm-up exercise (writing repetitive loops), the sentence **The quick brown fox jumps over the lazy dog** was written out as many times as possible in 30 s. Writing took place on unlined paper with the children using their preferred writing implement while seated at bench-style desks.

2.3 Handwriting measures

Handwriting samples were characterized in terms of the manner of the join between **th** in **the** (as indicated in Figure 1) and by the vertical extent (measured with a millimetre ruler) of **d** in the word **dog** (as in Figure 2), both words occurring at the end of the first completed sentence. The measurement and classification were carried out by a single research assistant without knowledge of the personality or intelligence profiles of the individual children.

In addition to the two detailed handwriting features, a broad characterization of the handwriting was obtained in terms of the average of two sets of rated legibility of the first sample. The ratings, which were made along a five-point scale, were provided independently by a research assistant and the first author. The judgements were very consistent as evidenced by an inter-rater correlation of .86. This consistency was probably aided by the fact that, at the time the subjective judgements were made, both individuals already had extensive exposure to the full range of handwriting samples. Thus, the estimates of legibility may have been influenced, not only by general neatness, but also by more local features such as slope, spacing, etc.

2.4 Personality and intelligence assessment

Two separate personality questionnaires were employed (see Table 1). One was the Jesness Behavior Checklist. Developed in California, it assesses 14 bipolar behavioural factors, of which the ten most reliable (combined observer and self-appraisal test-retest reliabilities, Jesness, 1971) are reported in the following. The other, the Eysenck Junior Personality Inventory, was developed in the UK and gives scores on two bipolar dimensions on the basis of yes-no responses to 57 questions (Eysenck, 1965). Two other tests were included to give an indication of intelligence. One test related to verbal ability (vocabulary Form B; Raven, 1982) and the other provided an index of visuo-spatial ability (digit-symbol sub-test, Wechsler; 1955). These are also listed in Table 1.

3.0 Results

On average 22.3 words were written at the first session. The amount written in the second session represented a small but statistically significant decrease of 10%. The proportion of different types of **th** join used at the two test session are summarized in the pie charts of Figure 3. The most common form of join was by the crossbar, followed by the base join with unjoined being the least frequent category. It will be observed that there was an overall gain in the frequency of crossbar-joined **th.**

The mean heights of the **d** base and staff were 2.8 mm and 5.4 mm respectively at the first test session. A reduction in size of the order of 10% from the first to the second session was not statistically reliable. The height of the **d** staff height expressed as a ratio of the base height and averaged over children was 2.0, a value that was unchanged over the two sessions.

The average scores of the schoolchildren on the various personality factors were generally within the normal range. Correlations between the scores on the various factors were

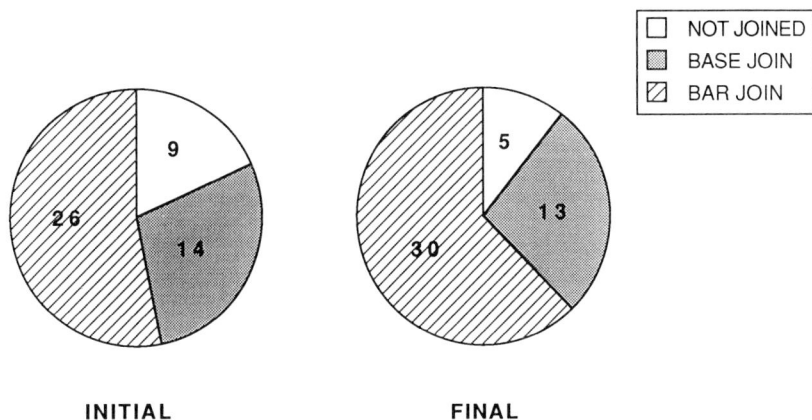

FIGURE 3: Changes in the proportion of children employing three different forms of **th** join over twelve months.

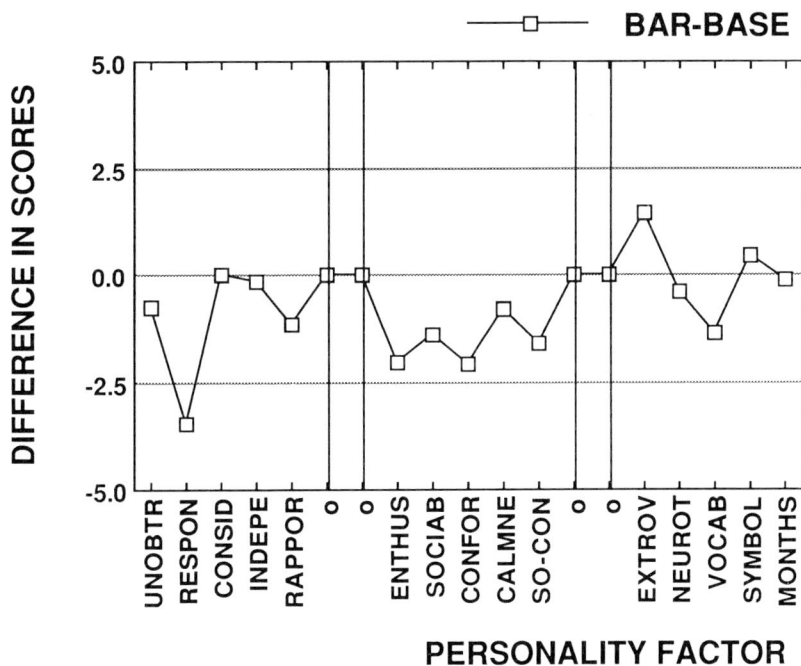

FIGURE 4: Average difference in personality factors, intelligence test scores and age of children employing crossbar and base **th** joins.

computed. With 49 subjects, correlations that differ from zero by more than $r=.27$ are statistically significant. Since some of the factors in the two personality tests manifested significant correlations, (extroversion with unobtrusiveness, $-.36$, and social-control, $-.50$; neuroticism with independence, $-.35$, enthusiasm, $-.30$, and calmness, $-.60$) it should be recognized that there is some degree of overlap in the personality tests.

The verbal and spatial intelligence test scores of the children were within the normal range. The two tests were uncorrelated, and there were no reliable correlations with any of the personality factors (with the exception of a correlation of .32 between vocabulary and social-control).

3.1 Dependence between handwriting and personality

In looking for correlations between handwriting, personality and intelligence, we first provide an account of the qualitative measure, **th** join. To evaluate whether the form of join was related to personality factors, a comparison was made betweenchildren who used a crossbar join in both years ($N=23$) and those children who used a base join in at least one of the two test sessions ($N=16$). The differences between the two sets of scores (which are depicted in the form of a profile in Figure 4) were small but several were statistically significant at the $p<.05$ level by individual t-tests. Those who used the base join were higher on responsibility, enthusiasm, sociability, and social conformity.

The dependence of the quantitative measure, vertical height of the **d** base, on personality is presented in Figure 5 in the form of two profiles over the same factors as in Figure 4. One profile shows the correlations over children's **d** base measurement expressed as an average over the two sessions. The other shows the correlations calculated on the change in each child's handwriting from one year to the next. There were statistically reliable correlations between **d** base vertical height and several aspects of personality (unobtrusiveness, considerateness, independence, conformity, social-control, extroversion). It will be observed that the change in the vertical extent of the base was no more reliably correlated with vertical extent than the average. Although not shown, an almost identical pattern of results was found for the **d** staff.

Handwriting features that are expressed in terms of absolute size are likely to be dependent on features of a document such as its shape and size (Harrison, 1966). For situations where paper size might not be controlled, it is thus useful to observe that there was a statistically reliable correlation of $-.43$ between extroversion and the size-invariant **d** ratio for the average over the two sessions. (In the case of correlation with the change in **d** ratio over the two sessions there was a non-significant correlation of $-.17$).

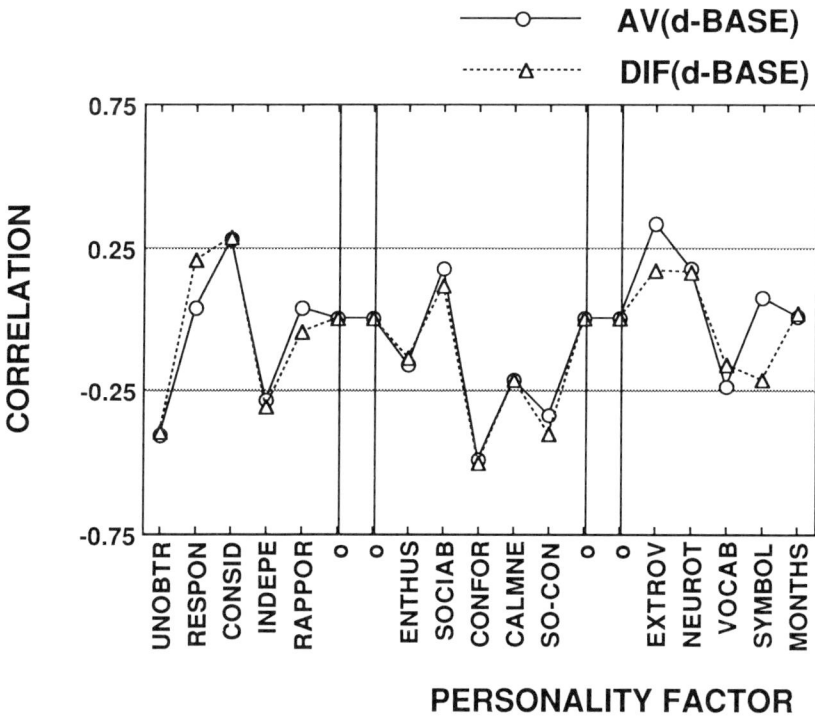

FIGURE 5: Correlations between **d** base height (for both the average and difference over the two sessions), personality, intelligence and age. With 49 subjects, correlations that differ from zero by more than 0.27 are statistically reliable.

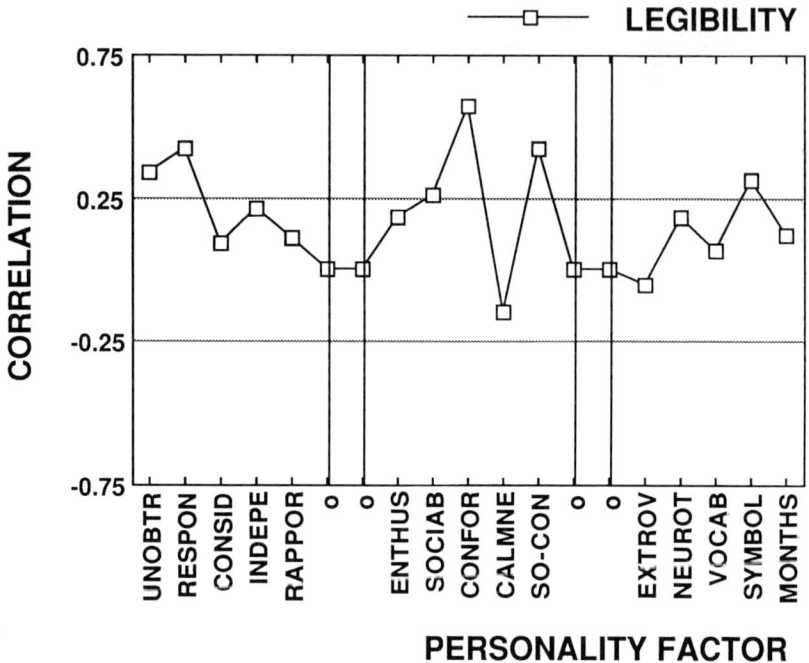

FIGURE 6: Correlations between rated legibility, personality, intelligence and age.

Both the qualitative and quantitative measures described above are precisely specified features that require careful assessment of handwriting. It is therefore interesting to note that personality is also related to legibility. The correlation profile in Figure 6 reveals significant correlations with unobtrusiveness, responsibility, sociability, conformity and social-control. In addition, legibility correlated reliably with the digit-symbol spatial intelligence sub-test.

Having treated each of the three aspects of handwriting separately with regard to the personality characteristics, we provide the following by way of summary. A child employing a *base-join* between **th** is likely:
- to be less of an attention seeker (social-control) (and this is also the case with *small **d** base* and *high legibility*)

- to have a good attitude toward work (responsibility) and get on with others in group setting (sociability) (as with *high legibility*)
- to be cheerful (enthusiasm).

With *small d base*, a child is likely:
- to conform to social conventions (conformity) and not be quarrelsome (unobtrusiveness) (as with *high legibility*)
- not to be impulsive (extrovert).

In addition, perhaps surprisingly, the *small d base* was associated with:
- lower scores on tact (considerateness) and on self-reliance in decision making (independence).

With regard to the personality factors it is worth noting that social control was reliably associated with all three of the handwriting measures employed in the study. As such, it would appear to be an aspect of personality that deserves particular attention in further studies of links between handwriting and personality.

4.0 Personality and the evolution of writing style.

There are two main findings in the present study. The first is that there are features in children's handwriting, both qualitative and quantitative, that are reliably related to personality (but not, for the most part, to intelligence). It therefore seems justifiable to contradict Furnham and Gunter (1987) and say that further research in the field of graphology is definitely warranted! However, we would urge that any such research be built on the approach we have outlined in the present chapter. We would ask for recognition that individuality evidenced in adult handwriting is a process of development from a common, or shared model taught in school and so the chances of finding links with personality might be expected to be that much greater in children's writing.

Our second major finding was that correlations between handwriting changes over the period of a year (in the quantitative **d** base measure) and personality were no stronger than the average of that measure over the two sessions. Our original reason for taking handwriting samples on two occasions twelve months apart was that, if children's writing is changing to meet educational demands, the extent of this change might relate to personality and/or educational ability. Certainly our negative finding in this regard is a disappointment and it might appear to go against our developmental approach to graphological research. However, two aspects of the present study suggest this conclusion may be premature. The first point is that, at fifteen years on first testing, the age of the children we tested may have been rather too old and the majority of handwriting changes may have already occurred. The second point is that, in looking for handwriting changes with age, we may not have spanned a sufficiently long time period.

One further aspect of our data deserves comment. Our findings of dependence between handwriting and personality, though statistically significant, were not large. Thus, for example, for the quantitatively defined **d** base and legibility, the strongest dependence involved the conformity factor. But even there, the correlations observed only accounted for approximately 25% of the variance. This low value might be taken to imply that trying to characterize aspects of personality on the basis of handwriting would be fraught with error. However, while this might be the case when the only handwriting sample available is a single instance of an isolated handwriting feature collected under speeded test conditions, the situation might improve for more extensive samples of writing collected under more normal conditions. Such conditions would increase the number of examples of each feature. Moreover several distinct handwriting features might be used simultaneously. Eldridge et al (1985) have shown that using several features in conjoint fashion allows better discrimination between the writing of different individuals. It is possible that this improvement might be related to underlying personality influences. Further improvements might also accrue if account is taken of general factors, such as sex or handedness, which are often identified as shaping handwriting but which, in the present study, have not been allowed for.

In bringing this discussion of our work to a close we now lay these qualifications to one side and return to questions of general interest that now arise. Given that statistically reliable relations between handwriting and personality can be demonstrated, how might these become established? What are the causal processes? In the introduction we discussed the pressure to write fast as contributing to the evolution of style. But writing faster is liable to make handwriting less legible. Does the influence of personality on handwriting arise, in part, from self-monitoring behaviour? Do personality-related differences in handling other people's comments, for example, about the legibility of one's handwriting also contribute to choice of writing style? Or is style determined primarily by aesthetic influences with efficiency merely a by-product. To the extent that personality characteristics contribute to friendship formation, the link between handwriting and personality might reflect the tendency of children to copy features of their friends' handwriting. Certainly aspects of these various pressures to develop handwriting style may be seen in the personality factors identified as relevant in the present study. Clearly, therefore, there are many potential avenues to explore in this fascinating area of research.

V: Dysfunction

One of the major incentives for studying the development of childrens' writing and drawing is that a significant number of children experience difficulty in mastering such skills. Flem Maeland and Karlsdottir *(Development of reading, spelling and writing skills from third to sixth grade in normal and dysgraphic school children)* provide a longitudinal perspective on such difficulties by following the same children over a 3-year period to document their reading, spelling and writing performance. Although dysgraphic children progressed substantially over the 3-year period, they continued to lag behind their normal peers after 3 years, which would seem to support the argument for the construction of remedial intervention programmes.

Before a remedial programme can be implemented, sensitive tools are required that can reliably identify children who are experiencing difficulties with graphic skills. The experienced teacher may be remarkably sensitive to subtle clues that lead to early recognition of problems, but it is not enough to rely purely upon teachers being able to judge by their experience. The three following chapters look at assessment tools for aiding such identification. Phelps and Stempel *(The identification of dyslexic handwriting through graphoanalysis)*, evaluate trained graphoanalysts' use of an evaluation scale, first to identify dyslexic children, then to construct a subset of the most diagnostic items. This scale was then used by a group of teachers in order to ascertain whether non-specialist raters could achieve the same degree of success as the graphoanalysts.

The use of dysfunctional handwriting as a diagnostic tool also underpins the chapter by Simner *(Estimating a child's learning potential from form errors in a child's printing)*. The chapter draws upon a wealth of previous research into the typical errors made by children in learning to print letters. The work includes a 6-year follow-up report that allows early printing performance to be correlated with subsequent scholastic record. Simner goes on to ask whether formal assessment of the errors made by children might be supplemented by teacher ratings, thereby providing a simple tool that could be used on a regular basis within the curriculum.

The final chapter in this section takes a different approach to identifying early problems in graphic skills by focusing on spatial variability in primary schoolchildren's handwriting. Wann and Kardirkamanathan *(Variability in children's handwriting: Computer diagnosis of writing difficulties)* describe a computer-based approach that allows variability to be estimated by computer scanning of children's work-books. One of the attractions of such a technique is that it affords the possibility of completely objective assessment that might, in the future, be related to a large national database.

Chapter 10

Development of reading, spelling, and writing skills from third to sixth grade in normal and dysgraphic school children.

Annlaug Flem Mæland & Ragnheidur Karlsdottir

1.0 Acquiring written language

Reading, spelling, and handwriting are complex skills that take years to master (Carroll, 1976). Theoretical models have been developed to explain the inter-relationships and the processes involved in the acquisition of these skills (Ellis, 1984). According to Sõvik (1987), reading and spelling are more strongly related to one another than reading and writing, or spelling and writing. Previous research has shown that many children fail to achieve the expected level of competence in reading, spelling, and handwriting (Rutter et al, 1970; Sõvik, 1987). In some children, difficulties in basic school subjects are related to low general abilities, environmental disadvantages, or neurological deficiencies. However, there are other children who suffer from specific reading and spelling disabilities (dyslexic children) or handwriting problems (dysgraphic children) which cannot be explained by neurological or intellectual deficiencies (Critchley, 1975; Sõvik, 1984b).

Two opposing models have been put forward to explain the development of dyslexic children. The *maturational delay* model suggests that dyslexic children are similar to young children and predicts that some of these dyslexic children will grow out of their problems (Satz and Van Nostrand, 1973). In contrast, the *deficit* model asserts that there is a failure in some aspect of

Development of Graphic Skills
ISBN 0-12-734940-5

cognitive functioning, and that dyslexic children will not necessarily catch up (Doehring, 1968).

In terms of the development of handwriting, de Ajuriaguerra et al (1979) studied both the product of writing and the development of the overt motor aspect of writing. In a cross-sectional study of children between the ages of 5 and 14 years, they found a clear developmental trend in writing behaviour, with respect to variables such as posture, muscle tension, and movement. They state that inadequate instruction and practice may hold up children in their writing development. Handwriting problems may therefore be due to a maturational delay in some children. In addition these authors also assumed that inadequate instruction and practice prevented children from developing their writing.

The characteristics of children's performance in reading, spelling and writing are thought to be acquired during the first years of schooling. It is therefore reasonable to believe that the relative performance level of a child in a lower grade will correlate with its later performance in these skills. In other words, children's reading, spelling, and writing performances are considered to be relatively stable over subsequent grade levels. A recent study by Undheim (1989) supported this point of view. An important aspect of a longitudinal study is therefore to examine the stability or change (relative performance-scores) of one or more variables over time (Magnusson, 1981).

2.0 A longitudinal study

So far, no longitudinal study has been undertaken to study how dysgraphic and normal children develop in reading, spelling, and handwriting. In order to examine this issue we conducted a longitudinal study over a period of three years. The main purpose was to investigate how dysgraphic children develop in these three school subjects in comparison to normal children. We were interested in investigating the possibility of predicting the performance of both groups of children in reading, spelling and writing in 6th grade on the basis of their 3rd grade performances. In addition, we also attempted to determine the relationship between reading/spelling/writing and perceptual-motor functions, and the possibility of predicting the children's performances in perceptual-motor functions from 3rd to 6th grade.

2.1 Subjects

A group of 12 normal children (9 boys and 3 girls) and a group of 12 dysgraphic children (5 boys and 7 girls) were selected randomly from nine school-classes in urban Norwegian public schools.

2.2 Tests

The following tests were administered to the children in both 3rd and 6th grade: 1. Silent Reading Comprehension (Solheim et al, 1984). 2. Word Spelling (Asheim, 1964). 3. Psychomotor Tests: (a) tracing, (b) finger tapping, (c) steadiness (Reitan and Davison, 1974). 4. (In 3rd grade only) Developmental Test of Visual-Motor Integration, VMI (Beery, 1967). In addition to the above, the children in the 6th grade were given the Southern California Figure-Ground (SCFG) visual perception test (Ayres, 1966). All tests, except the psychomotor and SCFG tests, were given as group tests.

2.3 Procedure

The silent reading comprehension test measured the children's ability to understand what they read. For 3rd-graders the test consisted of six short stories each followed by four questions regarding content with multiple-choice format (24 items). The 6th-grade version of the test consisted of 32 items. The first 24 items were identical to those in the 3rd-grade test. The word spelling test measured the children's ability to write single words correctly. It consisted of 50 words at both grade levels, but the 6th-grade test had more demanding words. The psycho-motor tests measured various perceptual-motor functions and were chosen from the tests in the Motor Steadiness Battery (Reiten and Davison, 1974). The tracing test measured vertical steadiness by moving a stylus through a gradually narrowing groove without touching the sides of the groove. The finger tapping test measured how quickly one can tap with the dominant hand. The steadiness test was used to measure steadiness of hand by holding a stylus steady in a hole for 10 seconds. The VMI-test measured children's coordination of eye and hand, and included 24 geometric figures which the children were requested to copy. The SCFG-test measured children's visual perception, and required selection of a foreground figure from a rival background. The handwriting performance of the children both in 3rd and 6th grade was rated on the same 0 to 7 point scale by two independent judges.The final performance score was taken as the mean value of their ratings. The validity and reliability of the tests above have been discussed previously (Asheim, 1964; Ayres, 1966; Beery, 1967; Reiten and Davison,1974; Solheim et al, 1984; Sõvik, 1975). The administration and scoring procedures were carried out according to the manuals.

3.0 Results

3.1 Means

Figure 1 shows the average reading, spelling and writing performances for normal and dysgraphic children in 3rd and 6th grade. The two groups of children showed different development in the three skills over a three-year period. With the exception of writing in the normal group, both groups improved their performances from 3rd to 6th grade. Overall, the normal group had higher scores in comparison to the dysgraphic children. The testing revealed that nine of the children in the dysgraphic group had dyslexic problems.

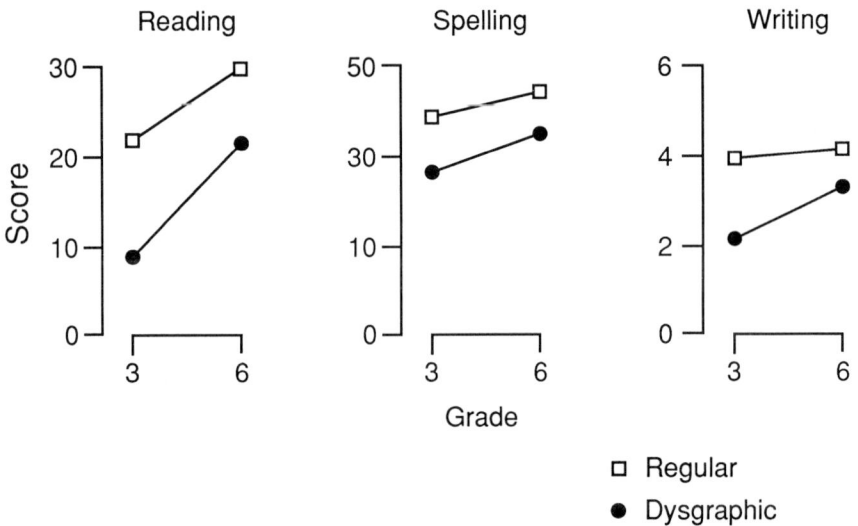

FIGURE 1: *Mean scores in reading, spelling, and writing in 3rd and 6th grade for 12 normal and 12 dysgraphic children. The scores are as follows: reading 3rd grade, 0–24; reading 6th grade, 0-32; spelling, 0-50; writing, 0-7.*

The mean scores of reading, spelling, and writing were analysed statistically by a mixed two-way analysis of variance. Significant main effects in favour of the normal group were found for reading [$F(1,22)=38.97$; $p<.001$], spelling [$F(1,22)=9.48$; $p<.01$] and writing [$F(1,22)=18.27$; $p<.001$]. Furthermore, the development of skills from 3rd to 6th grade showed a significant difference in favour of the 6th grade for reading [$F(1,22)$=113.48; p<.001], spelling [$F(1,22)$=9.86; p<.01], and writing [$F(1,22)$=12.05; p<.01]. The interaction effects between groups and skills were significant for reading [$F(1,22)$=6.70; p<.05] and writing [$F(1,22)$=10.12; p<.01], but not for spelling [$F(1,22)$=.62; p<.5]. However, a ceiling effect in the reading tests was observed for the regular group at both grade levels.

3.2 Correlations

Pearson product-moment correlations were calculated to test the relationship between reading, spelling, and writing on the one hand and the relationship between reading/spelling/writing and perceptual-motor functions on the other hand, within as well as between grades. In the Appendix Table I presents these correlations for the normal children and Table II presents the results for the 12 dysgraphic children.

For normal children significant correlations occurred between the 3rd and 6th grade scores in reading (r=.71), spelling (r=.81) and writing (r=.60), and for dysgraphic children significant correlations were found between the 3rd and 6th grade scores in spelling (r=.57) and writing (r=.77), but not in reading (r=.40). For normal children in 3rd grade significant correlations were found between reading and spelling scores (r=.67), between spelling and writing scores (r=.66), and in 6th grade between reading and spelling scores (r=.80). For dysgraphic children significant correlations occurred only between the reading and spelling scores in 3rd grade (r=.63). As Table I shows, the only significant correlation between the three skills and perceptual-motor functions for normal children was between the VMI scores and writing in 3rd grade (r=.62).

Table II shows that for the dysgraphic children the only significant correlation was between spelling and the SCFG scores in the 6th grade (r=.66). The results from perceptual-motor scores in 3rd and in 6th grade for normal children showed that only the scores from the two steadiness tests were correlated (r=.49). However, for the dysgraphic children tracing

($r=-.88$), tapping ($r=.69$) and steadiness tests were significantly correlated. The only significant correlations among the different perceptual-motor scores were between tracing and steadiness for the dysgraphic children in 3rd grade ($r=.60$) and in 6th grade ($r=.74$).

3.3 Commentary

In terms of predictions, the correlational results showed that the normal group was more stable than the dysgraphic group. In reading 60% and in spelling 65% of the variation of the performances in the 6th grade can be explained by the normal children's performances in 3rd grade. For the dysgraphic group the corresponding values were only 16% and 32%. However, in writing, the dysgraphic group was the more stable with an explained variation of 59%. The corresponding value in writing for the regular group was 36%. There was a closer relationship between the three skills of reading, spelling, and writing for normal than for dysgraphic children, and there were higher correlations between the three skills in 3rd than in 6th grade for both groups.

According to the results the relationship between reading/spelling/writing and perceptual-motor functions was low. The only significant correlation between writing and perceptual-motor tests was for VMI and writing in the regular group. There was a higher prediction for the performances in perceptual-motor functions from 3rd to 6th grade for the dysgraphic children. For the normal children the correlations among the different perceptual-motor functions were low. In the dysgraphic group the correlations were somewhat higher.

4.0 Discussion

Although the dysgraphic children progressed substantially in reading, spelling and writing from 3rd to 6th grade, the differences between them and the normal children were still significant in grade 6. This result is in agreement with previous studies on dyslexic children, which suggests that even if dyslexic children as a group progress substantially, the deficits persist with age (Trites and Fiedorowicz, 1976; Undheim, 1989).

Our findings indicated that the two groups differed in their development in the three subjects. With respect to reading and spelling, the results showed that in the normal group the development of these two subjects was more in line with previous studies. The reading and spelling performances of the normal group were more stable from 3rd to 6th grade, and the two skills were more strongly related to one another than in the dysgraphic group (Ellis, 1984; Sõvik, 1987; Undheim, 1989). Even if the dysgraphic group surpassed the normal group as to relative progress in reading, this difference might be due to a ceiling effect in the reading tests which inflated the scores of the regular group at both grade levels. Thus, with regard to reading and spelling, our results seem to support the deficit model.

The finding that only the dysgraphic group improved substantially in writing was surprising, and can perhaps be explained by the maturational delay theory. This theory implies that either there is a delay in neurological functioning which prevents early specialization of language functioning so causing written language problems, or that there is a delay in perceptual and motor skills which are of importance for written language learning in the early stages. It is reasonable to believe that reading and spelling are more closely linked to specialization of language functioning (Vellutino, 1978), and handwriting closer linked to perceptual and motor functions (Sõvik, 1975). This is supported by the fact that our results showed that reading and spelling were more strongly related to one another than spelling and writing or reading and writing. Because of this, handwriting might have a different development compared to reading and spelling. De Ajuriaguerra et al (1979) found that there is a clear developmental trend in handwriting behaviour, and the perceptual and motor functions which are important for the accuracy (legibility) of writing performances might therefore develop later in some children. Hence, normal children in 3rd grade are able to write with accuracy, whereas dysgraphic children develop slower. But even if the dysgraphics progress substantially, the deficits tend to persist with age. The correlational results also indicated that the two groups differed in the development of perceptual-motor functions. The dysgraphic group was more stable from 3rd to 6th grade than the normal group, and the correlations among the perceptual-motor functions were higher in the dysgraphic group. The relationship between perceptual-motor tests and writing was also different in the two groups, only the VMI test and writing were significantly correlated in the regular group. Thus, the maturational delay theory seems to be verified to some extent as far as writing is concerned.

One might also ask whether the normal group could have performed better than they did. According to de Ajuriaguerra et al (1979), in addition to maturation, training and practice are relevant for progress in handwriting. Traditional instructions given for handwriting in Norwegian schools probably do not encourage children once they have acquired a basic skill in writing. Our study suggests that normal children might also benefit from more systematic instruction and exercise in handwriting from 3rd to 6th grade.

The finding that no strong relationship existed between reading/spelling/writing and perceptual-motor functions in any of the groups was surprising. Although we expected a close relationship between handwriting and perceptual-motor functions, the prediction was verified only for the VMI test and writing in the regular group. The few significant intercorrelations between the perceptual-motor tests indicate that these tests measure different abilities and that these abilities may have different development, as suggested by Meulenbroek and van Galen (1986).

5.0 Appendix

Table I: Intercorrelations among reading/spelling/writing and perceptual-motor performance variables for 12 normal children. (Note: For all variables a high score is consistent with a good performance except for variables 5 and 7. The significance level is p < .05 for |r| >.49).

(a) in 3rd grade.

Variable							
	1	2	3	4	5	6	7
1 Reading	1.00	.67	.41	.16	.09	.28	.53
2 Spelling		1.00	.66	.22	−.37	.24	−.13
3 Writing			1.00	.62	−.40	.39	−.06
4 VMI				1.00	−.17	.12	−.07
5 Tracing					1.00	−.21	.28
6 Tapping						1.00	−.06
7 Steadiness							1.00

(b) in 6th grade

Variable							
	8	9	10	11	12	13	14
8 Reading	1.00	.80	.34	.05	.18	−.16	.08
9 Spelling		1.00	.33	.30	.31	.05	.16
10 Writing			1.00	.16	.20	.34	−.35
11 SCFG				1.00	.28	00	.47
12 Tracing					1.00	.04	−.12
13 Tapping						1.00	−.45
14 Steadiness							1.00

(c) 3rd (rows) and 6th (columns) grades compared

Variable							
	8	9	10	11	12	13	14
1 Reading	.71	.77	.16	.16	.01	−.25	.27
2 Spelling	.44	.81	.43	.34	.39	.10	.03
3 Writing	.31	.55	.60	.06	.06	.11	−.22
4 VMI	.24	.31	.19	−.29	−.36	.18	.03
5 Tracing	−.11	−.04	−.52	.24	−.27	.19	.14
6 Tapping	.38	.29	.42	−.48	−.08	.44	−.64
7 Steadiness	.36	.18	−.19	.23	−.30	−.47	.49

Table II: Intercorrelations among reading/spelling/writing and perceptual-motor performance variables for 12 dysgraphic children. (Note: For all variables a high score is consistent with a good performance except for variables 5 and 7. The significance level is p <. 05 for |r| >.49)

(a) in 3rd grade.

Variable							
	1	2	3	4	5	6	7
1 Reading	1.00	.63	−.14	.32	−.01	.13	−.39
2 Spelling		1.00	.02	.39	.29	.00	−.18
3 Writing			1.00	−.17	.30	.47	−.07
4 VMI				1.00	−.13	−.39	−.41
5 Tracing					1.00	.15	.60
6 Tapping						1.00	.11
7 Steadiness							1.00

(b) in 6th grade

Variable							
	8	9	10	11	12	13	14
8 Reading	1.00	−.15	−.22	.28	−.04	−.27	−.21
9 Spelling		1.00	.37	.66	.15	−.26	.25
10 Writing			1.00	.03	−.15	−.07	−.31
11 SCFG				1.00	.11	.00	−.08
12 Tracing					1.00	.19	.74
13 Tapping						1.00	−.02
14 Steadiness							1.00

(c) 3rd (rows) and 6th (columns) grades compared

Variable							
	8	9	10	11	12	13	14
1 Reading	.40	.43	−.18	.70	−.02	.01	−.13
2 Spelling	.32	.57	−.10	.65	.26	−.26	.35
3 Writing	−.05	.30	.77	.26	.14	−.12	−.10
4 VMI	.37	.14	−.43	.26	.08	−.56	.22
5 Tracing	.11	.11	−.07	.25	−.88	.25	.60
6 Tapping	−.07	.13	.58	.28	.20	.51	−.34
7 Steadiness	−.44	−.22	−.18	−.36	.77	.53	.69

Chapter 11

The identification of dyslexic handwriting through graphoanalysis

Joanne Phelps & Lynn Stempel

1.0 Handwriting and dyslexia

The Texas Education Code (1985: section 21.924) defines dyslexia and mandates a program of testing and treatment for the condition. "Dyslexia", the Code states, "is a disorder of constitutional origin manifested by a difficulty in learning to read, write, or spell despite conventional instruction, adequate intelligence, and socio-cultural opportunity." Identification of the disability has strained resources of many schools. The demands for evaluation have far exceeded the professional assistance available. At Texas Scottish Rite Hospital, applicants seeking diagnosis must wait six months to be tested. A method whereby the classroom teacher could gain insight and screen students prior to referral for special services would represent a significant saving of time and money for schools and frustrations for children.

The present study represents an effort to determine whether handwriting can furnish a key to the identification of dyslexic students in middle school, and whether the graphic signs can discriminate between dyslexic and normal pupils. Further, if handwriting differences do exist, graphoanalytic interpretation would offer insight into the personality of the dyslexics. Such understanding would serve as a tool for counselling and teaching and would provide a means for determining expediently and early in the school year what a teacher might otherwise discover over a period of many months.

Development of Graphic Skills
ISBN 0-12-734940-5

A review of earlier studies provides arguments for and against the validity of using handwriting as a projective technique. Brandstatter (1969), Jansen (1973), Eysenck and Gudjonsson (1986), and Furnham and Gunter (1987), found little or no correlation between graphologists' appraisals and other measures, such as the Eysenck Personality Inventory (1975) or classmates' judgements. On the other hand, Crumbaugh and Stockholm (1977), Pang and Lepponen (1968), Prystav (1971) and Silver (1984) found satisfactory confirmation of the value of graphoanalysts' interpretations. Some of the foregoing studies provided good controls for reliability and validity but others did not.

The handwriting characteristics of dyslexics, according to van Ness in the New York Times (1989), include varying degrees of letter reversals in words, poor reproduction of words, and improper sequence and spelling. Also, there is evidence of poor spatial orientation in judging distance and direction. Collette (1979), comparing dyslexic and reading-retarded students to adequate readers in grades 8 and 9, found that the former had more variability in letter size, reversals, rotations, and errors in forming loop letters than the latter.

Hearn (1969) stated that 50% of the dyslexics who have not received remedial treatment have behavioural problems, such as opposition, aggressiveness, inferiority feelings, fear, depression, and instability. He analysed 80 handwritings of dyslexic children and cited that some handwriting characteristics of dyslexics are also typical of the mentally retarded. These include: omission of words or letters, lack of rhythm, irregular writing, large width of or larger than average size letters, heavier than normal pressure which is often irregular, and inability to write in a straight, horizontal direction. Deviations in dyslexic writing show a preponderance of unembellished letters and misspelled words. A pilot study that we ran indicated that 69% of the dyslexic students wrote with poor or very poor legibility. This represented a higher percentage than was true of other diagnostic groups, including learning disabled, slow learners, and children with attention deficit disorder only.

Kimball (1973) studied handwriting samples of 12-year-olds and determined protocols that provided reliable and valid testing instruments to evaluate the personality of schoolchildren. He also found no difference between specimens copied from a standard text and those paraphrased from it at one time or with a five-week interval between. The present research tests the hypothesis that middle-school students diagnosed as dyslexic have handwriting characteristics which in toto and/or to a degree differ from those of subjects who do not have similar difficulties.

1.1 Overview

The study was conducted in several stages. The first part sought to establish graphic guidelines for differences in dyslexic and normal handwriting. The second part represented application of the rules to see whether they identified dyslexic writing. Graphoanalysts who had been certified by the International Graphoanalysis Society volunteered their services and participated in the first two parts. The next step was to extend the study to two groups of classroom teachers to determine whether the guidelines enhanced the accuracy of their judgements about the presence of dyslexia. The teachers were participating in a course at Texas Scottish Rite Hospital that would train them to be dyslexia therapists. One group was just beginning and the other completing the two-year requirements.

2.0 Establishing graphic guidelines

The initial part of this study was aimed at identifying subsets from the Children's Handwriting Evaluation Scale (CHES; Phelps et al, 1984) that have diagnostic potential in the identification of dyslexic children.

2.1 Subjects and procedure

Handwriting samples of previously administered tests were randomly selected from two categories of middle school students: a normal group of pupils in grades 6, 7, and 8 in mainstream classes of Dallas County Schools (collected by the authors during the norming of CHES) and a clinically diagnosed dyslexic group from the files at Texas Scottish Rite Hospital. The specimens were written on unlined 213 x 275 mm paper with a #2 pencil. The text comprised: **A boy named Jack lost a foot race at his school picnic. He ran home quickly to be comforted by his mother. "Mother," he said, "I will not race again if I can not win." "Son," said his mother, "you can not win if you do not race." Whatever you do, do with all your might.** The standardized directions given to each child were as follows: "I would like to see how well you write in cursive. After I have read this story aloud, I want you to copy it. Write as you usually do, and write as well as you can. Don't start writing until I tell you to."

2.2 Measures

Three graphoanalysts evaluated 10 dyslexics' and 10 normals' papers using the projective key of the CHES with several additions suggested by the research, for a total of 76 graphic indicators (see Appendix). The graphoanalysts were provided with a checklist and asked to rate the presence or absence of each sign based on the original writings.

The graphoanalysts were uncomfortable with a 0—1 rating and at their request the ratings were extended to a 4-point scale: 0, no indication; 1, just a little; 2, definitely present; and 3, strongly present. The analysts returned their appraisals within three weeks of receipt.

3.0 Results

Frequencies were counted for weights assigned by the three graphoanalysts to each of the 76 items on the two classes of writing. The 4-point rating scale did not show any clear-cut differentiation between dyslexic and normal writing. To sharpen the distinction, the two lower ratings were combined, as were the two higher ratings, to indicate either little to no or strong evidence of the sign. No formal method, even then, provided a meaningful subset. Percentages were calculated for the strong presence of each sign for each group and are shown on the right margin of the Appendix.

The 23 significant signs that seemed most able to discriminate normal from dyslexic writing and showed the highest correlation with the criteria are shown, with examples, in Figure 1. These indicators were abstracted and provided as a list of potential guidelines for graphoanalysts to use in the next step of the study. Additions made at the suggestion of the graphoanalysts were patching (soldering of lines) and lack of fluidity found in most dyslexic writing.

DYSLEXIC TENDENCIES

General Tendencies:

1. Slant - angled 60 degrees or less toward right
2. Baseline - uneven, irregular
3. Space - uneven between letters, words, or lines

Margins:

4. Left - wide
5. Right - crowded

Letters:

6. Transposed, substituted, or malformed *siad ram foot*
7. Variable size (not uniform) *Jack*
8. m's, n's, l's do not touch baseline *m n l*
9. Feathered finals *y e*
10. Rounded tops on m's and n's *m n*
11. Downstrokes weak and / or small *f y*
12. Flat - topped r's *r*
13. Dashes for i - dots *i*
14. Upstrokes beginning at base and breaking away *h le*
15. Loops left side of circle structure *o a*
16. Looped d's and t's *d t*

CONTRAINDICATIONS FOR DYSLEXIA

1. Baseline - downhill
2. Big buckle or printed K *Jack Jack*
3. Strong downstrokes below line, some incompleted loops *g — f*
4. Even letters and spaces *named*
5. Soft, rounded tops of letters, r's, s's *s n*
6. Breaks in words *ag an*
7. Hooks at beginning of words *race*

FIGURE 1: A characterization of dyslexic tendencies.

4.0 Determining the accuracy of the graphic guidelines

The next task was to determine the precision with which dyslexic children could be identified through the selected CHES items.

4.1 Procedure

Another group of papers were assembled. The authors divided dyslexics' writings into three groups: mild, moderate, and severe, and from the pool randomly selected 21 papers. Seven were of a mild degree, eight were moderate, and six were severe dyslexics. To make a group of 30, 9 papers were randomly chosen from the group of 75 papers previously used in the CHES norm study. Papers were photocopied and numbered 1 to 30. No other distinguishing marks were present. Three different analysts used the guidelines established earlier to determine the writer's category as normal or dyslexic. The analysts did not know how many normals or dyslexics were in the sample of 30. The task was completed within 2 months.

4.2 Measures

The graphoanalysts rated each of 30 papers as 0–1 (absent or present) on the checklist of 23 graphic guidelines. Summatively, each determined whether or not the writer of the sample was dyslexic.

5.0 Results

The overall judgements showed striking similarity and accuracy (see Figure 2).

In terms of a screening test, the specificity of this method resides in the percentage of normal samples selected from the normal pool by the graphoanalysts. This was 89%. The sensitivity of this method is the percentage of known dyslexic samples that were chosen from dyslexics by the graphoanalysts. This rate was 67% for mild dyslexics, 92% for moderate dyslexics, and 100% for severe dyslexics, with an overall rate of 86%. This combined rate reflects the fact that the mild, moderate, and severe dyslexics were about equally represented in the study. A population with a greater proportion of moderate and severe dyslexics would increase the sensitivity; conversely, a greater proportion of mild dyslexics would decrease the sensitivity.

In the present population of 24% mild, 27% moderate, 20% severe dyslexics, and 30% normals, the false positive rate was found to be 5% (i.e., about one out of twenty samples declared to be dyslexic would really have come from a normal). The false negative rate was 27% (i.e., about one out of four samples identified as normal would really have come from a dyslexic). In other words, any sample classified as coming from a dyslexic was quite likely to have actually come from a dyslexic, while there was a one in four chance that a sample declared to be from a normal might not be. While the false negative rate might seem high, it should be pointed out that seven of the nine samples incorrectly categorized as normals came from mild dyslexics, so a misclassification of normal in those cases would not be potentially catastrophic.

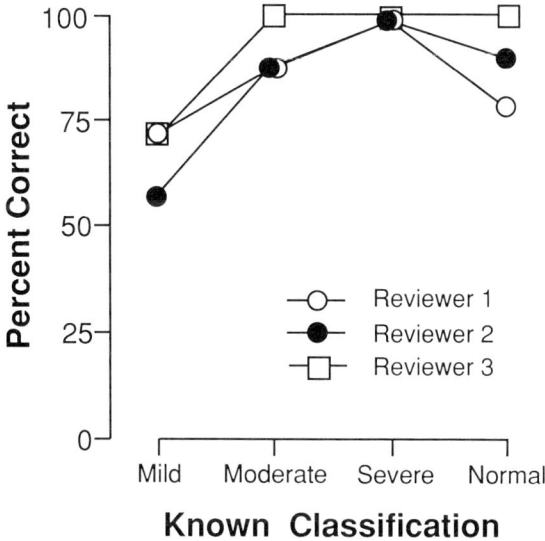

FIGURE 2: Predictive power of graphoanalysis in dyslexics and normals.

The graphoanalysts showed some variability in their use of graphic signs but in more than 72 out of 90 possible judgements, 80% or higher, they agreed upon the following indications of dyslexic writing: uneven baseline and spacing; crowded right margins; transposed, substituted or malformed letters; variably sized letters; feathered finals; rounded tops on m's and n's; weak downstrokes; flat-topped r's; dashes for i-dots; small kbuckles, and no breaks in words. The indicators coincided to a certain extent with Hearn's study (1969).

The graphoanalysts also concurred on personality traits prevalent in dyslexic students. These included: cumulative thinking (slow, gradual accretion of information to build conclusions); lack of perseverance, self-confidence, consistency, predictability, and rhythm; undeveloped talent for manual dexterity and difficulty adapting to change.

A one-way analysis of variance and the Tukey HSD multiple comparison procedure showed a significant difference between normal students and all levels of dyslexics for the number of dyslexic indicators that were marked by the graphoanalysts (Table 1). There was also a significant difference between the number of indicators for mild and severe dyslexic handwriting. The number of contraindicators, while significantly different between normals and all levels of dyslexia, did not reveal significant differences between the levels of dyslexia.

TABLE 1: Comparison of mean number of summed dyslexic indicators and contraindicators for dyslexic and normal handwriting.

Summed variable	Handwriting			
	Mild	Moderate	Severe	Normal
Indicator	12.7	14.3	15.4	8.8
Contraindicator	3.5	2.9	2.3	4.9

6.0 Applying the graphic guidelines in the classroom

Finally it seemed important to ascertain whether the guidelines established and validated through the earlier parts of this study could be used by teachers as a routine evaluation tool.

6.1 Procedure

Twelve classroom teachers completing classes and 10 teachers beginning classes in dyslexia remediation at Texas Scottish Rite Hospital were given identical copies of the handwriting used by the graphoanalysts and asked to judge whether or not the writer was dyslexic or normal. Half were asked to use their own experience to make decisions, and half were asked to use the rules established by the graphoanalysts. The samples were evaluated over a period of one week.

7.0 Results

The trained therapists (those with two years' schooling in dyslexia) identified mild dyslexics better than their counterparts beginning the course. Also, they were marginally more accurate in finding moderate dyslexics. Both groups tended to err in judging only the most deviant writing as severely dyslexic and the preponderance as normal, failing to recognize the mild and moderate.

The two groups were different in that the trained therapists (with the exception of one mother of a dyslexic child) all taught in elementary schools as regular or special education or

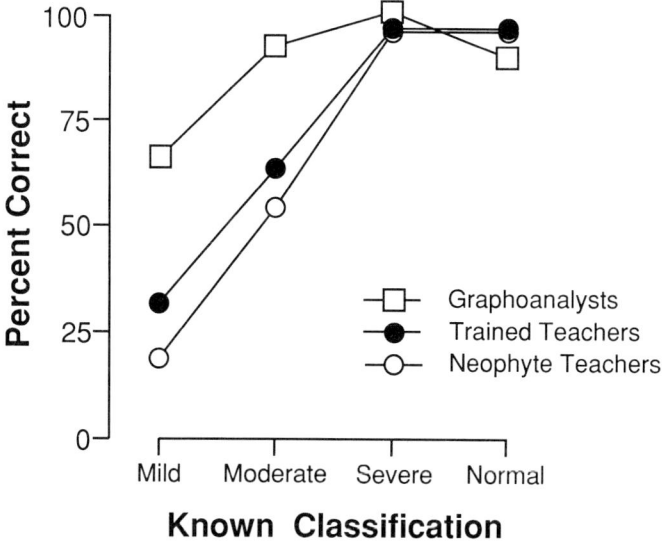

FIGURE 3: Comparison of diagnostic power for graphoanalysts vs teachers.

resource teachers. The beginning class was composed of three speech pathologists, a high school teacher, a college teacher, and the remaining five, elementary teachers. The focus and orientation of the trained individuals as well as their indoctrination in dyslexia possibly contributed to their superior performance.

Both groups of teachers registered 95% accuracy in selecting normal and severely dyslexic writing, but were significantly less accurate than the graphoanalysts (chi square, $p< .05$) in finding intermediate levels (see Figure 3). Neither group of therapists was affected or improved by being given the graphic guidelines.

8.0 Conclusion

This research indicates that it is possible for graphoanalysts to determine the presence of dyslexia in handwriting. Their discipline and training in careful discrimination enabled them to respond with sensitivity to the nuances of the writing line. Though they had no experience with dyslexia, when given writing cues they were able to select accurate designations for all levels of difficulty.

Teachers given the same set of rules as the graphoanalysts could not apply them meaningfully but did identify the extremes of normal and severely dyslexic writing. The relatively poor showing of the teachers may reflect the general standard and low expectations of handwriting found in the classroom and a customary emphasis on content rather than form. It appears unlikely that teachers who teach above the third-grade level will scrutinize individual letter forms. Also, research has brought out the information that many teachers are reluctant to teach or judge handwriting because they feel that their own is substandard. This attitude permits a broad area of acceptance and a lack of critical viewing. The trained therapists exceeded their neophyte counterparts — probably because part of the training for dyslexia therapy focuses on individual graphic symbols and instructions for teaching them through kinaesthetic and verbal cues. (It might also be noted that all but one of the group were experienced in teaching elementary school.)

The key problem for future effort if the technique outlined in this chapter is to be made practical and applicable is to make the graphic guidelines clear and understandable by teachers and to help them become keenly aware of the implications of writing strokes. An extension of this study is planned to discern and describe a set of rules that teachers can easily apply. If teachers can become sensitized to these graphic signs, the students will benefit. Their need for help, especially at the middle-school level, is acute.

"Middle schools", according to Robert F. Wagner Jr., president of the Board of Education of New York City, "are the forgotten weak link in the chain of reaching pupils at risk for dropping out" (Warren, 1989). The importance of finding and helping the student who has reached this grade level without needed remediation cannot be overemphasized. Handwriting can be a clue to an alert teacher that the student needs remedial help.

9.0 Appendix: CHES scoring sheet with presence of signs shown in percentages

Handwriting feature	Percentage of cases found in:	
	Dyslexics	Normals

1. *Slant* - Examine upstrokes. Determine region (relative to points of the compass) in which more than half of the strokes slant:

1. Between W and N or 2. Between N and NE	50	80
3. Between NE and E	47	17
4. Variable	3	3

2. *Pressure* — Rate as:

1. Heavy	3	3
2. Moderate	27	27
3. Light	10	0
4. Variable	60	70

3. *Baseline* — Rate as:

1. Uphill	17	17
2. Level	23	30
3. Downhill	20	47
4. Irregular	40	6

4. *Margins* — Rate as:

a. Left :		
1. Wide — inside printed paragraph	75	55
2. Narrow (or none)	25	45
b. Right :		
3. Wide	12	3
4. Narrow (or none)	38	92

5. *Global Impressions* — Indicate 0 = not present, 1 = weak, 2 = moderate, 3 = strong:

a. Cramped writing, retracted structures	80	77
b. Soft, rounded letters	40	67

c. Even letters and spaces	40	77
d. Letters on two writing lines overlap	0	0
e. Large middle zone letters, shortened upper and lower ones	52	50
f. Large writing, 1/4" or larger	52	48
g. Small writing, 1/16" or smaller	7	10
h. Variable letter size	70	33
i. Breaks in words	0	17
j. Misspelled words	17	0
k. Inverted or transposed letters	3	0
l. Omitted words or lines	0	3

6. *Circle Structures* — Indicate 1 = yes, 2 = no:

a. Loops right side of circle structures	20	30
b. Loops left side	70	30
c. Loops both sides	23	37
d. Very round circle structure	50	73
e. Closed circle structure	80	83

7. *Tall Letters* — Indicate 1 = yes, 2 = no:

a. Wide loops	10	10
b. Overstem t-bars	0	0
c. Low t-bars	41	63
d. Looped d and t	30	13
e. Wedge-shaped return strokes	17	10
f. Concave t-bar	13	17
g. Convex t-bar	7	13
h. t-bar on left side	0	7
i. t-bar on right side or tick stroke	13	3
j. Short t and d stems	67	73
k. Big buckle or printed k	10	43
l. High retraced d stem	20	20
m. Big tall loops	7	17
n. Weight of t-bar crossing — mark:	39	30
1. weak, 2. moderate, 3. strong	0	0
o. Tied strokes		

8. *Letters with Lower Extenders* — Indicate 1 = yes, 2 = no:

a. Wedge below line	10	7
b. Figure 8 letters	0	0
c. Strong down strokes	13	48
d. Large loops	10	0
e. Incomplete loops	3	27

f. Small loop cut off low	13	17
g. Small short loops	33	57
h. Hoops	0	0

9. *Middle Zone Letters* — Indicate 1 = yes, 2 = no:

a. Loops	17	3
b. Retraced to top (or almost to top)	63	73
c. Last hump higher	37	27
d. Rounded tops	80	67
e. V-shaped space between tops	40	40
f. U-shaped spaces between stops	3	0
g. Pointed tops	20	27
h. i dot omitted, t-bars uncrossed	0	0
i. Flat-topped r	53	27
j. Dashes for i dots	67	17
k. m, n or l not touching baseline	50	27
l. Upstrokes that begin at baseline, break-away to right	37	13

10. *Beginning and Ending Strokes* — Indicate 1 = yes, 2 = no:

a. Little loops on capitals	23	23
b. Straight, right beginning strokes	13	20
c. Hooks at beginning of words	10	40
d. Unnecessary beginning of words	37	23
e. Regressive strokes	13	20
f. Circle dots, decorative capitals, long upstrokes at word ends	10	17
g. Finals feather or do not touch baseline	70	43
h. Final hooks	47	47
i. Free flowing strokes	0	0

11. *Immaturity Index* — Add:

5e; 5f; 5h; 7n; 8g; 1 if 4	40	27

12. *Impulsivity Index* — Add:

1 if either 2 or 3; 2 if marked 3; 9, d,g,h, 5e	3	3

13. *Creativity Index* — Add:

2 if marked 1; 5c, 8, b,h, 9i	20	23

Chapter 12

Estimating a child's learning potential from form errors in a child's printing

Marvin L. Simner

Proponents of graphology have long defended the position that there are signs in cursive and printed script which may be employed for the purpose of assessing an individual's character, attitudes, personality and intelligence. The evidence obtained to date, however, seriously questions the legitimacy of this position (Ben-Shakhar et al, 1986; Eysenck and Gudjonsson, 1986; Lester et al, 1977; Rosenthal and Lines, 1978). In fact, some investigators even claim that there is so little evidence linking handwriting to behaviour that further research on this topic is probably unwarranted (Furnham and Gunter, 1987). For the most part, however, these negative findings have resulted largely from work with adults in which handwriting evaluations were confined mostly to the size, shape, slant, completeness and relative spacing of cursive letters within words.

In contrast to this work with adults, my findings have shown that there are certain components in a child's handwriting which can be very helpful in estimating a child's learning potential. These components, called form errors, result when children add, delete or misalign parts while printing individual letters and numbers, thereby distorting the overall shape or form of the intended letter or number (see Figure 1 for examples). In particular, my results indicate that preschool children who produce an excessive number of these errors are likely to experience serious learning problems once they enter school (Simner, 1982, 1985, 1986, 1989, 1990). In light of these findings, rather than discouraging further work on a possible tie between handwriting and behaviour, it would seem more

Development of Graphic Skills
ISBN 0-12-734940-5

appropriate to recommend instead that the focus of research
should be shifted from adults to children and that greater
emphasis should be given to examining this link between form
errors and school achievement.

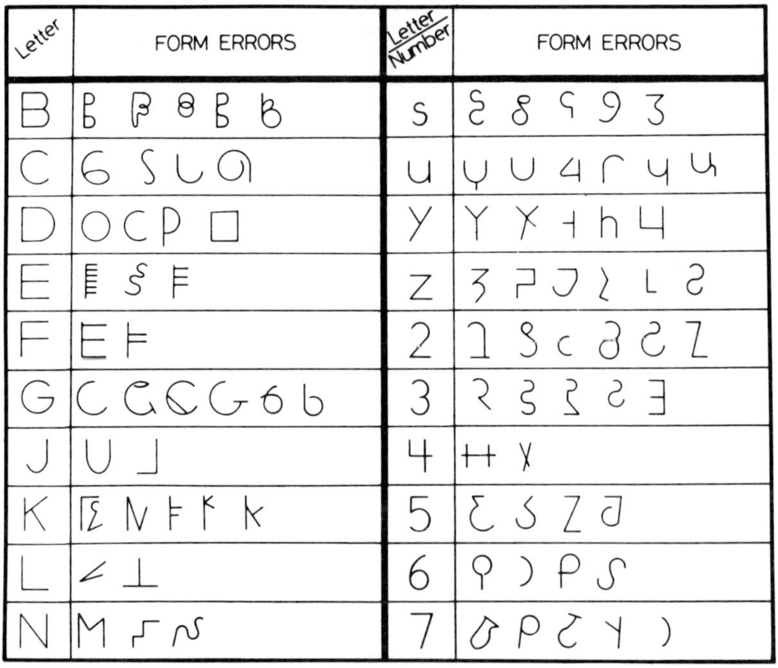

FIGURE 1: Examples of form errors in children's printing (from Simner, 1982, reproduced with permission).

To encourage such a shift in focus, the purpose of this chapter is
to review what is known about the relationship between form
errors and a child's learning potential and to direct attention to
some issues where future inquiry may be fruitful. In this
chapter I first describe a psychometric test that I developed to
measure form errors in 4- to 6-year old children. I then
summarize my previous findings with this test as well as some
recent findings obtained by others who have used the test. Next,
I report the outcome of a six-year follow-up investigation which
suggests that the link I initially obtained between form errors

and academic achievement might remain in effect well beyond the early school years. The material in the following section provides an extension to this work by demonstrating that formal testing might not be necessary to identify children who produce an excessive number of form errors. Instead, the longitudinal investigation reported here indicates that teachers' daily observations of children's classroom printing can be as successful as scores on my printing test in spotting children who are at risk for early school failure. Finally, I offer some thoughts on why these errors have a bearing on the preschool child's future success in school.

1.0 Printing Performance School Readiness Test

Several years ago I developed the Printing Performance School Readiness Test (PPSRT; Simner, 1985) to provide teachers with a systematic way to identify senior kindergarten children (age range: 51–77 months) who produce an excessive number of form errors. The PPSRT requires that children print a series of 41 letters and numbers from pictures presented one at a time on cards. If testing takes place in the fall or spring of senior kindergarten, the children print from memory immediately after seeing each letter or number for two to three seconds. If testing occurs in the spring preceding kindergarten entry, the children copy the letters and numbers from the cards while the cards remain in full view.

Although the PPSRT is quite appropriate for use at the senior kindergarten level, the task is too long and too demanding to employ with younger children. For this reason I developed an abbreviated version of the PPSRT (APPSRT; Simner, 1989) for use as early as the start of junior kindergarten, or in other words, with children as young as 45 months. Here the task consists of having the children copy 18 letters and numbers appearing on two response sheets in spaces provided directly below the letters and numbers.

Neither test is timed; however, testing averages about 10 minutes per child when the PPSRT is used and under 3 minutes per child when the APPSRT is employed. Once testing is

complete the protocols are scored by comparing each of the
child's reproductions against appropriate templates in the
PPSRT manual. Because each reproduction receives a score of
either zero (form error absent) or one (form error present), total
scores range from 0 through 18 when the APPSRT is used and
from 0 through 41 when the PPSRT is employed. The
psychometric properties (i.e. inter-rater reliability, test—retest
reliability and predictive validity) of both tests have been
extensively evaluated in a number of longitudinal investigations
which I now summarize.

1.1 Test reliability

To determine whether the form errors generated by these tests
can be readily identified I asked pairs of raters to score sets of
randomly selected protocols. The findings reported in the test
manual and elsewhere (Simner, 1982, 1986, 1989) show
considerable agreement among the raters. As one example, the
product-moment correlation between sets of scores submitted by
the pair of raters asked to evaluate protocols from the APPSRT
was .95. Moreover, the scores differed only by three points or less
in 90% of the cases.

In addition to obtaining information on inter-rater reliability,
five samples of randomly selected children were given either the
PPSRT or the APPSRT twice. When the interval between testing
was short (one month apart) the correlations averaged .87,
whereas when the interval was long (eight months apart) the
correlations averaged .74.

1.2 Test validity

Predictive validity was assessed by following eight samples
totalling nearly 800 children for periods of up to three years.
Thus, the children who received the APPSRT were tracked
through the end of first grade while the children who were given
the PPSRT were tracked through the end of second grade.
Criteria included measures like the Woodcock Reading Mastery
Test by Woodcock (1974, Form-B) and the Keymath Diagnostic
Arithmetic Test by Connolly et al (1971) as well as the children's

final report card marks and the teachers' end of year promotion decisions.

Representative findings from this work are illustrated in Table 1 which contains the results from the two samples of children who were given the APPSRT in the fall of junior kindergarten (Sample 1 and 2) and from two other samples of children administered the PPSRT in the fall of senior kindergarten (Sample 4 and 5). As the findings in Table 1 show, independently of when the printing task was administered, the sample of children to whom it was given, or the criterion measure employed, the outcome was similar, with the majority of the correlations ranging in the vicinity of −.50.

TABLE 1: Product-moment correlations (p < .001) between scores on the APPSRT (given in the fall of junior kindergarten) and on the PPSRT (given in the fall of senior kindergarten) and children's performances in school measured at the end of first and second grade. (a=Woodcock Reading Mastery Test; b=Keymath Diagnostic Arithmetic Test)

Test/ sample	School achievement					
	First-grade achievement test performance		Final first-grade report card marks		Final second-grade report card marks	
	WRMTa	KDATb	Reading	Math	Reading	Math
APPSRT						
1	−.40	−.49	−.42	−.44	-	-
2	−.57	−.60	−.58	−.51	-	-
PPSRT						
1	−.50	−.57	−.53	−.54	−.50	−.39
2	−.59	−.75	−.54	−.44	−.54	−.47

Through a further analysis of the follow-up data, I also found that both printing tests can be employed with reasonable accuracy as aids in identifying individual children who are likely to experience school failure. First I chose, as cutoff points, scores on the PPSRT and on the APPSRT that corresponded to about one standard deviation above the mean. The children whose scores were at or above these cutoffs were said to be at risk for failure. Next the children were divided into two categories reflecting the teachers' evaluations of the children's performances in class. Children who were placed in the poor performance category were the ones who either failed, were promoted to a slower or junior section of the next grade, or were recommended for some type of special education class. The second category, labelled good performance, contained children who received an overall rating of B— to A+ on their report cards at the end of the follow-up period. According to the children's teachers, these ratings were awarded only to children who were not experiencing any major problems with the core curriculum.

The outcome of this work revealed that, on average, 78% of the children whose work in school placed them in the poor performance category scored at or above these cutoffs and that 79% of the children in the good performance category had scores below these cutoffs. Of particular importance with regard to individual identification I also found that the children whose scores exceeded approximately two standard deviations above the mean had a 70—80% chance of failing or being placed in some type of special education class by the end of first or second grade. Thus, for the children who produced an excessive number of form errors, the chances of the children experiencing serious learning problems once they entered school were very high indeed.

1.3 Summary

The findings obtained thus far indicate that form errors produced by the PPSRT and by its abbreviated counterpart, the APPSRT, can be easily differentiated from other printing errors and that children who produce either a large number or very few of these errors on one occasion are likely to behave in a very similar manner when tested again even up to half a year later. Of greatest importance, follow-up evidence has clearly demonstrated that the number of form errors produced while the children were in preschool was closely tied to the children's command of the core curriculum. Although I do not advocate using either instrument as the sole means of identifying a failure-prone child, as noted in the manual, this follow-up evidence also compares quite favourably with the follow-up results reported by others using such traditional preschool screening devices as the McCarthy Scales of Children's Abilities, the Metropolitan Readiness Tests, and the de Hirsch Predictive Index of Reading Failure, to name a few. Hence, it would certainly seem that form errors in printing, as measured by both the PPSRT and the APPSRT, hold considerable promise as a means of aiding teachers in locating children who are at risk for early school failure.

2.0 Further follow-up studies

Recently I was able to review data provided by the Dryden and Fort Frances-Rainy River school districts in Northern Ontario (Simner, 1990). As part of a pilot project undertaken prior to adopting the PPSRT, all 353 senior kindergarten children attending school in both districts were tested by the children's teachers either in the fall or spring semester of kindergarten. The children were then followed through the end of first grade at which time information was gathered on the children's progress in school from the children's report cards. Like the data I obtained, the Dryden data yielded a product-moment correlation of $-.49$ ($p<.001$) while the data from Fort Frances-Rainy River produced a correlation of $-.51$ ($p<.001$) between the children's PPSRT scores and the children's final first-grade report card averages. Their data also showed a 60−70% chance of failure for the children whose form error scores were approximately two standard deviations above the mean.

Along with having access to these findings from Northern Ontario I was also able to collect further data on the senior kindergarten children in one of my original samples. This allowed me to extend my previous results well beyond the early school years. Specifically, I located all of the children who received the PPSRT in the fall of 1982 and who were still attending school in the same district six years later. The children were then assessed in terms of academic progress as well as in terms of handwriting skills.

2.1 Subjects

All thirty-four of the 132 children who had participated in my initial work in 1982 and who had not moved from the original school district were found in the fall of 1988. Although I was unable to track the remaining children due to budget restrictions, it is worth noting that the mean form error score (16.4) and standard deviation (11.1) produced by these 34 children were almost identical to the mean form error score (17.4) and standard deviation (12.0) produced by the sample as a whole. Therefore, it would seem that these 34 children were probably representative of the children in the original sample.

2.2 Task

To assess the children's progress in school at the end of this six-year period, I obtained information on the children's grade placements. That is, I asked whether the children were in the correct grade for their ages or whether they had failed and if so how often. The children were also tested in the areas of reading comprehension and arithmetic using the Comprehensive Inventory of Basic Skills (CIBS) by Brigance (1983).

In addition, and on the assumption that there might be a link between form errors and later handwriting difficulties, I administered the handwriting test from the CIBS. This test consists of having each child print, then copy in cursive script, a standard paragraph. The children's reproductions of this paragraph were then scored according to procedures given in the Test of Legible Handwriting (TLH) by Hammill and Larsen (1989). I chose to use the TLH scoring procedure rather than the procedure found in the CIBS manual because the TLH manual provided more detailed scoring instructions. Hence, each child's reproduction was assessed for speed, measured in terms of the number of letters copied within a two-minute period, as well as legibility. The legibility index was based on a composite score derived from values assigned to each of the following dimensions: letter formation, letter alignment, uniformity of letter slant, size of letters in relation to each other, size of letters in relation to available space, uniformity of spacing between letters, uniformity of spacing between words, and correct use of margins. To avoid bias, the three tests from the CIBS were given and scored by a person who was unaware of the children's performances on the PPSRT.

3.0 Results

Table 2 contains the outcome of this work. First in terms of academic achievement, as shown in Table 2, with the exception of the correlation between the children's scores on the PPSRT and the children's scores on the CIBS arithmetic test, the other two correlations are high enough to suggest that the children who produced the greatest number of form errors in the fall of senior kindergarten were still the ones experiencing the most difficulty in school six years later. In line with this point, five of the 34 children in this sample had PPSRT scores equal to or beyond two standard deviations above the mean. By the end of this six-year follow-up period, all five of these children had failed one or more times. In contrast, only one child whose score was less than two standard deviations above the mean failed a grade.

TABLE 2: Product-moment correlations between scores on the Printing Performance School Readiness Test administered in the fall of senior kindergarten and academic achievement as well as handwriting performance assessed six years later. (a =Comprehensive Inventory of Basic Skills; b=based on information provided by the children's schools; c=measured according to procedures in the Comprehensive Inventory of Basic Skills, scored according to instructions in the Test of Legible Handwriting; **p<.001;*p<.05)

Academic achievement			Handwriting performance (c)			
			Speed		Legibility	
Reading (a)	Arith- metic (a)	Grade place (b)	Cursive	Print	Cursive	Print
−.67**	−.26	−.67**	−.53**	−.36*	−.54**	−.73**

Next, in terms of handwriting, the findings in Table 2 suggest that an excessive number of form errors might also be predictive of certain writing difficulties. Regarding speed, both the magnitude and the direction of the correlation obtained with the cursive script task indicate that children who produce a large number of these errors in kindergarten, later write more slowly than other children. For example, the four children who produced the greatest number of form errors wrote half as fast (mean = 27 letters per minute) as the four children who produced the fewest form errors (mean = 62.3 letters per minute; $p<.05$, by two-tail Mann-Whitney U test). While the findings were similar when the children printed, as the size of the correlation in Table 2 indicates, here the difference was less striking. In particular, although the four children who produced the greatest number of form errors again printed more slowly (mean = 37.3 letters per minute) than the four children who produced the fewest form errors (mean = 55.5 letter per minute) the difference was not reliable ($p > .10$ by Mann-Whitney U test). Regarding legibility, however, the correlations for both tasks are high enough to suggest that children who produce the most form errors are likely to be more erratic or less controlled when writing and printing than children who produce very few of these errors.

3.1 Conclusions from the further follow-up studies

In short, the findings from this further follow-up work permit several conclusions. First, the Dryden and Fort Frances-Rainy River school districts in Northern Ontario, unlike the London school district in Southwestern Ontario where the PPSRT was normed, are largely rural and serve many native families. Thus, in addition to providing independent confirmation of my results, the similarity between their results and mine suggests that the findings that I obtained with the PPSRT are likely to apply to children from backgrounds that are quite different from the backgrounds that characterized the children I employed when I standardized this instrument. Second, from my extended follow-up data it would also seem that form errors might be predictive, on a long-term basis, of learning problems as well as certain handwriting deficiencies. This second conclusion must be viewed as tentative, though, because the evidence on which it is based stems from a relatively small sample.

4.0 Form errors generated during normal classroom printing exercises

The evidence summarized above demonstrates that form errors produced under standard testing conditions can be quite helpful in identifying preschool children with potential learning problems. From a practical standpoint, however, if teachers, through their normal observations of children's printing in class, already know which children make an excessive number of form errors, formal testing with the PPSRT might not be necessary. Hence, the aim of the work reported in this section was to determine whether teachers' appraisals of children's everyday printing leads to findings similar to the findings summarized in the previous section.

Twenty-seven teachers were asked to rate the senior kindergarten children in their classes on a five-point scale in terms of the frequency with which form errors occurred in the children's normal classroom printing. The ratings were conducted in the early spring of kindergarten to provide the teachers with ample opportunity to observe the children. The children were then followed for one year though the end of first grade and evaluated on their command of the curriculum.

4.1 Subjects

As in all of my previous work I employed two samples of teachers for the purpose of replication. Sample 1 contained 11 teachers while Sample 2 consisted of 16 teachers.

4.2 Writing samples

The 417 children whose printing was evaluated were obtained as part of another investigation (Simner, 1987, 1988) by distributing permission forms through the public school system in London, Ontario, and requesting parental approval to collect information on the children. Approximately 70% of the forms were returned and, with few exceptions, all of these gave approval for the children to take part in this study. Because the total number of children employed in Sample 1 was 127, each teacher evaluated, on average, 12 children. In Sample 2 the total number of children was 290 and so here each teacher evaluated, on average, 18 children. The mean age of the children at the time of the evaluations (March of senior kindergarten) was 69 months.

4.3 Rating task

The teachers were shown the examples of form errors in Figure 1 to guide them in judging the frequency with which these errors occurred in the children's normal classroom printing. As anchoring points the teachers were told that a rating of 1 signified that a child produced form errors very often, a rating of 3 indicated the occasional appearance of form errors in the child's printing, and 5 meant that the child never made form errors. The teachers were also asked not to confine their judgements to name printing alone if other printing exercises were regularly employed. Instead, they were requested to keep in mind the children's general printing habits over the previous two to three months when deciding which values on this five-point scale were the proper ones to employ.

4.4 Rater reliability

Seven of the classes had a teacher and an assistant teacher, both of whom had equal access to the children's printing throughout the year. Therefore, I was able to obtain sets of ratings on 113 children. To guard against bias, each teacher was requested not to discuss her ratings with the assistant teacher. The results yielded a product-moment correlation of .76 (p <.001) between the pairs of ratings. Moreover, in 90% of the cases the ratings were either identical or differed by only one point. In addition, 82 other children were given the PPSRT by a person who was unaware of the teachers' ratings. Here the correlation between the children's PPSRT scores and the teachers' ratings was $-.64$ (p< .001). Together these findings indicate that teachers show considerable agreement with one another when asked to judge the frequency with which form errors take place during classroom printing exercises and that their judgements are also likely to match the evidence obtained through formal testing.

4.5 Follow-up

Both samples were followed through the end of first grade. To assess the children's academic achievements at the end of this period and to permit a direct comparison between the present findings and my previous results, I employed the same sets of criteria used in my earlier investigations. The first set made use of the children's report card marks in the two major areas of the curriculum, reading and math. These marks ranged on a 12-point scale from D− to A+ and reflected the teacher's appraisals of the children's command of the core curriculum established by the board of education. According to the teachers, the children whose marks were in the D− to D+ range were having considerable difficulty mastering the curriculum. As mentioned above, marks in the B− to A+ range were only awarded when there was reasonable certainty that the children were not experiencing any serious learning problems.

The second set of criteria consisted of the children's raw scores on the standardized achievement tests used before. Hence, in May of first grade I administered grade-appropriate sub-tests from the Woodcock Reading Mastery Test and from the Keymath Diagnostic Arithmetic Test to approximately 85% of the children in each sample. Both tests were given by personnel who were unaware of the kindergarten teachers' ratings of the children's printing and of the children's progress in school.

5.0 Results

The outcome of this follow-up work can be found in Table 3. As the results in this table indicate, the correlations, which were similar for both samples and for all of the criteria, once more ranged in the vicinity of −.50. Hence these findings are certainly in line with the correlational evidence that I obtained with both the PPSRT and the APPSRT (see Table 1).

TABLE 3: *Product-moment correlations (p < .001) between teachers' ratings of form errors in senior kindergarten children's classroom printing and the children's performances measured one year later at the end of first grade. (a=Woodcock Reading Mastery Test; b=Keymath Diagnostic Arithmetic Test)*

Teachers	First-grade achievement performance		Final first-grade report card marks	
	WRMTa	KDATb	Reading	Math
Sample 1	−.57	−.61	−.58	−.47
Sample 2	−.42	−.52	−.45	−.43

Table 4 provides a more detailed breakdown of the data by presenting the findings in an expectancy table format in order to show more clearly the relationship between each value on the five-point rating scale used by the kindergarten teachers and the children's progress in school. To construct this table I followed a procedure discussed by Brown (1983). First, I combined the information from the two samples to produce a more stable estimate of this relationship. Next, I separated the children into either a D− to D+, C− to C+, or B− to A+ category based on the children's average in-class performance in reading and math at the end of first grade. I then distributed the children who were placed in these three categories according to the ratings the children received from their kindergarten teachers on the five-point scale.

Inspection of the findings in Table 4 shows that 36 of the 417 children in the combined sample were given a rating of 1. By the end of first grade, of these 36 children, 78% were performing poorly enough in school to warrant being placed in the D− to D+ category. As the kindergarten teachers' ratings of the children's printing neared 5, though, the percentage of children in this category diminished substantially. For example, only 4% of the children who received a rating of 4 and none of the children with a rating of 5 appeared in the D— to D+ category. On the other hand, of the 65 children who were rated 5 by their kindergarten teachers, by the end of first grade 82% were performing well enough in class to justify placement in the B— to A+ category. Moreover, the percentage of children in this category diminished substantially as the teachers' ratings neared 1. In short, the evidence in Table 4 reveals that the odds of a child experiencing a serious learning problem once that child enters school increase dramatically as the teacher's rating of the child's printing in kindergarten becomes lower. This evidence, then, illustrates far more effectively than does the correlational evidence, the very close fit which exists between the kindergarten teachers' evaluations of form errors in children's everyday printing and children's subsequent progress in school.

TABLE 4: Expectancy table showing the number and percentage (in parentheses) of children in the three first -grade report card mark categories according to the form error ratings awarded the children by their teachers when the children were in senior kindergarten.

Form error rating	N	First grade report card mark categories		
		D— to D+	C— to C+	B to A+
1 Very often	36 (9%)	28 (78%)	5 (14%)	3 (8%)
2 Often	57 (14%)	26 (46%)	20 (35%)	11 (19%)
3 Occasionally	103 (25%)	23 (22%)	52 (50%)	28 (27%)
4 Rarely	156 (37%)	7 (4%)	51 (33%)	98 (63%)
5 Never	65 (15%)	0 (0%)	12 (18%)	53 (82%)
Total	417	84	140	193

6.0 Why form errors relate to academic achievement

The major findings that have emerged thus far from my work on form errors indicate that these errors, whether assessed

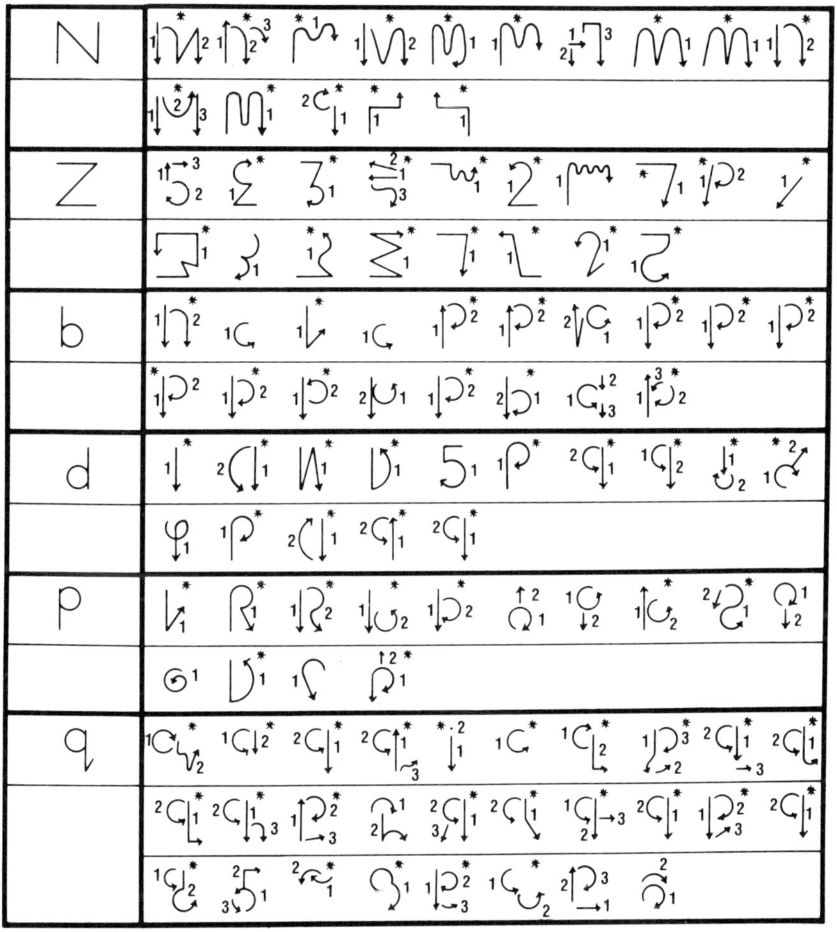

FIGURE 2: Form errors generated by six letters showing the pencil strokes employed by the children when the errors occurred. The numbers indicate the order of the strokes while the arrows designate the end point in the construction of each stroke.

using the PPSRT, the APPSRT, or through a teacher's every-day observations of a child's classroom printing, can provide important information about the at-risk status of a child. Two closely related questions now remain, namely, what causes form errors to take place and why do these errors provide so much insight into a preschool child's learning potential?

Several explanations come to mind, the first one having to do
with a memory problem, the second one having to do with a
planning problem. Both explanations stem from an additional
finding that I obtained as part of my earlier investigations of
children's printing (Simner, 1979). Briefly, 79 senior
kindergarten children, tested individually, were asked to
reproduce the 41 letters/numbers in the PPSRT shown one at a
time on slides. The pencil strokes used by the children as the
children constructed the letters and numbers were recorded by
an observer standing behind the children while the children
printed. The outcome of this work showed that when the
children made a form error the error itself took place reliably
more often during the final stage, rather than during the initial
stage of letter construction.

Figure 2, which illustrates this finding, contains the stroke
patterns used to generate all of the form errors produced by the
children for six of the letters employed in this study. The
numbers indicate the order of the pencil strokes, the arrows
designate the end point in the construction of each stroke. As the
material in this figure shows, for the most part, the children
began constructing the letters with strokes that were
appropriate for producing proper renditions of the letters. As the
children proceeded, however, it was the remaining feature(s) of
the letters that became distorted thereby causing the finished
products to differ from the original. An asterisk appears next to
each error in Figure 2 where this process is evident.

Based on this finding, one way of explaining the occurrence of
form errors is to suggest that these errors might take place due
to a poorly developed or unstable memory image which
gradually fades and then disappears as children print.
According to this account, then, children start a letter with the
proper visual image of the letter in mind. As printing proceeds,
however, this image fades leaving the children without an
appropriate model to follow. This could be why, for example, the
alphanumeric characters in Figure 1 that have curved features
(eg **C**, **G**, **3**, **6**) tend to generate form errors that are largely
curved, whereas the ones with linear features (eg **E**, **F**, **4**, **7**) tend
to produce mostly linear form errors. Thus, according to this
first explanation, it could be that form errors relate to school

achievement because these errors are symptomatic of an underlying memory problem and it is this memory problem which persists and subsequently interferes with the child's learning in school.

I hasten to add, however, that by raising the possiblity that form errors might result from a memory problem, it is not my intention to suggest that children who produce many form errors necessarily suffer from a serious deficiency in the capacity to remember or to retrieve information. Rather, I believe that if these errors are indeed caused by a memory problem, in all likelihood this memory problem stems from difficulties the children experienced during the early stages of acquiring a memory image. That is to say, because my findings also show that children who produce many form errors are easily distracted (Simner, 1982), it is certainly possible that when these children were exposed to the letters initially they might not have been able to focus their attention on the shapes or forms of the letters long enough to develop memory images that would remain intact throughout the course of printing. Hence, when I use the term memory problem, I employ this term only to convey what I feel might be the immediate or direct cause of the error and not because I feel that these children have a truly deficient memory system.

The second explanation which stems from this stroke pattern evidence is that form errors possibly result from the children's difficulty in organizing or planning the sequence of strokes needed to generate a proper rendition of the letters. My reason for offering this other explanation is that for the preschool child the act of printing itself is a complex task which involves the need to make decisions at a number of choice points using what must be an extremely intricate processing system (Simner, 1981, 1984). Furthermore, it is well known that many preschool children need to actually observe the sequence of movements required to reproduce a letter in order to carry out this sequence themselves. That is, they must see someone perform the stroke sequences, then they must learn the rules that govern these sequences, and finally, they must practise implementing these rules if they are to print without error (Furner, 1983). Thus, for some children, to engage in printing before they receive any formal training in printing might simply be overwhelming, and so for these children form errors could result from an inability to decide where or how to connect the individual pencil lines that go toward making up a letter. According to this second explanation then, it could be that form errors are tied to school achievement because these errors result from an underlying problem-solving or strategy-planning difficulty and it is this difficulty which lingers and subsequently affects the child's school performance.

In essence, my first explanation holds that it could be an underlying memory problem which is responsible for the relationship between form errors and school achievement, whereas according to my second explanation this relationship might stem from an underlying planning problem. At present it is not possible to say which of these two explanations best accounts for all of the available evidence. For example, I also found that children who produce an excessive number of form errors make fewer of these errors when they trace than when they copy letters and numbers (Simner, 1986). Is this reduction in the number of form errors during tracing due to the lower demand that tracing places on the child's memory system or is it due to the lack of a need to plan the stroke sequences? Independent of the outcome of future work on this matter, it is worth noting that many young children who do have learning problems in school also often experience memory as well as planning problems that frequently interfere with their ability to master the curriculum (Hughes, 1988; Smith, 1981). I mention this final point because I believe it provides still further reason for suggesting that the tie between form errors and school achievement might very well be a memory or planning problem (or a combination of the two) that surfaces at an early age, disrupts the child's printing, then resurfaces at a later age and disrupts the child's learning.

Chapter 13

Variability in children's handwriting: Computer diagnosis of writing difficulties

John Wann & Maha Kardirkamanathan

1.0 Technology and children's handwriting: Unfulfilled promises

Despite numerous predictions during the past 20 years that handwriting would become diminished in importance, these idle dreams of a microcomputer on every desktop have not been realized. Technology has not replaced the need for written script in education. Such simplistic predictions also ignored that the acquisition of written script can provide a landmark in each child's acquisition of fine manipulative behaviours and may have significant diagnostic potential. The acquisition of cursive handwriting not only provides a significant hurdle to most children but a conspicuous stumbling block to some. It is likely that such children have stuttered if not stumbled at similar fine motor hurdles prior to their identification as poor writers (Wann, 1986, pp 207–209)

The promise that technology has fulfilled is the ability to study writing skills with remarkable precision. It would be complementary to believe that technological evaluation of written script is a product of twentieth century ingenuity. A brief historical review, however, reveals that Jack (1895) used a novel apparatus that threw written records into waves so that pen velocity could be deduced. Binet and Courtier (1893) employed an Edison pen, which punctured the paper at high speed, to quantify the production of writing strokes. It is interesting that, a hundred years later, such technology can still be usefully employed (see Vinter and Mounoud, Chapter 6). It would be

Development of Graphic Skills
ISBN 0-12-734940-5

attractive to imagine that it was the same pen, discovered in the store-room of a French laboratory that made its centenary reappearance, but Annie Vinter suggested that this was not the case.

The real explosion of technologically driven research into handwriting began at the end of the 1970s; Teulings and Thomassen (1979) outlined advanced techniques for recording handwriting; Wing (1980) explored time-keeper models of stroke production; Viviani and Terzuolo (1980) proposed invariant temporal programming of letter sequences, while Hollerbach (1981) outlined a coupled cyclic oscillator model for the same task; and Wing and Baddeley (1978) braved "evenings of social drinking" to document the effects of alcohol on handwriting.

What was particularly surprising was that there was a paucity of research applying such advanced techniques to children. Meulenbroek and van Galen (1986) and Wann (1986) presented a comprehensive appraisal of developmental trends and delayed performance in the patterning of children's handwriting, using techniques similar to those outlined by Teulings and Thomassen (1979). These studies concentrated in particular upon the control of pen speed by children to highlight the process rather than the product of handwriting. Such work has continued and a broader understanding of the control problems in handwriting is evolving as a result of computer-aided analysis.

What has not been realized has been the diagnostic potential of computer analysis in identifying children with handwriting difficulties. Both the technology and techniques are well refined; what seems insurmountable is the interface between the computer and the child. The present technology requires that data is collected on-line, such that every child has to be brought to the apparatus, made to feel comfortable, told what to do, allowed to practise and then perform the task. This performance is then recorded, stored, transformed, analysed. In the case of diagnosis it would then be desirable to go back to the child and repeat the procedure in more detail. It is not surprising, therefore, that where a large sample of children are to be studied, simpler techniques are used such as the Edison pen of Vinter and Mounoud or that analysis concentrates upon human judgements of the graphic product (eg, Simner, Chapter 12; Phelps and Stempel, Chapter 11). What is outlined in this paper are computer-based techniques for the analysis of children's handwriting that may allow off-line identification of writing difficulties. The goal is to develop techniques that allow children's school books to be scanned by computer and appraise writing variability without having to access the child in person.

1.1 The variability variable

"What is wrong with my son's/daughter's handwriting?" Such a question from a concerned parent inevitably makes the researcher squirm. There is no simple answer to why a particular child displays difficulties with handwriting. The aetiology is heterogenous and it would be a bold scientist who suggested a singular cause for all writing dysfunctions. Interpreting the question literally, however, we would suggest *variability*. Not the variability introduced by context or individual style, but the random variability from the "inherent unreliability of the neuromuscular system" (Wing, 1979, p.286). What singles out careless from dysgraphic writing is the cause of the degraded legibility. Directly equating low legibility with writing problems according to a popular myth would classify the whole of the medical fraternity as having writing difficulties. It is obvious that a large number of motor-competent adults have poorly legible writing, due to choice carelessness or ignorance of the ambiguities within their script. The essence of writing difficulties lies in the source of degraded legibility. Where an ambiguous form is consistently produced, it may be assumed that attention to form may remedy the problem. When poor quality is due to variability in the size, form and orientation of letters across repetitions, however, the problem may go beyond the need for greater care (Wann, 1986, p 220).

Variability in stroke length, timing and pen speed are hallmarks of control problems. At the diagnostic level the problem is marked by a lack of what Keogh and Sugden (1985) have termed "consistency and constancy" in motor control. We propose that, although the cause of a particular child's problems may require detailed and extensive screening, the initial identification of such children should focus on techniques that will quantify the so-called random variability within a child's writing.

1.2 Variability in the time domain

As a precursor to application of an off-line (spatial) analysis of handwriting we will outline some of the most salient features gleaned from an on-line (temporal) analysis of childrens' writing (Wann and Jones, 1986). The sample group included two age groups; children just commencing cursive handwriting and those with 1 year (3 school terms) of experience. The groups were selected from a large sample of children on the basis that they displayed either advanced writing skills or delayed writing skills for their age (judged upon graphic quality).

One initial observation from the analysis of the children's data at both ages, was that although there was no significant difference in the average writing time of letters and words, the poor writers were significantly more variable in the time taken to write the same letters over a number of repetitions (Wann and Jones, 1986). This initial finding partially confirmed the idea that it was the stability of performance that differentiated between children of differing skills.

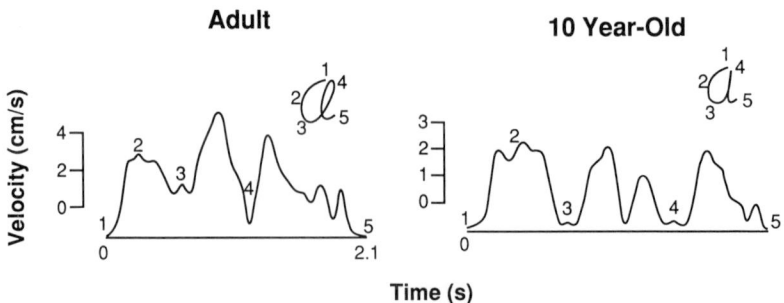

FIGURE 1: Form-related features in the velocity profile of a letter **a**, written by an adult (left) and a 10-year-old (right), illustrating the occurrence of pauses and the somewhat longer periods during which the pen is stationary in the child's writing. (From Wann, 1986.)

A second area of investigation was the factors that could contribute towards changes in the writing time of letters. In particular, pauses between writing strokes, often termed breaks, were analysed by calculating the pen speed for each trial by each child. Figure 1 demonstrates this approach.

A third level of analysis was the control of individual strokes, and in particular the control of pen-speed (tangential velocity). The length of a writing stroke is closely linked to the velocity and duration of the stroke.

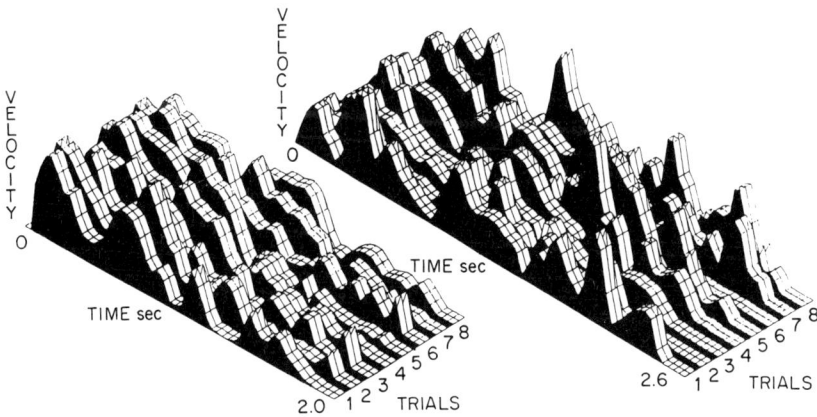

FIGURE 2: Velocity profiles for repeated trials of the letter **a**; those of a good writer (left) display some correspondence across trials in the height and location of the main features; whereas trials by a poor writer (right) have a more disparate organisation. (From Wann, 1986.)

It is, in principle, possible to produce the same stroke with different times and velocities (by moving at a higher speed for less time, for instance), but in practice the independent scaling of velocity and time requires highly skilled performance. Figure 2 displays the velocity profiles for a number of trials of the same letter by both good and poor writers to again underline the principle that *variability* in the control of velocity was what marked the performance of less able writers.

2. 0 Spatial variability

The foregoing analysis outlines some of the measures that could be used for the on-line (temporal) identification of writing problems. The next issue is to consider whether an off-line system can catalogue related variability purely from the spatial domain.

2.1 Methods

The data used for this study were the writing records collected by Wann and Jones (1986). The writing quality of children (N=197) in Australian primary school grade 4 (mean age 109 months) and grade 5 (mean age 123 months) was appraised using the Rubin and Henderson (1982) protocol, which assessed legibility and constancy of size and form. The 10th and 90th percentiles were then identified as children displaying advanced or retarded handwriting skills with respect to their peers. The final sample was 32 children (8 good and 8 poor at each of the two grades). The handwriting of these sub-groups was then recorded using an on-line digitizer during their performance of familiar letters and letter strings. In this analysis only the letters a and w will be used to provide suitable multisegment tasks which also are typical examples of both closed-curve and linked-line letter formation. In each case the analysis is over 8 repetitions of each letter by each child. For full details see Wann and Jones (1986).

2.2 Processing

The records from Wann and Jones (1986) were used to allow comparison between time domain estimates and those of spatial processing. The data therefore underwent two stages of processing. Initially the spatial segmentation routines were applied to the data. A time domain analysis was then applied to calculate the velocity for each trial (Wann, 1987). The velocity estimates were then matched up with each spatial point to provide a comparative analysis.

2.3 Spatial segmentation

The scale space approach was developed by Kardirkamanathan (1989) and is designed to work upon spatially sampled data (eg the spatial layout of a letter measured from a writing sample, photograph or computer scan of a letter or word). The first stage in the processing of the Wann and Jones (1986) data was to throw away the time domain information and resample each letter purely as a series of equidistant spatial points as seen by the human observer.

A smoothing filter is then applied to this spatial record. This has the effect of diminishing the prominence of the various features of a letter. A metaphor might be that of a mis-shapen pebble flung onto the beach. The gradual lapping of the waves begins to round off the corners and features of the pebble, until the final result is a smooth elliptical stone. In a similar way the technique of Kardirkamanathan (1989) explores how strong the smoothing has to be (or how many waves are needed in our pebble example) before a particular feature, such as a cusp, disappears. An illustration of this technique is provided in Figure 3.

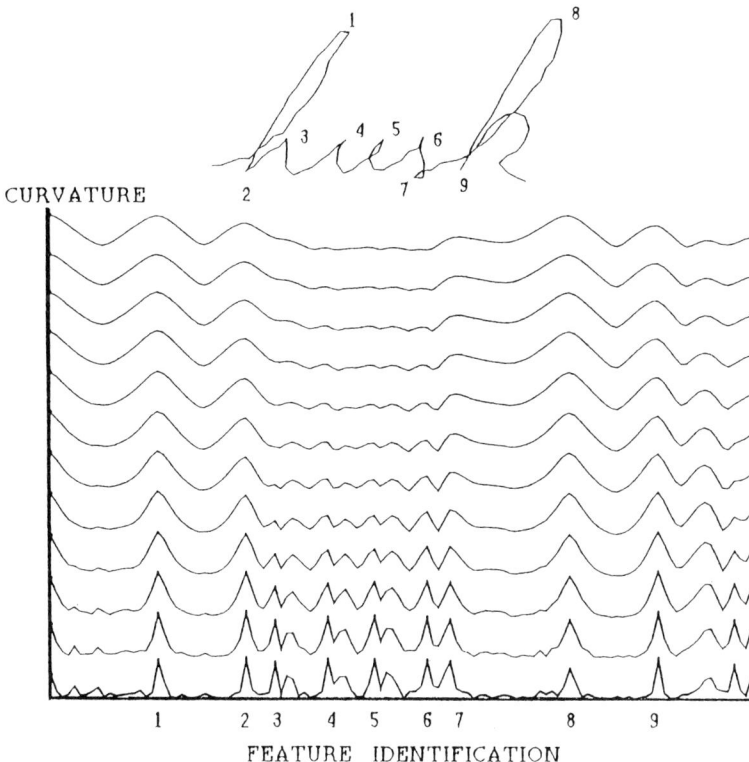

FIGURE 3: Displacements for the word **husk** due to context smoothing. The bottom curve displays a curvature estimate, such that each peak can be identified as arising from features of the written word (numbered). Each curve set above the original displays the relative smoothing effect at different levels of application of the filter.

The approach in this study used 12 levels of smoothing (Figure 3), to provide each curvature feature with a number from 1 to 12, indicating the prominence or robustness of that feature. Having discerned the major features (those that can resist a high level of smoothing) from minor fluctuations in the writing stroke, these segmentation points can be used to chart the variability in spatial production across repetitions.

One approach is to count the number of features detected. In principle the number of major features should not vary, otherwise a **v** might actually look like a **w** or vice versa, but the number of minor features is a measure of how straight a line or how smooth a curve was produced. Analyses of variance performed upon the average number of features observed within **a** and **w** for each child indicated that there was no significant difference in the number of major features produce by good and poor writers, but that poor writers generally produced more minor features (line fluctuations) on both letters, $[F(1,28)=4.57, p<.05; F(1,28)=7.75, p<.01]$. A significant interaction for the letter **a** indicated that the difference between good and poor writers on this task was predominantly between the grade 5 children $[F(1,28)=8.98, p<.01]$. These results are discussed in more detail in the next section.

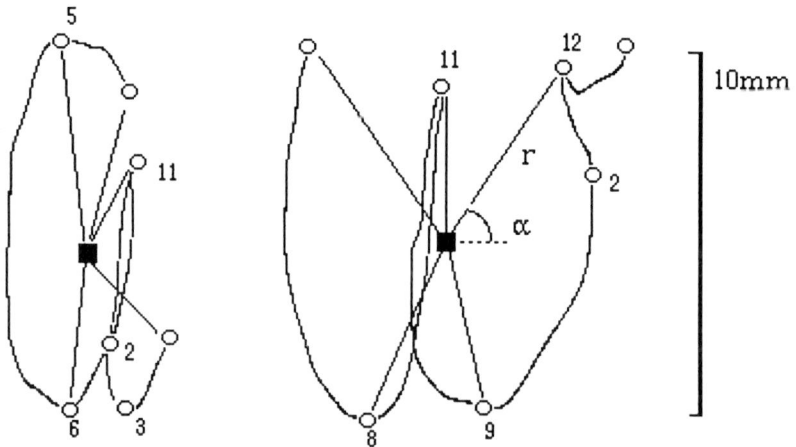

FIGURE 4: Two letters **a** and **w** written by a child, with scale-space features (circles) identified through sequential smoothing. The number next to each circle indicates the robustness of each feature (see text). The main features (high number) can be expressed on a polar coordinate system, such that each has a heading angle (α) and radius (r) with respect to the centroid of the letter (square). The tail of the **w** is ignored.

A second approach is to take the major features and use them to calculate an estimate of subtle changes in the written form. The approach used in this study was to transform the location of each point into polar coordinates, with the coordinate centre being the centroid of the letter (Figure 4)

The attractive feature about using a polar representation of the letter features is that a linear scaling of both horizontal and vertical extent of a letter (writing proportionally bigger) will scale the radius but not affect the heading angle of each point. A change purely in orientation will change the absolute heading angles, but not the relative heading angles or the radii. A variation in the letter form, however, will change both the heading angles and radii. In principle, therefore, simple transformations, such as changes in size or orientation can be dissociated from form changes. The measure used in this study was to calculate the root mean squared error (RMSE) on each parameter for each child as a measure of variability across letter repetitions (N=8):

$$\text{RMSE} = \text{SQRT} \left(\Sigma \, \sigma^2 / N \right)$$

3.0 Results: Exploring diagnostic parameters

The technique outlined in the methods allowed an off-line analysis of the data of Wann and Jones (1986). The written letters of each child could be split into a series of major features (turning points, cusps) and minor features (fluctuations in the writing line) using purely the spatial information.

3.1 Feature numbers

The initial analyses examined whether poorer writers displayed more features or discontinuities in their writing. Figure 5 graphs the mean number of features (segmentation scores >1) and the mean number of major features (segmentation scores > 5).

It would be surprising if there was a difference between children in the number of major features, as this would generally be equivalent to the letter having an extra stroke. There is the possibility, however, of a child changing writing direction too early and then correcting to produce an addition sharp feature and elevating this score. In general, however, the letter **a** has 5 major features (start; top turning-point; bottom turning point; cusp and finish; Figure 4) although particularly rounded letter

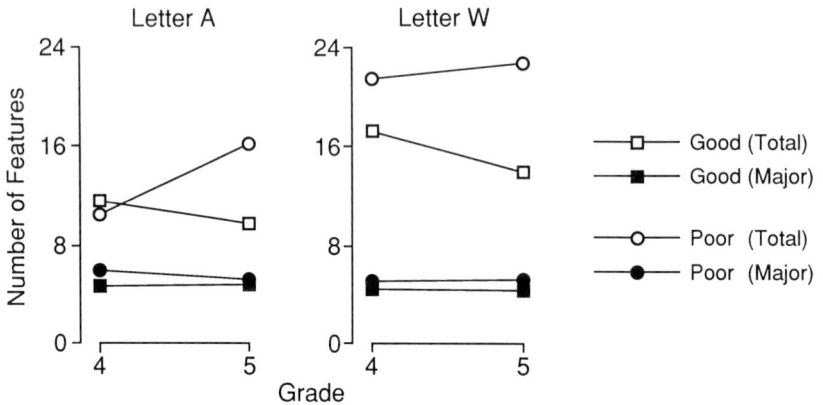

FIGURE 5: *Mean number of major features and total number of features identified for each repetition of letter **a** and **w** written by each child within the four groups.*

forms may reduce the salience of the top and bottom turning points. The letter **w** has 5 major features (Figures 4 and 5).

The total number of features (major+minor) provides a more insightful measure than the number of major features. In all cases, both good and poor writers seem to have a number of extra minor features within their writing strokes, indicating discontinuity that is perhaps predictable for children at the early stages of cursive acquisition. Furthermore, poorer writers in both grades displayed significantly more features than their more accomplished peers ($\alpha < .05$). This difference was predominantly due to the large number of minor features found within the letters written by older (grade 5) poor writers, (Figure 5). This finding is in agreement with some of those of Wann and Jones (1986) which suggested that poor writers in grade 5 lagged behind their peers to a greater extent than their younger counterparts in grade 4.

Having established some diagnostic potential within the total number of features observed, a prudent question to ask is how these features relate to the motor processes involved in letter production. When children's data is collected on-line, a widely used criterion for segmenting a letter sequence into strokes is pen velocity (horizontal or vertical) or pen speed (Teulings and Thomassen, 1979; Wann, 1987). The data used within this study was originally collected on-line, hence allowing recourse to the time-domain information to compare the features extracted from the scale-space approach with the segmentation points that might have been used with time-domain records. Figure 6 graphs the respective pen velocities observed at each identified spatial feature.

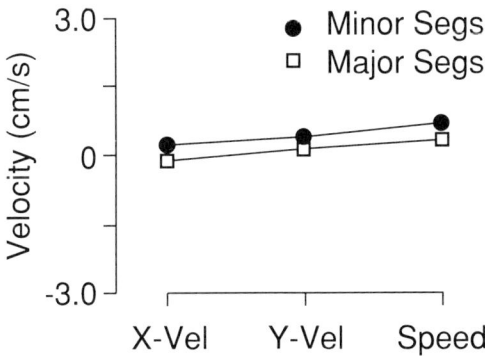

FIGURE 6: Average pen velocity at both minor and major features. X-Vel is the horizontal velocity and Y-Vel the vertical velocity. The scale has been selected to set the results in the context of the average peak speed (3 cm/s).

It may be observed from Figure 6 that the average velocity at each of the segmentation points is generally very low (0.25 cm/s), indicating that the points identified purely from the spatial records were close to those that would have been identified form the time-domain records. This is not too surprising as a reversal of pen direction physically requires a point of zero-velocity and it has generally been observed that pen speed drops around points of high curvature (Jack, 1895; Lacquaniti et al, 1983; Wann et al, 1988). It is pleasing, however, that a measure of dysfluency extracted from the spatial trace should closely approximate that which might have arisen from the time-domain (eg the number of low velocity points or re-accelerations).

3.2 Feature orientation

A second level of analysis concentrated upon the orientation of the major features and their variability across repetitions. As outlined in the Methods section the two polar parameters α (heading angle) and r (distance from the letter centre: radius) are independently affected by proportional scaling and re-orientation, but generally commonly affected by form changes. Figure 7 displays root mean squared errors (RMSE) for both of these parameters as a measure of variability across repetitions for each child.

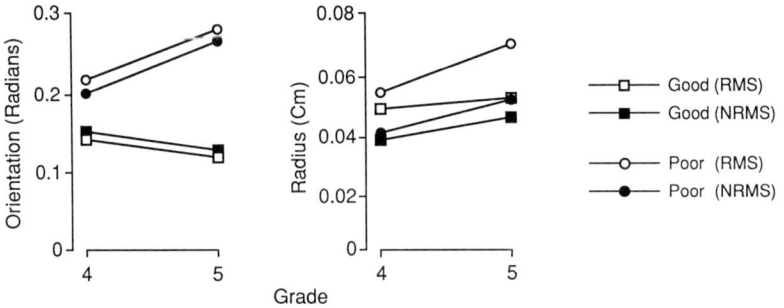

FIGURE 7: Root mean squared error scores for the orientation (heading angle) and radii (distance from centre) calculated across repetitions and averaged over subjects. A higher RMSE is equivalent to greater variability across repetitions.

In line with the previous discussion it can be observed that, if the letter size is normalized before analysis (NRMS), the variability of the heading angle is generally unaffected but the radius variability is reduced. When considering the heading angle there is a significant difference in the variability displayed by good and poor writers, but this is most marked in grade 5, which agrees with earlier findings. The radii RMSE (prior to normalization) suggested that the poor writers were generally more variable in letter size (despite size being cued on all trails) although such differences are not statistically significant. When the radii NRMS (normalized) is compared with the heading angle results, the indications are that the radius measure is not particularly sensitive to letter distortions and therefore has less diagnostic potential.

4.0 Conclusions: Selecting diagnostic measures

The conclusions that arise from the small-scale analysis undertaken in this paper are twofold. Firstly, it seems that the scale-space approach to the analysis of handwriting can identify features or segments that are remarkably similar to those that may have been used with a more demanding on-line (time-series) approach to analysing children's writing. Secondly, at least two measures of spatial variability appear to have diagnostic potential, in that they differentiated between the performance of good and poor writers in the present study, and such groupings had already been confirmed by previous qualitative and quantitative (time-domain) appraisals. These measures were the number of features (discontinuities) in the writing line and the variability in orientation (heading angle) of major features across letter repetitions.

Both the discontinuity of strokes and form variability may be appraised through a subjective rating by a teacher, and one might question why a computer-based technique is necessary. It is unlikely that there would be any time-saving advantage as the time required to scan with a computer and select parts of a child's script is likely to be longer than any subjective rating procedure. Such preprocessing does not need to be done by teachers, however, and may become a secretarial task. The real advantage, however, lies in the objectivity of the technique. A valid and reliable human rating scheme relies upon the observer remaining objective and assigning scores to each script that are balanced across the whole class, school or population. Anyone who has attempted a large-scale rating study will know how difficult objectivity becomes after only a short period of studying scripts. A computer-based approach allows the construction and updating of a normative database that can provide mean and standard deviation estimates for each diagnostic measure. In principle this could allow each child to be compared to a class, a school, a national or a cultural norm, thereby providing early identification of children lagging behind their peers as well as re-appraisal facilities to examine the efficacy of remedial measures.

The adaption of the scale-space approach to the diagnosis of children's writing difficulties is still at its nascent stage. Work has yet to be undertaken to adapt the procedures to the computation facilities available within schools. It is also envisaged that a more rigorous test of its potential would be a larger-scale project to try to identify poor writers from their peers in a post-hoc fashion. The intent would be to look back over the previous years' records to establish whether children could have been identified at an earlier stage through appropriate computer-based techniques. Should this potential be realized, then such an approach would enable the routine scanning of children's practice books during the early years of handwriting instruction. The goal would be to identify any child who was displaying variability in letter formation that fell outside the school/regional norms, so that respective teachers were aware of the possible need for additional aid and early remedial activities might be considered.

VI: Remedial issues

The previous section included various approaches to identifying dysfunctional handwriting. Once such difficulties have been identified, it is important that remedial work be undertaken in order to minimize the effects of a child's delay in skill acquisition. A key component in designing effective remediation is recognizing particular sources of difficulty. Van Doorn and Keuss *(Dysfluency in children's handwriting)* suggest that the use of vision (rather than body sense) to control pen movements may be a mixed blessing for some children and develop ideas about the difference between controlling whole arm and finger—hand movements.

Maarse, van de Veerdonk, van der Linden and Pranger-Moll *(Handwriting training: Computer-aided tools for remedial teaching)* ask whether the remedial role can, in part, be taken by computer-based packages. They compare computer-based measures of dysgraphia with ratings from a standardized scale, then monitor changes in the computer-based measures as the children undergo a conventional therapy programme. Recommendations on the role of computers in a therapy programme are then made.

Laszlo and Broderick *(Drawing and handwriting difficulties: Reasons for and remediation of dysfunction)* have a long-term involvement in an extensive research programme examining children's perceptual-motor difficulties. In the final chapter of the book they develop specific hypotheses on the potential causes of children's difficulties in graphic skills. The suggestion is that specific deficits in body sense (kinaesthetic sensitivity) and motor planning contribute to many children's difficulties and that remedial programmes should focus upon such skills.

Chapter 14

Dysfluency in children's handwriting

Robert R. A. van Doorn & Paulus J. G. Keuss

Contemporary handwriting research is becoming computerized to an increasing extent. For example, movements can be recorded during the act of writing and stored by means of special digitizing equipment linked to a computer. An essential contribution of this relatively new technique to handwriting research is that, after recording, the properties of the movements, underlying the writing product, remain fully accessible (Teulings and Maarse, 1984). Dynamic properties have to do with the rate and speed of the writing act, which provide insight into movement regulation and movement problems. It is our aim to illustrate the usefulness of this approach in the present study using children with prolonged writing problems. By looking at the dynamics of the writing performance we hope to identify the causes underlying the writing deficiency of these children. First, however, it makes sense to focus on adults and to explore their movements, because the imitation of the behaviour of the adult is the endpoint in the motor development of the child.

1.0 Fluent writing

Skilled, adult writers are able to produce strokes and patterns of strokes in a fluent way. The successive movements are made very rapidly while the consistency of form that contributes to legibility is maintained. Looking at the velocity pattern of their performance, one can infer that a minimum of force impulses are used in their writing movements. In general, every letter stroke is characterized by one major impulse which is associated with one velocity peak. In other words, one force impulse suffices to produce a letter stroke. This type of movement may be referred to as *ballistic*. The biomechanical components are launched towards the goal without subsequent corrections. In this respect, adult handwriting is characterized by the succession of ballistic movements, resulting in a coherent series of letterforms and words.

To attain the goal of fluent writing, advance planning is indispensable (cf van Galen and Teulings, 1983). This implies that before the start of the movement, a movement plan has to be ready. Such a plan has to incorporate various types of information about the movement. One type of information is about the letterform, in particular the specification of the trajectory for the movement in space. The second type of information is related to the forces with which movements are made, which become manifest in the size, speed and duration of the movements. Finally, muscle groups have to be specified and activated for movement execution. For example, a writer can either employ the finger-thumb in coordination with the wrist muscle system, as is usually done, or in the case of writing with chalk on a blackboard, use arm and shoulder muscles.

The question arises of whether advance planning renders superfluous external information during writing? This does not appear to be the case. When skilled writers are deprived of visual information, errors like omissions, transpositions and repetitions of strokes and letters become manifest (Smyth and Silvers, 1987). Furthermore, adult writers try to compensate for the lack of vision. They use as few penlifts as possible (Smyth, 1988), lengthen movement duration (van Galen et al, 1989), and increase the size of the writing movements (van Doorn and Keuss, submitted). Because these studies addressed the total absence of vision, no conclusions can be drawn about the delicate balance of vision and advance planning, except for the general assertion that vision is somehow needed in adult handwriting.

2.0 Non-ballistic writing

In children, the development of motor control evolves continuously. The use of ballistic movements for strokes and letters is preceded by a period in which slow, non-ballistic movements predominate (Meulenbroek and van Galen, 1988).

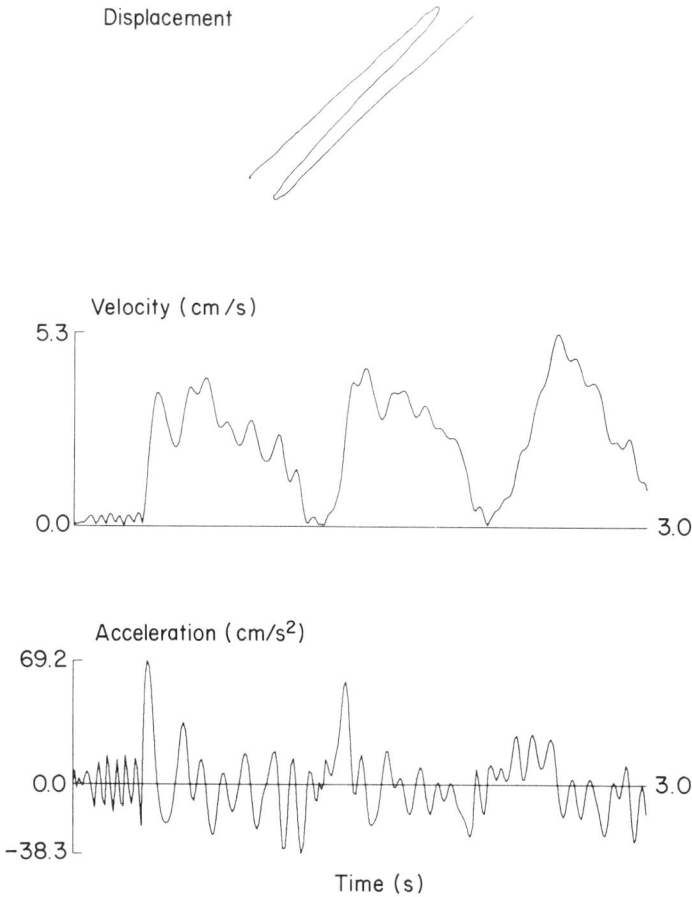

FIGURE 1: Illustration of the wrist task. The trajectory of three successive pen strokes produced by the wrist is depicted in the upper panel, the first derivative (velocity pattern) in the middle panel and the second derivative (acceleration pattern) in the lower panel.

Figures 1 and 2 illustrate non-ballistic strokes along with the underlying velocity and acceleration patterns. It is evident that non-ballistic writing shows several velocity peaks (as stated already, the fluent stroke is characterized by only one velocity peak), accompanied by several acceleration zero crossings. Such a dynamic pattern is typical of non-ballistic strategies and

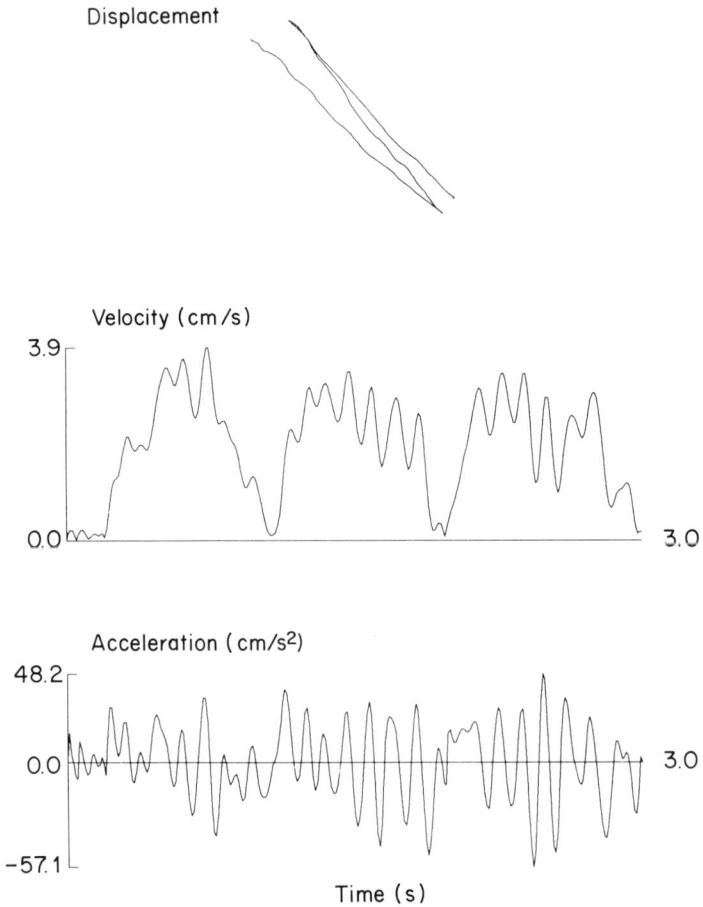

FIGURE 2: *Illustration of the finger-thumb task. The trajectory, of three successive pen strokes produced by the finger-thumb muscles is depicted in the upper panel, the first derivative (velocity pattern) and the second derivative (acceleration pattern).*

indicates movement (re-)adjustments or corrections during the execution phase. The hypothesis put forward in the present study is that too much visual information may be responsible for these corrections. In this respect it is relevant to notice that visual information is indispensable at school when the pupils do not possess a mental picture of letters. Then children are forced to adopt a copying strategy to reach adult levels of accuracy and neatness, the primary goals of most education programmes.

Another cause of deficiencies in children's handwriting may be the inadequate control of the various muscles involved in the movement execution. Ontogenetic development of movement control begins with more proximal muscle structures near the body and ends with distal structures distant from the body (Gesell, 1940; Touwen, 1982). In the period in which non-ballistic movements are predominant, the control of the distal muscle system (in handwriting, the finger-thumb muscles) is still not perfect, as compared to the proximal system (in handwriting, the wrist). But to produce fine motor patterns, as needed in handwriting, the development of motor control of the distal muscles has to be completed. In the period of pre-ballistic movements, during which more than one force impulse is applied, the pupil may rely upon external information conveyed by vision to correct movements which are under the control of the finger-thumb muscles. To test this hypothesis, we submitted our subject group to a finger-thumb task which had to be done, once with vision and once without vision. The expectation is that vision improves the writing performance, since vision supports the functioning of the distal system. The control situation was a wrist task for which the more proximal system is responsible. In this case the advanced level of motor control of the proximal system may profit less from visual information than the finger-thumb task.

As stated already, adult handwriting can be regarded as a goal for children to meet, irrespective of their course of development. The majority of children are able to learn to write rapidly and fluently, and go through a period in which less fluent writing is normal. But the present investigation is focused on the 10% of children in the Netherlands who have major writing problems (Hamstra-Bletz and de Bie, 1985). Most problems are characterized by very slow and inaccurate handwriting, accompanied by inappropriate body postures (Borysowicz and Blöte, 1985) and pen-grip (Sassoon et al, 1986).

2.1 Subjects

A subject group of 10 children aged from 9 to 11 years was chosen from the Paedologisch Instituut in Nijmegen. They were selected by the teachers using their own criteria of poor, inaccurate, slow writing style, often accompanied by cramping postures and musculature. In addition, our subjects often had individual problems concerning learning capacity, language comprehension or emotional responding. Recognizing the heterogeneity of the subject group, one needs to be cautious in extrapolating the results to the wider population of retarded children. In passing it is noted, however, that the writing style of our pupils corresponds to children who are two years younger. A major feature of the writing style of such children is inadequate control of the distal muscle-joint structure (observation from the teachers).

2.2 Apparatus

Writing data were recorded and stored using a Calcomp digitizer connected to a PDP-11/45 computer. Writing movements were made with a normal-sized writing stylus connected to the tablet. Sampling was carried out with a frequency of 105 Hz and with a tablet resolution of .025 millimetre. A forward and backward Fourier transform was employed to filter the raw data (Teulings and Maarse, 1984) with a cut-off frequency of 12.5 Hz.

2.3 Tasks

To find out which muscle system contributed to writing deficiency all pupils undertook two separate tasks. In one task they made wrist movements, in the second task finger-thumb movements. Wrist movements resulted in right up and left down pen strokes, whereas the finger-thumb movements produced pen strokes in the left up and right down directions (Figures 1 and 2). In both tasks, strokes had to be written in a continuous fashion for a period of thirteen seconds. Writing duration was indicated by a metronome. This produced one high pitch tone per second in which one stroke had to be performed. The speed of the test was chosen in accordance with the children's normal writing production. The time reference was given to ensure an equal number of strokes per subject. Writing size was unconstrained, resulting in a rather large script for all subjects. The position of the writing arm on the table was marked by tape. We did not employ a cuff to fixate the arm because of undesired spasms which could be elicited in the more hyperactive children.

There was a vision condition and a no-vision condition. Under both conditions both tasks had to be performed by all subjects. In the vision condition the children were free to use visual information about writing hand and writing performance. In the no-vision condition a box was placed over the writing hand as well as the stylus, which also prevented vision of the resulting writing trace, but allowed normal free-floating writing behaviour.

The pupils were asked to draw the strokes within the time limits given by the metronome. Neatness of form was not evaluated, and pupils were made aware of this. (Note that the drawing tasks were simple so as to avoid problems related to the form of the trajectory).

2.4 Measurements

In Figures 1 and 2 the trajectories of three successive pen strokes resulting from respectively wrist- and finger-thumb movements are depicted together with the first (velocity) and second (acceleration) derivatives of pen position. The figures illustrate that the number of force pulses (velocity peaks and zero crossings of the acceleration) are rather large. Because of our focus on the dynamic properties of the writing movements we measured the number of zero crossings present in the acceleration function derived from the writing movements. This dependent variable is the index of the number of consciously controlled adjustments and the number of distortions, the latter probably due to cramp-like manifestations (Hornsveld, 1983). As a consequence, the number of zero crossings in acceleration can be used as a measure of dysfluency in the writing movements.

3.0 Results

The main finding was the differential effect of vision on the two writing tasks. The interaction of the condition (vision versus no-vision) with task (wrist versus finger-thumb) significantly contributed to the variance [$F(2,20)=5.05$, $p<0.05$].

3.1 Wrist task

When the pupils made movements with the wrist, the number of zero crossings in the acceleration function became larger when vision was available than when vision was unavailable, as Figure 3 illustrates. In other words, dysfluency in wrist movements increased when the children were allowed to visually monitor their writing performance. One may infer that visual information exerts a detrimental effect on on-line writing when muscle control is rather good, as is the case with the proximal muscle system involved in the wrist task. Vision entices the children to make additional corrective adjustments in the movements.

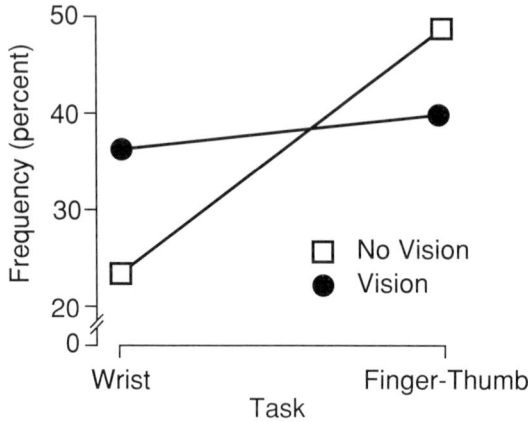

FIGURE 3: *The number of zero crossings in acceleration on the vertical axis, as a function of vision and task.*

3.2 Finger-thumb task

An opposite picture emerged from the finger-thumb task, wherein dysfluency decreased when vision was allowed. Figure 3 illustrates that more distortions (indicated by the number of zero crossings on the vertical axis) occurred when the children were forbidden to look at their writing patterns than when they were allowed to use visual information. We suggest that the negative vision effect on the finger-thumb task is due to the pengrip employed by the children. The reasoning is that when vision is absent, the control of the pengrip, for which the finger-thumb musculature is mainly responsible, becomes worse than when vision is allowed. One may infer that the distal musculature of our pupils was still not able to cope with the demands imposed by the writing stylus. Visual information is helpful in this respect. Absence of vision does not increase the demands of the pengrip.

4.0 Discussion

A peculiar finding of the present study was that our pupils were more fluent without vision when making writing movements for which the relatively well-controlled proximal muscle system of the wrist is responsible. It is as if the allowance of vision invited the pupils to continually adjust their writing movements. In order to avoid a negative influence of visual information, it may be that training programmes should incorporate tasks in which writing of patterns and strokes is performed without the presence of visual information, wherein the fluent writing of letter and word patterns should be the primary concern.

In the case where no visual information is provided during the writing act, information afterwards becomes relevant to evaluate the writing performance. When giving knowledge of results, two approaches are imaginable. The first is to show the subject the writing trace and to emphasize that the letter must be drawn as a series of ballistic strokes which constitute the letters. The second approach, which would be in line with the work of Sõvik and Teulings (1983) on computer applications in handwriting, is to make dynamic properties of the writing act available to the subject. One could, for example, show the relation between dysfluency and the number of hesitations in execution, which is characteristic of non-ballistic movements. In a similar vein, the teacher might demonstrate the ballistic nature of mature adult writing and show examples of the underlying time and force characteristics, as depicted in the figures of this chapter.

The present study also led to the conclusion that visual information was fruitful in the finger-thumb task to maintain an appropriate pengrip. This task imposed more on the distal muscle system which is required by the pengrip than the more proximal system used in the wrist task. The control of the finger-thumb system is needed to produce fine motor behaviour. It is clear, however, that the pupils in the present study were not yet ready to produce a series of strokes (or letterforms) under the fine motor requirement of the finger-thumb instruction, which is the normal paper-and-pencil situation of the school. Thus, in a teaching programme our pupils might be submitted to a training procedure that keeps the involvement of fine motor control at minimum, for example, by practising on the blackboard. In that case there would be nearly no involvement of the distal muscle system, since the whole arm functions as the main controlling mechanism. As a further step, children might then be invited to produce strokes and letters in paper-and-pencil tasks, as required in school. Distal muscles of finger-thumb would then be involved, but in the instruction emphasis should be laid on fluency rather than on neatness of form.

To conclude, examining the dynamic properties of the writing act is fruitful and provides a valid tool for discovering writing problems that are based on a distinction between the wrist versus finger-thumb involvement in movement execution. The positive versus negative effects of vision on wrist and finger-thumb tasks, respectively, have been suggested as the basis for specific training methods that might be suited to overcome writing problems exhibited by pupils. In spite of the simplicity of the movements, inference from the results to a novel approach of teaching children in writing letters and words is a challenge. The view that the problem pupils of the present study tend to behave as normal children of a younger age, suggests that the latter might also benefit from the training programmes proposed.

Chapter 15

Handwriting training: Computer-aided tools for remedial teaching

Frans J. Maarse, Jos L.A. van de Veerdonk,
Marijke E.A. van der Linden & Winifred Pranger-Moll

1.0 Computer analysis of handwriting

During the last ten years digital computers with specific software, methods and apparatus have become available for handwriting research. Teulings and Maarse (1984) describe several specific signal processing techniques for handwriting. Digitizers with a pressure-sensitive pen (Maarse et al, 1988) allow automatic recording of handwriting samples whether for a few seconds or for several hours. Using this software, it is possible to carry out handwriting experiments and analysis not only on laboratory computers, but also on personal computers. Both spatial (static) features such as size, width, slant, and height and temporal (dynamic) features can be determined. Some examples of temporal features are pen velocity, pen pressure, ballisticity and dysfluency (Maarse, 1987).

The insights thus obtained and the methods developed in handwriting studies may be helpful in the design of drawing and writing exercises to be used in the primary school prior to the actual handwriting lessons (Maarse, 1987; Meulenbroek, 1989). They may also promote the development of diagnostic instruments for handwriting education, such as maturity tests to assess the child's ability to meet the fine-motor control required in handwriting and achievement tests to assess progress. Furthermore, computer-assisted exercises could be developed for children and adults with specific handwriting problems requiring remedial teaching.

The general question behind this study is to what extent the methods and apparatus developed for laboratory handwriting research can be used by a writing therapist. This study focuses on the more specific question: Can real-time computed global features such as pen pressure, pen velocity, ballisticity and writing slant be used as feedback in a writing exercise and can they help an individual to improve handwriting performance?

2.0 Handwriting therapy study

In order to answer this question an experiment was carried out in the first-year classes of a secondary school. Thirteen subjects with writing problems formed the experimental group, which received writing therapy for 4 months. Every week they had 30 minutes' private training which used Heermann's (1985) method. In a relaxed atmosphere, the subjects first learned about pen grip, writing position and paper placement. The exercises consisted mainly of simple movements such as arcades, clockwise and anticlockwise springs, factory rooftops, etc. No specific attention was paid to letter form or other typical handwriting features.

A handwriting sample with Heermann's movements was recorded for each child before starting, after 2 months, and again after 4 months. All specimens were first judged by the two therapists involved in the writing training with respect to spatial features such as size, page layout, irregularities, ratios of height and width, and corrections. For this judgement the therapists used the table of Borysowicz and Blöte (1984). This table is based on the observations table of de Ajuriaguerra et al (1978, 1979). Then 10 other individuals were asked to select the best handwriting specimen from each child's writing samples. Finally, pen velocity, width of the handwriting, pen pressure, ballisticity and roundness were computed.

It would be expected that if handwriting improved following therapy sessions, one would observe:
- a better score on the observation table of Borysowicz and Blöte (1984),
- a high correlation between the scores of the two writing

therapists and the 10 other judges,
- a lower pen pressure,
- a higher pen velocity,
- an increase of the ballisticity
- a more or less spontaneous normalization of writing the slant
  to a value between 70 and 90 degrees.

If there is a high correlation between the computer derived features and the Borysowicz and Blöte score the computed values might then be used as feedback during computerized remedial teaching exercises.

2.1 Subjects

124 children (59 boys and 65 girls) from a first-year class in a secondary school were asked to write a small essay (about 100 words). The handwriting of these essays was roughly scored by two writing therapists. Selection criteria included irregularities, page layout, letter forms, writing pressure and so on. Thirty children were selected, of whom 17 finally took part in the experiment, 13 children as subjects in the experimental group (3 girls and 10 boys, 2 left-handed) and 4 (boys) as subjects in a control group. All the subjects were between 12 and 14 years old. As can be seen in Table 1 all the subjects of the experimental group as well as of the control group have a high score on the dysgraphia scale and have obvious writing problems.

2.2 Training

The subjects of the experimental group received an individual weekly half-hour training session. During the training attention was given to ensuring a relaxed atmosphere while the basic writing movements and writing posture, pen grip, and paper placement were taught as described by Heermann (1985). No specific attention was given to letter form or other typical handwriting features such as writing slant, pen pressure, and cursive versus non-cursive script.

2.3 Tasks

At the beginning, after 2 months, and again after 4 months, a maximum of 5 minutes of handwriting (see Figure 1) and 11 movement patterns (see Figure 2) were recorded by and stored in a personal computer. The 11 movements shown in Figure 2 are:
-factory rooftops (normal and rapid tempo),
-garlands (normal and rapid tempo),
-arcades (normal and rapid tempo),
-anticlockwise coils (normal and rapid tempo),
-clockwise coils (normal and rapid tempo), and
-alternating clockwise and anticlockwise coils (normal tempo only).

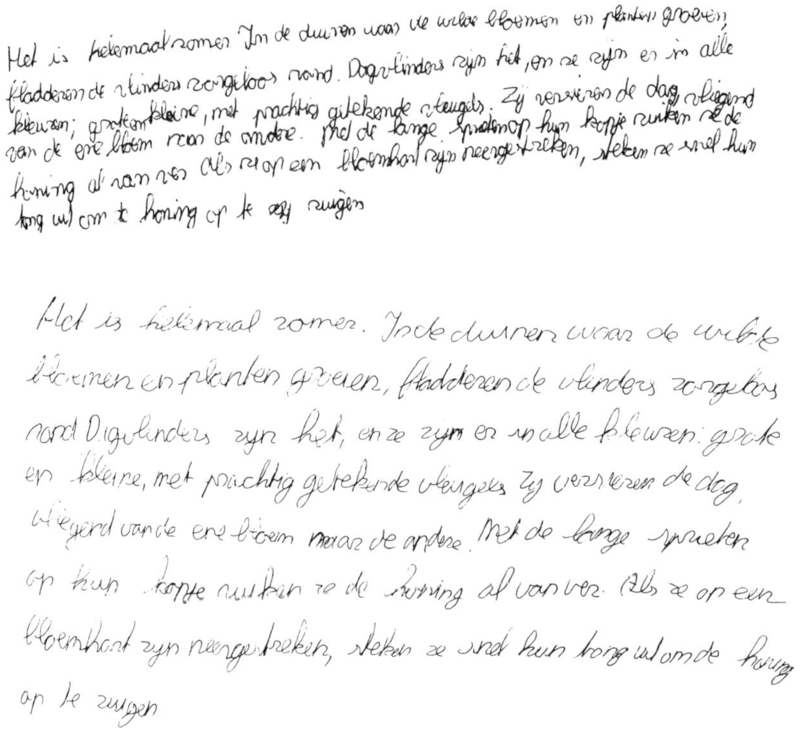

FIGURE 1: An example of the handwriting of one of the experimental groups at the beginning (upper panel), and after 4 months (lower panel) of training. The time taken to write each sample was about 5 minutes.

2.4 Apparatus

To record the handwriting and movement data, a Calcomp 23180 digitizer connected to and controlled by an Olivetti M280 computer was used. By means of the digitizer with a resolving power of 0.025 mm, the X and Y coordinates were sampled at a frequency of 100 Hz. The accuracy was about ±0.1 mm. The pressure (P) along the axis of the pen was recorded with a miniature load cell in the stylus (Maarse et al, 1988); the signal of the pressure cell was sampled by means of an AD-converter. The sampling of the digitizer and the AD-converter were synchronized. The range of the pressure was 0 to 10.23 newton. The pen had an ordinary ballpoint refill.

2.5 Subjective scoring

From all the handwriting specimens, the following scores were collected:
- BB, according to Borysowicz and Blöte, using the whole observation table.
- BBO, according to Borysowicz and Blöte, but using only those scores concerned with motor behaviour. Items concerning page layout,

FIGURE 2: The handwriting movements practised by the experimental group with examples before (left panel) and after (right panel) handwriting training.

produced errors and letter forms were skipped. BBO is a subset of BB.

- Rank, the ranking by 10 individual judges of the handwriting produced by the subjects. The task was to select the better handwriting specimen: the one produced at the beginning or that produced at the end of the training.

2.6 Data processing and analysis

In order to compute the needed features the data was filtered with a low-pass filter with a cutoff frequency of 10 Hz and a transition band between 10 and 25 Hz. Frequencies above 25 Hz were attenuated more than 40 dB. Subsequently the following features were computed for each handwriting

specimen:
- Pen velocity (*V*). The average absolute velocity of the pen when on the paper.
- Writing pressure (*P*). The average pen pressure on the point of the pen as measured along the pen axis.
- Writing slant (*Phi*). This feature was computed from a distribution of the distance with the pen on paper as a function of movement direction (see Maarse and Thomassen, 1983).
- Width (*W*). This was defined as the average length of the strokes in the positive horizontal direction with the pen on the paper. The measure *W* was an indication of the width of the letters.
- Roundness (*Rnd*). For circular movements Rnd is maximal 1.0 and for to and fro movements minimal 0.0.
- Ballisticity (*B*). This measure of the fluency of the handwriting was defined as the ratio between the number of zero-crossings in velocity in the vertical direction (the beginnings and the endings of the vertical strokes) and the number of zero-crossings in vertical acceleration (velocity extremes in vertical strokes). This ratio is maximal 1.0 for ideal writing. For a skilled writer a value of 0.9 is attainable.

Using SPSSX, the Pearson-product correlations were computed between changes in BB, BBO, *V*, *P*, *Phi*, *W*, *Rnd*, and *B*. The analysis of variance program MANOVA was used to verify to what extent these variables were affected by training.

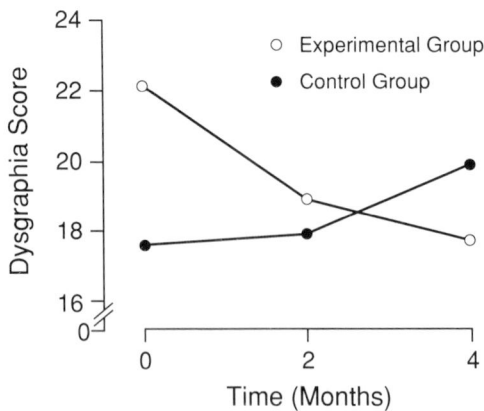

FIGURE 3: *Dysgraphia scores, using the method of Borysowicz and Blöte (1985), of the 13 subjects of the experimental group and the 4 subjects of the control group.*

TABLE 1: *Dysgraphia scores before training and at 2 and 4 months.*
The values are the averages of two judges. Subject numbers starting with
P and C correspond to the experimental and control group, respectively.
Rank gives the number of judges who selected the post- training sample as
being of better quality. BB categories: equal to or more than 19 = dysgraphic
(bold faced in table); 14.0−18.5 = high probability of being dysgraphic;
10.0−13.5 = "suspect"; further examination is necessary

Subject	Test interval						Rank
	Before		2 months		4 months		
	BB	BBO	BB	BBO	BB	BBO	
P1	**20.5**	11.7	17.0	6.8	13.8	4.2	3
P2	16.5	7.5	10.2	5.2	7.7	4.5	10
P3	**23.0**	13.7	**19.2**	10.5	**22.0**	11.5	2
P4	**24.5**	12.2	**20.5**	10.0	18.2	7.7	10
P5	**21.5**	12.7	**21.5**	11.0	**19.2**	10.7	10
P6	**23.0**	10.0	**19.7**	8.7	14.7	7.0	10
P7	**20.5**	7.7	**20.0**	8.2	14.2	4.2	10
P8	**19.2**	9.5	**19.0**	10.0	18.0	10.0	5
P9	**23.7**	12.0	17.7	9.0	18.7	9.0	10
P10	**26.0**	14.7	**23.2**	13.0	**21.0**	13.2	9
P11	**23.7**	12.2	**20.2**	10.5	17.5	7.5	9
P12	**23.7**	12.7	**20.0**	11.7	17.5	8.2	8
P13	**21.7**	9.0	17.0	7.7	14.7	4.5	6
C1	15.2	6.0	16.7	6.5	17.2	8.7	4
C2	**19.2**	9.0	**19.0**	8.7	**22.0**	10.7	2
C3	13.7	7.7	14.5	8.7	17.7	8.7	0
C4	**22.0**	10.2	**21.0**	9.2	**22.0**	9.7	6

3.0 Results

After 4 months of training, the handwriting of the experimental
subjects showed a significant improvement: the subjects were
less dysgraphic as seen in the Borysowicz and Blöte score (Table
1 and Figure 3). The control group showed a significant increase
in dysgraphia. The subset BBO, which can be considered to be a
sort of clumsiness scale, showed a significant decrease for the
experimental group and a (non-significant) increase for the
control group. Independent judges can correctly distinguish
between the handwriting before and after the training period

(78%: Table 1). It seems obvious that this score confirms the results of the Borysowicz and Blöte scores.

The computer analysis of the handwriting samples, recorded at the beginning and during the training period, showed that the pen pressure decreased and the pen velocity increased as expected.

From the correlations given in Table 2, it may be seen that the handwriting of the experimental group BBO correlated significantly with Rnd, P, and of course with BB. The velocity V correlated significantly with pressure P and with width W. It is clear that P ought to correlate with V negatively, because it is difficult to write rapidly with a high pen pressure. Also it is clear that V ought to correlate with W as V depends to a high degree on the size of the handwriting produced.

TABLE 2: Correlations between handwriting specimens of the experimental group. Number of subjects: 13. Relevant and significant correlations are marked with *

Variable								
	BB	BBO	V	P	Phi	W	Rnd	B
BB, full	1.00							
BBO, subset	* .62	1.00						
V, velocity	−.15	−.45	1.00					
P, pressure	.27	* .56	*−.75	1.00				
Phi, slant	.27	.51	.52	.46	1.00			
W, width	−.23	−.06	*−.62	−.40	−.54	1.00		
Rnd, roundness	.23	* .68	−.56	.64	.39	−.11	1.00	
B, ballisticity	.55	−.05	.20	−.15	.20	−.49	−.23	1.00

The non-significant decrease in pen pressure and the increase in roundness for the control group were probably caused by learning and habituation effects during the experiments itself. We observed in the third and last measurement session that the subjects were more relaxed.

In Table 3 the average values for the handwriting features are given for all the variables investigated during this study. It appears that after handwriting training the BB and BBO decreased significantly: the resultant handwriting showed improvement in the spatial features. Another finding is that the subjects wrote larger. An unexpected outcome is the small but significant decrease in ballisticity. Only in the control group was there a significant increase in BB. This means that the handwriting of the subjects of the control group deteriorated.

TABLE 3: *Values for handwriting features from experimental and control groups before training and at 2 and 4 months. In each row, underlined values indicate scores that were NOT significantly different.*

	Experimental group			Control group		
	Before	2 months	4 months	After	2 months	4 months
BB	22. 14	18. 89	16. 72	17. 56	17. 81	19. 75
BBO	11. 23	9. 40	7. 87	_8. 13_	_8. 19_	_9. 5_
V	_29. 12_	_30. 19_	_32. 65_	_32. 20_	_34. 82_	_35. 05_
P	2. 69	1. 84	1. 38	_3. 23_	_2. 22_	_1. 55_
Phi	_80. 85_	_75. 52_	_73. 91_	_81. 06_	_80. 48_	_78. 18_
W	2. 48	2. 81	2. 77	_2. 88_	_2. 28_	_2. 23_
Rnd	_0. 16_	_0. 12_	_0. 15_	0. 07	0. 07	0. 14
B	0. 84	0. 79	0. 80	_0. 81_	_0. 85_	_0. 84_

4.0 Discussion

The expected result of this experiment, that the handwriting would be improved at the end of a training period, was verified. Secondly, a change in the computed features of velocity, pressure, size and ballisticity was expected. This was not found for ballisticity. As seen in an earlier study of Maarse (1987), ballisticity changes only after an extended period of practice. Greater changes may be expected only as a function of age. In this experiment no explicit attention was given to improve the handwriting. This could explain the absence of an improvement in ballisticity. Usually a training period lasts almost a year with weekly training sessions of an hour. The children in the experimental group received 10 training sessions of half an hour, which is significantly less training than would usually occur.

Another finding of this experiment was that computed values for slant and ballisticity were not sensitive to short-term handwriting training. This result stood in contrast to changes in global features such as width and pressure. For handwriting exercises more specific tasks and corresponding features have to be used. For example, the more local features of dysfluency, stroke length, and line quality would seem more appropriate.

The significant increase in the handwriting size (W) and the significant decrease of pen pressure (P) were the most important objective (as well as subjective) findings of this experiment.

Several problems arose in connection with our use of the Borysowicz and Blöte (1984) method: Firstly, the method was only developed for right-handed subjects. Two of the subjects in the experimental group were left-handed. Secondly, scoring large groups of subjects was very time consuming. Thirdly, for some of the items on the scoring list, the description lacks precision, and this led to differences between judges (eg for subject P9 in Table 1 at 2 months there was a difference of 4.5).

In conclusion, the use of global and local features as feedback in a computer-aided writing exercise seems difficult. We would suggest that only specific exercises and tasks should be implemented. If writing therapists and researchers continue their cooperation, the first computer programs should be on the market within the next few years. This does not mean that writing therapists can be replaced by computers, but that the use of computers can be meaningful in predefined exercises. Computers do not have the creativity and flexibility of a therapist. For some exercises computers can give fast and objective feedback, but they do not have capabilities to create a relaxed atmosphere necessary for a therapy session.

Chapter 16

Drawing and handwriting difficulties: Reasons for and remediation of dysfunction

Judith I. Laszlo & Pia Broderick

Efficient and effortless handwriting is essential in many educational activities. We expect children to acquire, in the first three years of schooling, a level of proficiency which enables them to use handwriting as a tool in their school work. Yet, despite considerable effort by both child and teacher a significant number of children do not learn the skill adequately.

The development of handwriting skill has been extensively reviewed (Askov et al, 1970; Peck et al, 1980;) and investigated in terms of pencil grip (Sassoon, 1983; Ziviani and Elkins, 1986), form and letter production (Lally, 1982; Meulenbroek, 1989; van Sommers, 1984), and timing (Wann, 1986).

We are interested in paper-pencil skills from a process-oriented perceptuo-motor viewpoint. We have investigated the processes which contribute to the acquisition and performance of these skills and isolated the causes which explain why some children find it difficult or even impossible to learn to write. We argue that once the underlying perceptual and motor processes which contribute to the skill are defined and measured, dysfunctional processes can be diagnosed. Following diagnosis the dysfunction can be alleviated and the difficulties in learning and performing the skills will be reduced or eliminated.

Development of Graphic Skills
ISBN 0-12-734940-5

1.0 Processes underlying perceptuo-motor skill

The following processes have been found to underlie perceptuo-motor skills: kinaesthetic information processing, spatial and temporal programming and motor planning (Laszlo and Bairstow, 1985a). We now briefly review each component in turn.

Kinaesthesis — the sense modality often overlooked — was established as one, if not the most important factor underlying efficient perceptuo-motor performance. Kinaesthesis is the sense of movement and position of body parts and limbs. It conveys information about the extent and direction of movements, the timing of the movement — whether fast or slow — and the force produced by the muscles. Kinaesthesis is a complex sense served by four types of receptors: the muscle spindle, tendon organ, joint receptor and receptors in the skin over the joints (McCloskey, 1978). Kinaesthesis provides ongoing information from every part of the body, about the prevailing posture, the tension in the muscles which maintain the posture and about movements superimposed on the posture. This intricate and finely graded sensory input is monitored continuously.

All skilled movements are flexible and goal directed. In order to perform a movement appropriate *motor units* must be activated in the relevant muscles. Motor units are the smallest independent building blocks of the motor system. Muscles are composed of many motor units. These can be activated individually and in various combinations according to the motor tasks. Movements differ from each other in terms of the extent and direction in which body parts and limbs are to be moved, *spatial programming*; whether the movement is to be fast or slow, *temporal programming*; and the amount of force necessary to overcome external resistance such as in lifting a weight, *force programming*. These movement parameters can be combined in ways appropriate for reaching the goal. The term motor programme refers to the selective activation of appropriate motor units.

The three *programming* processes — spatial, temporal and force — are relatively independent from each other as has been reviewed in Laszlo and Bairstow (1985a). Evidence for this independence can be observed in some children. For instance, a child might be able to move in the right direction but his/her movements could be either too fast or too slow or jerky. Spatial programming problems might be the reason why a child knocks over his/her glass of milk if his reaching movement is too long, or why the line he/she draws is going in the wrong direction. Excessive force production can lead to unnecessary tension when grasping the pencil. As kinaesthesis is generated throughout the movement, any divergence from the goal can be detected, provided the kinaesthetic information is processed adequately.

Motor *planning* relates to goal attainment. It is the process by which the starting point, the direction and speed of the movements are chosen, the point where the changes in direction should be made and how the movement should be terminated. Motor planning is an integral part of the perceptuo-motor system and is not a conscious process. The more appropriate the motor plan is the more accurate the movement will be. The motor plan is formulated according to information stored in memory about the movement. Previous attempts at the task are stored kinaesthetically. Thus the effectiveness of the motor plan depends on efficient processing and storage of the relevant kinaesthetic information.

1.1 Motor planning in drawing

Following the process-orientated analysis of drawing and writing skills (Laszlo and Broderick, 1985), we turned to investigate these skills in an attempt to define the specific role of some of the contributing perceptuo-motor processes. The importance of each process can be studied in two ways: by systematically varying process demands or comparing the performance level of subjects with different levels of process development. At the same time one needs to eliminate, or at least minimize the factors which are not under investigation. In all our drawing studies we minimized cognitive demands by placing the model in front of the child, leaving it in full view throughout the copying attempt. This way the child's knowledge of the figures could not influence his performance.

From our previous work (Laszlo and Bairstow, 1985a) we obtained evidence which confirmed findings already reported in the literature (Freeman, 1980) that oblique figures and lines are more difficult to draw than figures and lines in the horizontal/vertical orientation. This difference, according to our data, persists across all age groups tested, from 5 years to adults. We also knew from the earlier studies (Laszlo and Bairstow, 1985a) that this differential difficulty between drawing horizontal/verticals versus obliques is not due to spatial programming. Even 5-year-old children can trace a square or the same square placed in the oblique orientation with similar accuracy. In tracing, the motor planning demand is minimal, and obliques posed no greater difficulty than horizontal/vertical lines, in contrast to drawing, where the differential difficulty is evident even in adults. Thus it can be argued that rather than spatial programming, motor planning might be the decisive variable here.

This chapter presents results from two studies on drawing in which we examined the role of motor planning. The first study, which has been published elsewhere, is briefly reviewed in the next section. In this, and the second study, which has not previously been reported and which we describe in full, we used figures and lines in either the horizontal and vertical or oblique orientation.

In addition to the drawing studies carried out with children who had no known perceptuo-motor problems we will present results obtained while working with children who suffered from perceptuo-motor dysfunction (clumsiness). We will describe how alleviation of process dysfunction can lead to remediation of writing difficulties.

1.2 Guidelines assist motor planning

In the first study (Broderick and Laszlo, 1988) we varied planning demands systematically using components of a square, orientated either in the horizontal/vertical or oblique orientation. Three hundred and twenty children, attending mainstream schools, took part in this experiment. Four age

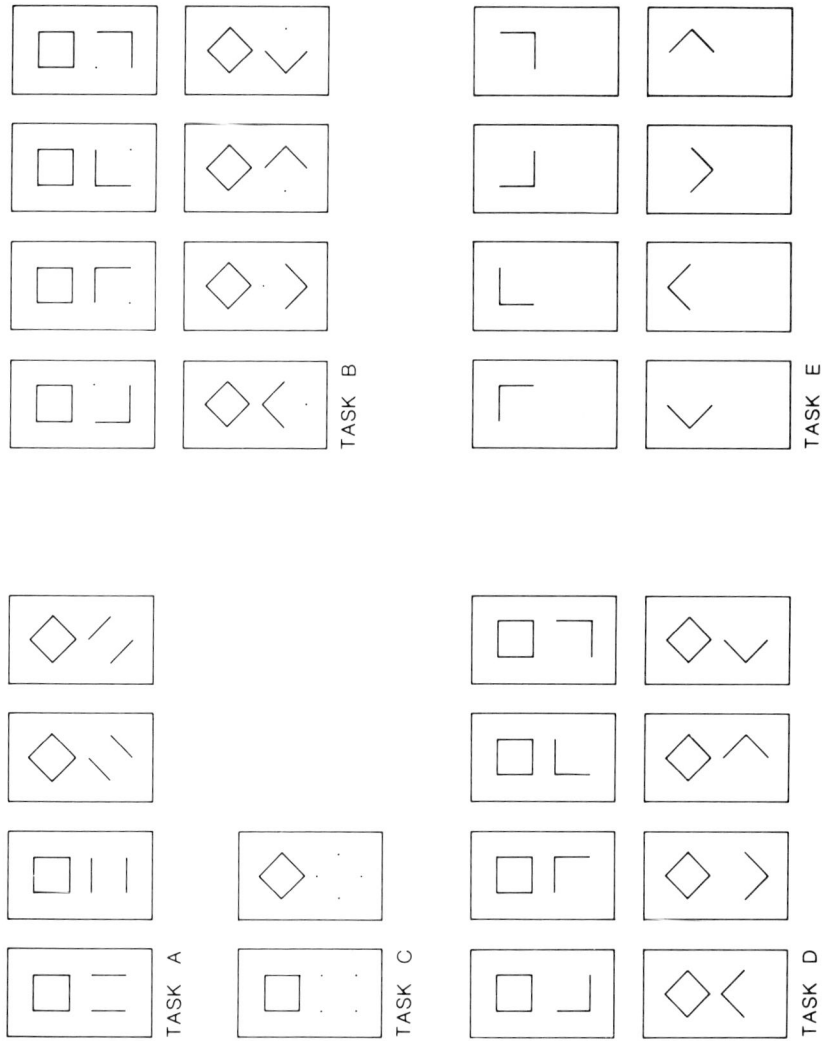

FIGURE 1: The experimental tasks used in the first experiment on motor planning.

groups were used: 6-, 7-, 8- and 10-year-olds. The experimental tasks are shown in Figure 1. Each child completed one task only. From each age group 16 children performed each task. The children were presented with one worksheet at a time. Eight children started with the horizontal/vertical figure components, the other eight with the oblique components.

Motor planning demands were increased gradually across the tasks. In Task A both start and endpoints were given and planning of angles was not required. In Task B the planning of the required angle was facilitated by the printed dot which defined the point where the change in movement direction was to take place. In Task D this dot was omitted, thus the angle had to be planned fully. Task E presented the highest planning demand as here, beside the angle, the start and end points needed planning as well. Task C was included as a control task with minimal planning demand but increased motor programming demand, ie four rather than two lines had to be drawn.

We scored performance accuracy by measuring each drawn angle and calculating the mean deviation of these angles from 90 deg. As predicted, overall accuracy decreased as planning demand increased. Task C was performed as accurately as Tasks A and B. It was found that obliques were more difficult to plan than horizontal/verticals. Only the 6-year-olds improved markedly across the tasks when drawing horizontal/vertical lines, while the three older age groups could plan these lines with similar accuracy regardless of planning difficulty. In the oblique orientation, however, accuracy decreased as planning demands increased. With age, over all tasks, performance improved: 6-year-olds were the least accurate, 7- and 8-year-olds performed similarly, while the 10-year-olds were the most accurate.

These results strongly support our prediction that motor planning is of crucial importance in drawing; that motor planning efficiency increases with age; and finally, that 6-year-old children, as a group, have developed motor planning ability to a low level only, as for this group even tasks with low-level planning demand presented difficulties. (For a detailed description of this study please see Broderick and Laszlo, 1988).

2.0 Continuous versus discrete movement and planning

In the second study, still keeping motor planning as the central variable, we compared continuous with discrete straight line patterns in both horizontal/vertical and oblique orientations. Three tasks were used. In two of these (A and B) connected patterns were to be copied, in the other (C) discrete patterns were copied (see Figure 2). Tasks A and B differed from each other in the level of motor planning demand only. In Task A printed dots defined both the direction of each movement and the point where the angles had to be formed, that is the motor planning demand

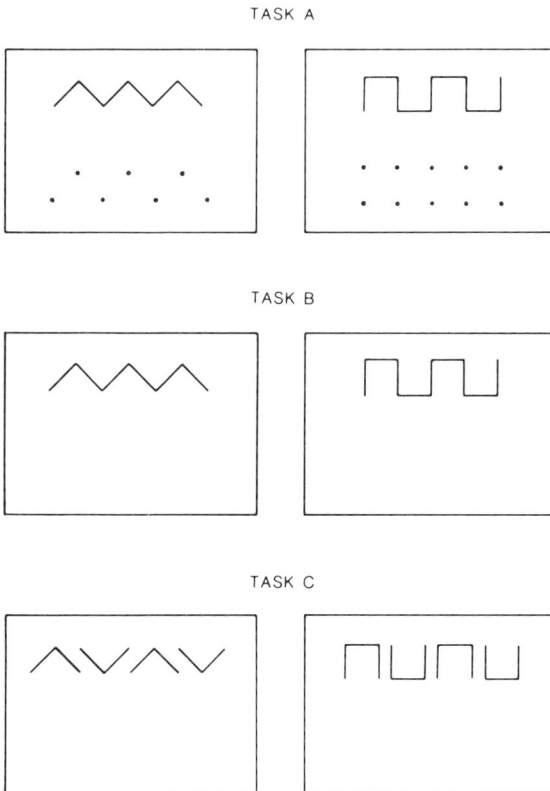

FIGURE 2: The experimental tasks used in the second study on motor planning with continuous and discrete patterns.

was minimal. In Task B, by omission of the dots the planning demand was increased considerably. By breaking up the continuous pattern into discrete units (Task C) the planningdemand was maximal. For each unit the start and endpoints had to be planned here, while in Task B only one start and one endpoint had to be planned.

2.1 Subjects

240 subjects participated in the study. 48 children, 24 girls and 24 boys, from each of four age levels were included. The age ranges, and means were as follows: 5.7 − 6.7 years, 6.2 years; 6.7 − 7.9 years, 7.2 years; 7.7 − 8.8 years, 8.2 years; and 9.7 − 10.9 years, 10.2 years. As well, 48 adults, all students of The University of Western Australia, served as subjects. Their ages ranged from 17 to 58 years, with a mean age of 20 years.

All the children tested were attending one of three state-run schools in the metropolitan area of Perth, Western Australia, both of which served areas incorporating wide ranges of socio-economic levels. Subjects within each age level were randomly assigned to one of three groups, with the single restriction that there were equal numbers of males and females in each of the three groups.

2.2 Apparatus

White unlined rectangular sheets of paper, 295mm x 210mm, were used (worksheets) and all subjects used soft lead pencils in the drawing tasks. A large sheet of stiff white cardboard was placed over the entire working surface and the worksheets were placed on this as required. A table and two chairs completed the apparatus.

2.3 Tasks

Three copying tasks were used. Each task entailed the completion of two worksheets, one containing a pattern of horizontal and vertical lines, and one containing a pattern of oblique lines. The three tasks were as follows (see Figure 2 for examples of the worksheets):

Task A: Connected pattern with dots. The required task was to draw straight lines to connect a series of dots, 40 mm apart, which became the vertices of 90 deg angles in a straight line pattern. The model was given in the upper half of the worksheet, and the pattern of dots was given in the lower half of the worksheet.

Task B: Connected pattern. The task was to copy a pattern constructed of 40-mm lines. The two models were designed and presented in the same way as for Task A; however, the lower section of the worksheet was left blank for the copy.

Task C: Discrete unit pattern. The task was to copy two models of several discrete units, each comprising a series of 40-mm lines. The upper half of each worksheet contained the model units and the lower half was left blank for the copy.

2.4 Procedure

Each age level was divided into three independent groups of 16 subjects each. Each of the groups were required to complete one task, either A, B, or C. Within each task, alternate subjects were given the worksheet of the pattern of horizontal and vertical lines first, or the pattern of oblique lines first, in order to counterbalance the effects of the initial exposure to the pattern orientations. Subjects were tested individually by one experimenter, seated opposite the experimenter on an appropriately sized chair. The experimenter described the task required, and then presented first one worksheet to be completed, and then the other. There was no time limit imposed on the completion of any of the tasks.

2.5 Scoring

Each angle of the drawing was measured and the absolute deviation from 90 deg (the size of the angles of the model pattern) was calculated. The mean deviation of all the angles from 90 deg was used as the score, providing a measure of the accuracy of the angular shape of the pattern. A second score was used to give a measure of the orientation of the pattern compared to the model. The initial direction of each line of the copied pattern was scored in terms of its deviation in degrees from the orientation of the corresponding line of the model pattern. The mean orientation error of all the lines in each pattern was used as the score. (If the child extended the pattern to include more lines than the model the additional components were not scored.)

Together, these two scores described the accuracy of the copied pattern.

3.0 Results

3.1 Orientation error

The first score considered is orientation error, describing the deviation of the lines of the copy from the orientation of the lines of the model. In Task A, the overall orientation of the pattern was predetermined by the given dots. However, the direction in which the subject started to move was taken as the chosen orientation of each line. A four-factor analysis of variance (3 Tasks x 5 Age Levels x 2 Genders x 2 Patterns, repeated on the variable of patterns) was performed on these scores. Only first-order interactions will be considered here. The main effects are clearly shown in Figures 3 and 4, which combine the scores of male and female subjects, as there was no main effect of gender. Effects of tasks [$F(2,210)=45.66$, $p<.001$], and age levels

$[F(4,210)=74.74$, $p<.001]$ were found as well as an interaction between them [Tasks x Age Levels, $F(8,210)=2.37$, $p<.05]$. Up to age 8 years Tasks B and C differed in accuracy, but these differences decreased in the older subjects. An interaction between the tasks and gender was also found $[F(2,210)=3.3$, $p<.05]$ due to less accurate performance by females on all tasks with the exception of Task A.

The oblique patterns were less accurately orientated than the horizontal-vertical patterns $[F(1,210)=400.46$, $p<.001]$; and the task variations differentially affected orientation error scores on the two patterns [Tasks x Patterns, $F(2,210)=33.04$, $p<.001]$. This was the result of a decrease in accuracy for the oblique patterns over all three tasks from A to C, contrasted with a steady level of performance for the horizontal-vertical patterns. The two patterns were performed with differing degrees of accuracy at the various ages [Age Levels x Patterns, $F(4,210)=18$, $p<.001]$, the result of overall performance on the oblique patterns showing a strong and consistent developmental trend, while performance on the horizontal-vertical patterns showed a distinctly less pronounced increase in accuracy with age.

Two further analyses of variance were performed, one for the oblique patterns and one for the horizontal-vertical patterns (3 Tasks x 5 Age Levels x 2 Genders). Significant task differences were found for both the horizontal-vertical patterns $[F(2,210)=3.1$, $p<.05]$, and the oblique patterns $[F(2,210)=47.97$, $p<.001]$. Newman-Keuls post hoc analyses (significant at $p<.05$), for the horizontal-vertical patterns, established that orientation on Task C (discrete unit pattern) was less accurate than on Task A (continuous pattern with dots). Differences between the tasks for the oblique line patterns were such that Task A was the most accurately orientated, followed by Task B (continuous pattern), while Task C was the least accurately orientated.

Age level main effects were found for both the horizontal-vertical $[F(4,210)=31.94$, $p<.001]$, and the oblique $[F(4,210)=51.37$, $p<.001]$ patterns. Newman-Keuls post-hoc tests (significant at $p<.05$) showed that, in the case of the horizontal-vertical patterns, orientation accuracy scores formed four age categories. The adult group orientated their copies the most accurately, followed by the 10-year-old group. The 7- and 8-year-olds were less accurate than the 10-year-olds in orientation, but more accurate than the youngest age level (6 years of age). Adults were again the most accurate in orientating the oblique pattern copies, followed by the 10-year-olds and then the 8-year-old group. There was no difference evident between the two youngest groups (6- and 7-year-olds), together, the least accurate of the age levels.

Interactions between the age levels and tasks were found for both the horizontal-vertical $[F(8,210)=2.1, p<.05]$ and the oblique patterns $[F(8,210)=2.68, p<.01]$. This interaction for the oblique patterns was a reflection of that found in the main analysis; until 8 years of age Tasks B and C differed in accuracy, but these differences decreased in the older subjects. The interaction for the horizontal-vertical patterns was due to the developmental trend of Task A.

3.2 Angles

The angle deviation data was subjected to a four-factor analysis of variance (3 Tasks x 5 Age Levels x 2 Genders x 2 Patterns, repeated on the variable of patterns). Significant main effects were found for tasks $[F(2,210)=46.89, p<.001]$, and age levels $[F(4,210)=46.1, p<.001]$ as well as an interaction between tasks and age levels $[F(8,210)=2.63, p<.01]$.

Angles of the oblique patterns were significantly less accurately formed than those of the horizontal-vertical patterns $[F(1,210)=222.86, p<.001]$; and tasks, age levels, and sex were found to differentially affect performance on the two patterns. The task by pattern interaction $[F(2,210)=44.28, p<.001]$, was a result of the same circumstances found for the orientation score; there was a noticeable difference in accuracy for the oblique patterns over the three tasks, consistent with motor planning demands, while accuracy differed less over the three tasks for the horizontal-vertical patterns.

The age level by pattern interaction $[F(4,210)=11.94, p<.001]$, was the result of a significant developmental trend for accurate angle formation for the oblique patterns which was not matched for the horizontal-vertical patterns. An interaction, between gender and the two patterns [$F(1,210)=4.29$, $p<.05$], was due to females drawing angles of the oblique patterns less accurately than males, while there was no difference between males and females drawing the angles of the horizontal-vertical patterns.

Two further analyses of variance were performed, one for the oblique pattern data, and one for the horizontal-vertical pattern data (3 Tasks x 5 Age Levels x 2 Genders). The analysis for the horizontal-vertical patterns revealed only an age level difference [$F(4,210)=24.63$, $p<.001$], a result of increasing angle copying accuracy with age. Newman-Keuls post hoc tests (significant at $p<.05$) established three distinct age groupings for the horizontal-vertical patterns; adults were the most accurate; there was little difference between the 7-, 8-, and 10-year-olds, together forming the second grouping, which was significantly more accurate than the 6-year-olds.

The age level differences for the oblique patterns [$F(4,210)=30.56$, $p<.001$] were the result of four groupings, identical to the pattern established for the orientation error score. The adult group was the most accurate, followed by the 10-year-olds and then the 8-year-olds. The 6- and 7-year-olds together were the least accurate in angle formation. In contrast to the horizontal-vertical patterns where there were no significant task variations, there were significant differences between tasks for the oblique patterns [$F(2,210)=54.16$, $p<.001$]. Newman-Keuls post hoc tests indicated that Task C (discrete unit pattern) was the least accurate, followed by Task B (continuous pattern). Task A, with dots to guide the required movements, was the most accurate. This task differentiation structure for the oblique patterns was identical to that found using the orientation error score. The task differentiation structure for the horizontal-vertical patterns varied slightly when measuring angle deviation compared to orientation.

A main effect of gender was found for the oblique patterns [$F(1,210)=4.69$, $p<.05$], accounting for the interaction between gender and patterns in the main analysis; females drew angles of the oblique pattern less accurately than males. At present, no explanation can be offered for this isolated and unexpected sex difference.

Performance on the three oblique pattern tasks was differentially affected by the age levels, [Age Levels x Tasks, [$F(8,210)=3.56$, $p<.001$]. This reflected the interaction found in the main analysis; while Task B (continuous pattern) was more accurately performed than Task C (discrete unit pattern) at 6- 7 and 10 years of age, the difference was not present at 8 years of age or in the adult group.

3.3 Summary

A summary of the results is presented in Figures 3 and 4.

Again, as in the earlier study reviewed in Section 1.3, accuracy of performance decreased as motor demand increased. Oblique patterns were more affected by planning demand manipulations than were horizontal/vertical patterns. Overall there was improvement with age. Of specific interest is the finding that the 6-year-old children performed worse than the older age groups

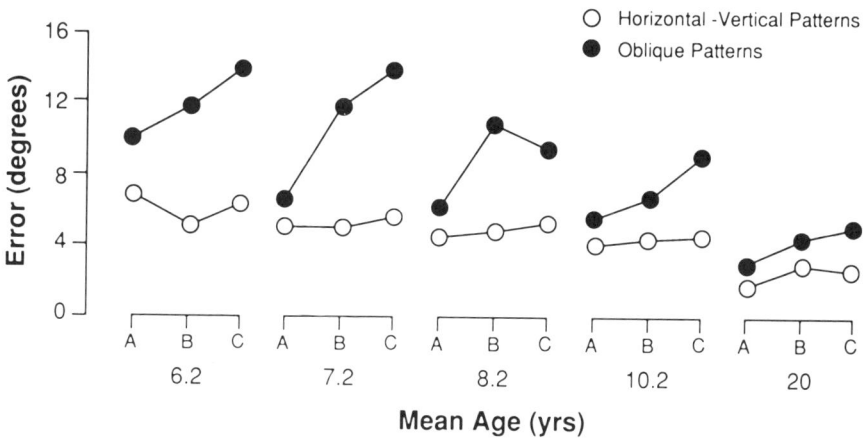

FIGURE 3: Summary of the orientation deviation results.

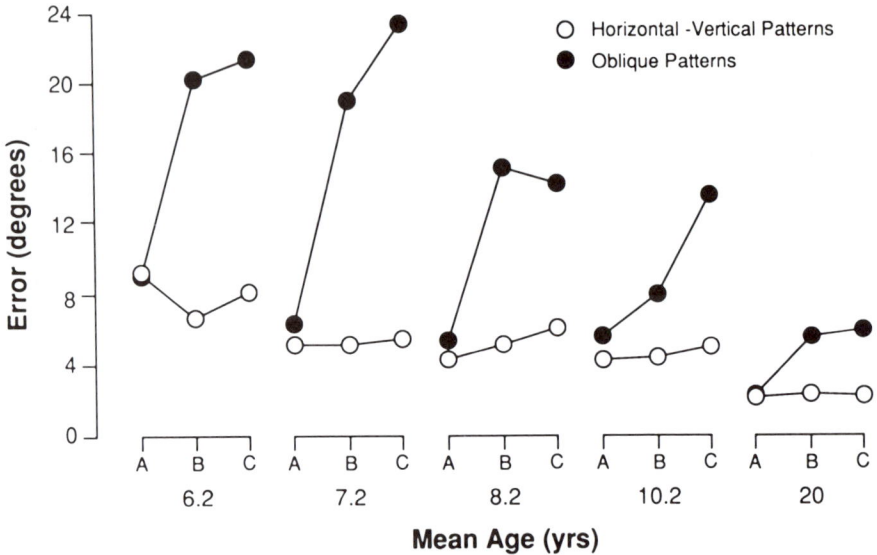

FIGURE 4: *Summary of the angular deviation results.*

in all tasks, on both scores, including the low planning demand
dot-to-dot drawing. Oblique patterns were copied less accurately
than horizontal/verticals at all ages. Task B was performed
better than Task C. Figure 5 gives some examples of the copies
children have produced.

4.0 Implications for teaching handwriting

What are the theoretical and applied implications which can be
drawn from the results of these studies? Do they have relevance
to the teaching of handwriting?

Drawing of both horizontal/vertical lines and oblique lines,
indeed all paper-pencil skills require a high level of spatial
programming ability. With the aid of the Perceptual-Motor
Abilities Test (Laszlo and Bairstow, 1985a) it has been
established that this ability develops rapidly up to 8 years of age.
Although 6- and 7-year-old children cannot be expected to
generate finely graded spatial programmes, they can control
both horizontal/vertical and oblique movements with equal
accuracy, that is, spatial programming ability cannot be the

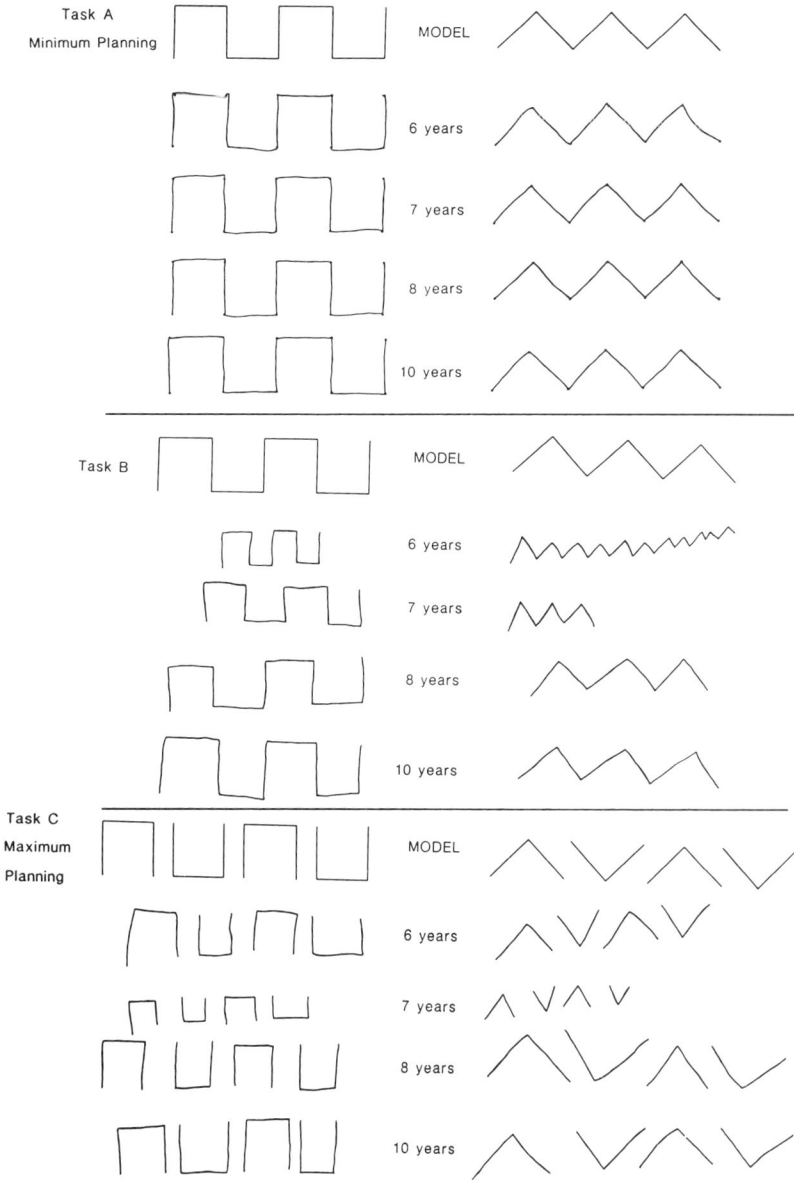

FIGURE 5: Examples of the performance of children from each age group on the three experimental tasks.

reason for the difficulty experienced with oblique lines. The evidence points to motor planning as the determining factor.

Motor planning is not an isolated process, but, as was mentioned in the Introduction, depends on memory traces stored from previous attempts of the same or similar tasks. As movements are remembered in kinaesthetic terms, that is we remember what a movement felt like, adequate processing and storage of kinaesthetic information is a necessary prerequisite for generating effective motor plans. The dependence of motor planning on kinaesthetic processing can be considered as the reason for the difficulty experienced when drawing oblique lines and figures. Observational data shows that many dys-kinaesthetic children can recognise kinaesthetically presented horizontal and vertical lines, but are unable to recognize obliques as the kinaesthetic feedback generated by movements in the oblique direction is more complex than that generated by horizontal or vertical movements.

The close relationship between motor planning and kinaesthetic processing is further supported by the finding that developmental trends in these two processes are similar. Kinaesthesis develops at a slow rate and, as a group, 6- and 7-year-olds have developed kinaesthetic ability to a relatively low level. Development accelerates from 8 years onwards, with improvement continuing into adulthood. The same developmental trends were obtained in the studies where motor planning was examined. Here again 6- and often 7-year-olds found it difficult to plan even easy movements.

4.1 Pre-writing exercises

Some of the methods used in teaching handwriting can now be considered in the light of the reported findings. Firstly, the effectiveness of pre-writing exercises can be discussed. Do our results lend support to dot-to-dot and tracing exercises as useful prewriting tasks? Dot-to-dot drawing, in motor skill terminology is an aiming task, dependent, primarily, on spatial programming, as is the tracing task, with minimal motor planning demands. While a few children might need training in spatial programming, our normative study has shown (Laszlo and Bairstow, 1985a) that this process is relatively well developed in most normal children, certainly to a level where line orientation does not effect performance accuracy. Most 6-year-olds, entering school, need to improve kinaesthetic processing and motor planning, processes not involved in these exercises. Thus, for the vast majority of children, exercises such as Task A will not be beneficial in preparing them to acquire handwriting skills.

Another type of exercise is copying continuous patterns, as in Task C. The main purpose here is described as focusing the child's attention on what the movements feel like, with accuracy of the copied patterns being of secondary importance. With the introduction of this task educators tacitly acknowledge the importance of kinaesthesis in handwriting. However, in our opinion, this exercise is unnecessary for those children who can feel their movements, that is, whose kinaesthetic development has reached the level where the intricate, finely graded kinaesthetic information generated during these exercises is perceived and processed. Moreover, it is of no help for the 30 per cent of the normal 6-year-old population who have not reached this level of kinaesthetic processing ability, that is, the children who would need kinaesthetic enhancement.

The transition from these exercises to letter production creates an unexpected difficulty. The goal in the pattern copying task is to feel the movement, while in writing the goal is the accuracy of the movement or letter. Motor planning is goal directed and the two tasks have different aims. When feeling the movement is set as the aim, the child at a low level of kinaesthetic development might attempt to increase the clarity of the kinaesthetic signal by involving more motor units in their motor programme than necessary. This can result in an increase in the tension with which the fingers grab the pencil, or the pressure the pencil exerts on the paper, or even in producing unwanted movements. These learnt adjustments will affect writing efficiency in an adverse way when the goal is changed from feeling to accuracy. There is no way in which we can predict whether transfer will occur here, that is, we cannot predict whether the exercises help or hinder the acquisition of the writing skill. Yet we know of no published transfer study which would give us evidence for or against the use of these exercises. We have heard of one unpublished study, in which zero transfer was found, showing that drawing continuous patterns has no effect on the acquisition of handwriting.

Secondly, our results indicate that printing is a more difficult task than cursive writing. Yet in many educational systems printing is taught before cursive writing, not withstanding the fact that many children find it very difficult to learn to connect the letters correctly. Indeed, we have shown that discrete units are less accurately reproduced than continuous patterns constructed of the same units, due to the increased planning demand from continuous to discrete patterns. In addition, the order in which the tasks are taught is not strictly logical. Continuous pre-writing exercises precede the discrete printing task, which is followed by continuous cursive writing. It seems that printing is an unnecessary step, especially as the final aim is to teach children cursive writing.

Some readers might level the criticism against the arguments presented on teaching methods as unwarranted generalization from the experimental setting to the applied field. After all, we have investigated only a selected sample of all possible line combinations and did not include curved lines. However, our reasoning can be extended to these handwriting components. Curved lines are more difficult to perceive kinaesthetically than obliques. Again, we have observed this gradation during kinaesthetic training. The kinaesthetic difficulty is, in turn, reflected in motor planning difficulty. There is no reason to assume that the different types of lines are processed and/or planned in qualitatively different ways. The production of any and all lines is dependent on the same perceptuo-motor processes. Only the level of demand placed on these processes will vary according to the type of line combinations of which a given letter or word is composed.

5.0 Handwriting difficulties: Causal diagnosis and remediation

Achieving an adequate level in handwriting is not only difficult for many 6—7-year-old children but poor handwriting skill is also a prevalent symptom of perceptuo-motor dysfunction (clumsiness) in the 8−12-year-old age group. In a recent study (Laszlo et al, 1988; Laszlo, 1990) children, aged 7−12 years of age were chosen by teachers from mainstream primary schools. Teachers selected children who they considered to be abnormally clumsy. Forty children were included in the study who, on testing, were diagnosed as suffering from perceptuo-motor dysfunction. Of these 40 children the teachers rated 32 as having very poor to poor handwriting. It would be inappropriate to discuss this study in detail here, thus only aspects relevant to remediation of handwriting difficulties will be described.

5.1 Kinaesthetic training

The children were tested on the Perceptual-Motor Abilities Test (Laszlo and Bairstow, 1985a) in order to obtain each child's perceptuo-motor profile. This test includes the Kinaesthetic Sensitivity Test (Laszlo and Bairstow, 1985b), which assesses two aspects of kinaesthesis, namely, acuity, and perception and memory. The children who scored significantly lower than expected for their age in one or both aspects of the test were given appropriate kinaesthetic training. Kinaesthetic training is based on principles similar to those applied in many sensory modalities such as in wine tasting. First, easily discriminated stimuli are presented. When these are differentiated confidently, task difficulty is gradually increased until fine discrimination is reached. Most children achieved better than age-related levels in kinaesthetic sensitivity within 5−10 sessions, each session being of approximately 15 minutes duration. The sessions were spread over a two-week period. Spatial programming dysfunction can also be alleviated by gradually increasing the difficulty level of specific tasks which are chosen for their reliance on spatial programming. From the time children entered the study their remedial training in handwriting was discontinued.

The relevant findings of the study will now be reported. All 30 children who had handwriting difficulties and were suffering from dyskinaesthesia at the beginning of the study showed dysfunction in programming as well. Some of the children were trained in kinaesthesis alone, others in kinaesthesis and motor programming. It was found that kinaesthetic training alone was as effective in alleviating perceptuo-motor dysfunction as the combined training regime. On the other hand, children who were trained in programming processes alone did not improve. Only when programming training was supplemented by kinaesthetic training did the children improve in motor skill performance.

Improvement in relatively simple motor skills, such as ball skills, occurred in parallel with the progress in kinaesthetic processing. Complex skills, such as handwriting, improved more slowly, over a 2–12-week period after training was completed (Laszlo, 1990).

The importance of kinaesthesis in acquisition and performance in every-day motor skills has been shown clearly by our results and supported by research workers and practitioners who are using our process-orientated diagnostic and treatment methods. An example using short sightedness as the cause of perceptuo-motor dysfunction might clarify the reason underlying the success of the treatment of dyskinaesthesia. A myopic child might present as clumsy because he cannot perform skills in which far distance vision is important. He would be unable to catch balls or copy material from the blackboard. Remedial training in these tasks cannot be expected to improve his performance. However, once the visual problem is diagnosed and the dysfunction is alleviated by the use of suitable spectacles the child will be able to learn the skills, and will be "cured" of clumsiness. But far distance vision, though of great importance in some skills, is not essential in others. On the other hand, kinaesthesis is essential in all perceptuo-motor behaviour. It is necessary for maintenance of posture, for error detection and hence error correction in goal-directed skilled movements, and is the major source of information in memorizing movements. The role of kinaesthesis in memory explains why motor planning, a crucial process in handwriting skill, cannot develop in the dyskinaesthetic child, and why inadequate kinaesthetic development adversely effects the performance in a variety of skills. It is predictable that successful treatment of kinaesthetic dysfunction will improve the child's overall motor performance.

5.2 Learning to write: the concept of kinaesthetic readiness

During the collection of the normative data for the Kinaesthetic

Sensitivity Test (Laszlo and Bairstow, 1985a, 1985b), 30 percent of 6-year-old children were found to show kinaesthetic sensitivity at a level below that necessary for the acquisition and performance of finely graded motor skills such as drawing. Kinaesthetic training of these children led to improved drawing performance (Laszlo and Bairstow, 1983).

In the educational setting it is often assumed that children who are ready to learn to read are ready to learn to write as well. There is a high degree of commonality in cognitive terms between reading and writing, but in addition to cognitive factors, in writing, adequately developed perceptuo-motor abilities are also necessary prerequisites. Of these perceptuo-motor processes kinaesthesis is a crucial one. Yet 30 percent of 6-year-olds have not reached kinaesthetic readiness at the time they are expected to learn to write. The concept of kinaesthetic readiness should be taken into account when the age at which handwriting instructions are introduced is decided on.

What are the consequences of disregarding the problems of the children who have not reached kinaesthetic readiness yet are trying to master the skill of writing? These children are exposed to failure at the very beginning of their school career. Failure to succeed in an important part of school work can undermine the child's self-confidence and self-esteem. Criticism from the teachers would further aggravate their problems. The child would appear careless and lazy in the eyes of the teacher and would be urged to be more diligent and to practise more. The assumption that lack of application is the cause of the child's slow progress was understandable before the importance of kinaesthesis in motor skills became established, and before kinaesthetic developmental trends have been charted. The slow kinaesthetic development should not be regarded as perceptual retardation but should be accepted as the normal, albeit slower end of developmental variance, which is entirely outside the child's control.

Many of these children are aware that practice is of little help to them without knowing why this should be so. To us the reason is obvious. The child who cannot process kinaesthetic information adequately and hence cannot store it in memory, will, in effect face a new task every time he repeats previous attempts. As the child cannot advance in writing he might assume that he cannot handle printed material in general and consequently develop a dislike of reading and number work as well. A further aggravating problem is the difficulty he might experience in spelling. While concentrating on the mechanics of letter formation, correct spelling must take a secondary place in the scheme of things. These seemingly insurmountable problems can be sidestepped by opting out or giving up trying to succeed. By adopting this course of action, children learn a maladaptive behaviour pattern which can impair their school progress and their psychological well-being.

Three possible solutions can be suggested to either eliminate or at least lessen the difficulties encountered by these children. We could start the instructions in handwriting at age 8 by which age kinaesthetic readiness would be reached by most children. We could introduce handwriting at 6 years of age, but refrain from assessing the performance, thus possibly avoiding the far-reaching psychological problems generated by loss of self-esteem and self-confidence. Finally, we might introduce routine kinaesthetic testing early in the first year of schooling for those children who exhibit difficulties in performing paper and pencil exercises and, if a low level of kinaesthetic sensitivity is diagnosed, accelerate their kinaesthetic development by kinaesthetic training. This would eliminate the need for lengthy and often ineffectual remedial handwriting training at a later stage, and prevent the development of the psychological problems associated with perceptuo-motor dysfunction.

6.0 Conclusions

Evidence was presented, based on our experimental findings, which showed that kinaesthetic sensitivity and motor planning are essential processes in acquisition and accurate performance of handwriting skills. We have made an attempt to present a cohesive picture based on both theoretical and applied research. It seems to us that by establishing close communication between research workers and educators the optimal method of developing good handwriting skills in the large majority of children would be advanced and accelerated.

Glossary

This glossary is intended as a rough guide for the reader with a limited background in research. It covers a number of the terms used by authors within their chapters. Although it may sometimes oversimplify meanings, it should enable some appreciation of unfamiliar terminology and procedures.

Acceleration: Pen-point acceleration is normally calculated by recording pen position during handwriting with a digitizer and then calculating the second derivative with respect to time. The first derivative is velocity (rate of change of position) and the second derivative is acceleration (rate of change of velocity).

Age groups: In this volume various terms are used to refer to different age groups. Approximate equivalents are primary = kindergarten = nursery = 3—5 years; junior = 6—10 years; secondary =11—16 years; adult = 17+ years.

Analysis of variance (ANOVA): A statistical test that evaluates the difference in the average scores or measured values of two or more groups of subjects (eg novice vs skilled writers) perhaps experiencing contrasting sets of experimental conditions (eg hard vs easy tasks). Using F-ratios, the analysis determines the likelihood that differences could have arisen as a result of chance factors in sampling.

Ballistic: Strictly, a ballistic motion is one in which all the energy is imparted to an object at the beginning of its movement (eg a bullet or arrow). In a handwriting context, ballistic is generally used to refer to movements where no adjustment or shaping of the stroke takes place subsequent to its initiation.

Chi-square: A statistical test that compares the relative frequency of observations across a number of categories with theoretically expected frequencies to determine the likelihood that the differences could have arisen as a result of chance' factors in sampling.

Correlation (r): A summary statistic that estimates the extent to which two measures of performance vary in similar ways. A value of $r=1$ indicates perfect correlation (eg volume of water and weight); $r=0$ indicates that there is no correlation (eg hair length and shoe size). A negative value (eg $r=-.5$) indicates the same strength of relationship as the corresponding positive value ($r=.5$), except that the variables change in opposite directions (eg as writing speed increases, legibility decreases).

Cross-sectional study: In the study of developmental changes in handwriting, a cross-sectional study is one that examines the differences in performance of children of different ages.

Digitizer: An electronic device, also referred to as a *graphic tablet*, that allows pen movements in handwriting to be recorded by computer. Normally, pen position is sampled at regular intervals of one hundredth of a second with a spatial accuracy of the order of one tenth of a mm.

Distribution: The spread of scores around some central value (mean or median). For many statistical tests the theoretical distribution of the measure of interest is assumed to have a particular bell-shape, termed *Normal* or *Gaussian*, in which the frequency of occurrence of scores diminishes smoothly on either side of a central maximum at the mean.

Dysfluency, dysgraphia, dyskinesia: Loss of (or disorder in) fluency, graphic skills, movement.

F-ratio: In the analysis of variance, ratios of the variance measured over conditions and the variance occurring within conditions are used to assess the statistical significance of differences in mean between the conditions. These are termed *F*-ratios.

Factor analysis: A statistical technique that uses patterns of correlation between a number of variables to group them into clusters of variables that are closely related and may be presumed to be influenced by an underlying common *factor*.

Feedback: Any human action generates perceptual consequences that can be monitored and used to guide future action. Information about movement arises in the visual system, vestibular system, proprioceptive system (muscles and joints) and the tactile (touch) system. The use of such cues to determine future action is generally referred to as feedback control.

Filtering: Data collected with a digitizer usually contain small random recording errors, often termed *noise*. The noise is generally of a much higher frequency than the frequency (speed) of human movements and mathematical techniques may be used to filter out the noise distortion. This results in a smoother-looking spatial handwriting trace.

Grammar of action: A theoretical suggestion that certain movement sequences are guided by general principles that dictate the ordering of components within the sequence. In handwriting it is proposed that a child learns principles such as "start at the top", "move left to right" and that these govern the acquisition of skill.

Graphic tablet: See *digitizer*.

Graphology: The study of handwriting with the aim of discerning personality characteristics of the writer.

Hypothesis: Formal scientific method follows a procedure of examining previous evidence, generating an experimental hypothesis (eg girls will be neater and faster writers than boys), then collect data to examine that hypothesis against the *null* hypothesis (there is no difference between girls and boys). In practice, many researchers do not state their hypotheses explicitly; the reader is left to assume that the researchers examined girls' and boys' writing on the assumption that there would be some differences.

Interaction: An experimenter may choose to assess the effect on performance of more than one experimental factor at a time. It is then relevant to ask whether differences due to one factor are affected by a change in the other factor, in which case the two factors are said to interact in their effects on performance. The statistical significance of such effects is commonly assessed with the Analysis of Variance.

Isochrony: A number of human actions appear to be performed in approximately the same time despite moving through a different distances. If you wrote your signature in the same amount of time, irrespective of whether it was 2 cm or 5 cm high, then the movements may be described as isochronous.

Kinaesthesis: The sense of movement of the body and limbs arising primarily from joint and muscular sensors. The term is often taken to include the sense of position and used interchangably with *proprioception*.

Kinematics: The position, velocity and acceleration of an object taken with respect to time.

Longitudinal study: In the present context, a study that examines handwriting development by following a specific group of children as they get older and testing them repeatedly at pre-specified intervals.

Mann-Whitney U: A statistical test used to appraise the difference in central value between two sets of data when the data cannot be assumed to be samples from a Normal distribution (see Distribution). In practice this type of test (called non-parametric) is most often used when the data comprises rank-ordered information or subjective ratings of behaviour.

Mean: The average of a series of measurements, calculated as the sum of all the measurements divided by the number of observations.

Monotonic development: A constantly increasing (or decreasing) trend in development. If children wrote progressively faster each year from 6 to 10 years, then writing speed would be described as following a monotonic trend. If, however, speed increased from 6 to 8 years but then decreased between 8 and 10 years, this would be described as a non-monotonic relation between handwriting speed and age.

Motor plan: A specification of how a goal for action may be achieved that is phrased in broad spatio-temporal terms rather than in terms of commands to particular muscles.

Motor programme: A set of commands prepared by the brain for the selective activation of specific muscles in order to achieve some movement goal.

p-value: There is a certain probability, *p*, that the value of any test statistic (eg chi-square, *F*, *t*, *U*) could have occurred through random sampling fluctuations from subject to subject, or trial to trial. For example, *p*=.01 indicates that there is a one in a hundred chance of this happening. A convention in behavioural science is that *p*<.05 is an acceptable level at which to claim the results of an analysis as *statistically reliable*.

Pen pressure: This term is generally used to refer to the force with which the pen tip is pressed against the paper (strictly, pen-axial force). A less common usage of the term refers to the pressure on the pen barrel arising from the pengrip.

Process variable: This term is commonly used in handwriting research to refer to measures that relate to the action of writing (eg pen speed, pressure). Process variables contrast with *product* variables that relate to the end-product of the action of writing, namely, the written trace (eg style, size).

Proprioception: See *kinaesthesis*.

Proximal, distal musculature: The proximal muscles are those closer to the trunk such as the shoulder and elbow (for the arm). Distal refers to the wrist and particularly fingers.

Resolution: The accuracy of measurement resulting from limitations of the experimental equipment. In handwriting research, the latter normally means a digitizer. Good spatial resolution is important for accurate measurement of height and length of strokes, good temporal resolution is important for the estimation of velocity and acceleration.

Sampling frequency: The rate at which data points are collected in time. In handwriting this is normally 50-200Hz (50-200 points per second). The reciprocal of the sampling frequency is the temporal resolution (50-200Hz = .02-.005 sec per point).

Standard Deviation (SD): A measure of the dispersion of values around the average (mean). If the data originate from a Normal distribution, in principle 68% of the observed scores should fall in a region 1 SD above and below the mean and 98% within 2 SDs on either side of the mean. The SD is used as a general measure of the variability of performance.

Statistical significance: See *p-value*.

t-test: A statistical analysis that compares the difference between two mean scores with the variability that occurs within each group of observations. This allows an estimate of the probability that such a difference could have arisen by chance.

Trajectory: The spatial path followed by an object. In the case of handwriting the trajectory usually refers to the shape or form of the successive *strokes* that comprise letters. The term trajectory is often used to include the time-course of the movement (ie kinematics).

Variance: The dispersion of a set of values around the average, it is computed as the mean sum of squared deviations of the individual observations about the mean. The standard deviation is the square root of the variance.

Velocity: The speed of an object in a particular direction in three-dimensional space. With 2-dimensional X-, Y-position data from a digitizer, velocity can be calculated for both X and Y directions. *Speed* is the combination of both X and Y velocities without regard to direction.

X, Y, Z variables: Simple letter codes that are used to refer to movements in three-dimensional space. In handwriting research these are generally taken to refer to the following directions: letter width across the page, movements along the writing line (X), letter height, movements down the page (Y), pen pressure, movement into the page (Z).

References

Ajuriaguerra, J. de (1964) *L'écriture de l'enfant (Children's handwriting).* Paris.

Ajuriaguerra, J. de, Diatkine, R. & Lebovici, S. (1961) *La Psychiatrie de l'enfant: Vol 3 (Child Psychiatry).* Paris: P.U.F.

Ajuriaguerra, J. de, Auzias, M., Coumes, F., Denner, A., Lavondes-Moaned, V., Perron, R. & Stambak, M. (1978) *L'écriture de l'enfant, Vol II.* Paris: Delachaux et Niestlé.

Ajuriaguerra, J. de, Auzias, M., Coumes, F., Denner, A., Lavondes-Moaned, V., Perron, R. & Stambak, M. (1979) *L'écriture de l'enfant, Vol I (The handwriting of children).* Paris: Delachaux et Niestlé.

Alston, J. & Taylor, J. (1987) *Handwriting.* London: Croom Helm.

Arnheim, R. (1956) *Art and visual perception: A Psychology of the creative eye.* London: Faber & Faber.

Asheim, S. (1964) *Standpunktprøver i skolen. Orddiktat 2.-6.kl. (Achievement tests. Word Dictation for 2nd—6th grade).* Oslo: Universitetsforlaget.

Askov, E.N., Otto, W., & Askov, W. (1970) A decade of research in handwriting: Progress and prospect. *The Journal of Educational Research, 64,* 100-111.

Athenes, S. (1984) *Adaptabilité et development de la posture manuelle dans l'écriture (Adaptability and development of hand posture in handwriting).* Master's thesis, University of Marseille.

Ayres, A.J. (1966) *Southern California figure-ground visual perception test manual.* Los Angeles: Western Psychological Services.

Ayres, L.P. (1912) *A scale for measuring the quality of handwriting of school children.* New York: Russell Sage Foundation.

Bard, C., Fleury, M., Carrière, L. & Bellec, J. (1981) Components of the coincidence-anticipation behavior of chilren aged 6 to 11 years. *Perceptual and Motor Skills, 52,* 547-556.

Beery, K.E. (1967) *Developmental test of visual-motor integration.* Chicago: Follett.

Beetsma, I. (1980) *Schrijven als motorische vaardigheid (Writing as a motor skill).* Groningen.

Ben-Shakhar, G., Bar-Hillel, M., Bilu, Y., Ben-Abba, E. & Flug, A. (1986) Can graphology predict occupational success? Two empirical studies and some methodological ruminations. *Journal of Applied Psychology, 71,* 645-653.

Beusekom, M.F. van & Versloot, J. (1982) *Ik schrijf zo (I write so).* Zutphen: Thieme.

Binet, A. & Courtier, J. (1893) Sur la vitesse des mouvements graphiques (On the velocity of handwriting movements). *Revue Philosophique de la France et de l'Etranger, 35,* 664-667.

Blöte, A.W., Zielstra, E.M. & Zoetewey, M.W. (1987) Writing posture and writing movement of children in kindergarten. *Journal of Human Movement Studies, 13,* 323-341.

Borysowicz, B. & Blöte, A. (1984) *Beoordelingsmethode voor de schrijfhouding en de schrijfbeweging (Evaluation method for the writing position and the writing movement).* Lisse: Swets & Zeitlinger.

Borysowicz, B.A. & Blöte, A. (1985) De ontwikkeling van het schrijfgedrag: Een onderzoek met de bewegingsschaal voor de schrijfhouding en schrijfbeweging (The development of writing behaviour: A survey of movement skill for writing posture). In Thomassen, A.J.M.W., Galen, G.P. van & de Klerk, L.F.W. (Eds.) *Studies over de schrijfmotoriek: Theorie en toepassing in het onderwijs.* Lisse: Swets en Zeitlinger.

Brandstatter, H. (1969) On diagnosing personality from handwriting. *Psychologische Ruiadschau, 20,* 159-172.

Brigance, A. (1983) Comprehensive inventory of basic skills. North Billerica, MA: Curriculum Associates.

Broderick, P. & Laszlo, J.I. (1987) The drawing of squares and diamonds: a perceptual-motor task analysis. *Journal of Experimental Child Psychology, 43,* 44-61.

Broderick, P. & Laszlo, J.I. (1988) The effects of varying planning demands on drawing components of squares and diamonds. *Journal of Experimental Child Psychology, 45,* 18-27.

Brooks, V.B., Cooke, J.D. & Thomas, J.S. (1973) The continuity of movements. In Stein, R.B., Pearson, K.B., Smith, R.S. & Redford, J.B. (Eds.) *Control of posture and locomotion.* New York: Plenum Press.

Brown, F.G. (1983) Principles of educational and psychological testing (3rd edn.) New York, NY: Holt, Rinehart and Winston.

Brown, F.M. (1985) Teaching English in an English inner-city area. *Journal of the Forensic Science Society, 25,* 313-321.

Bruckner, L.J. & Bond, G.L. (1955) *The diagnosis and treatment of learning difficulties.* New York: Appleton, Century, Crofts.

Brugsch, H. (1848) *Scriptura Aegyptiorum Demotica ex Papyris et Inscriptionibus Explanata.* Berlin: R. Gaertner.

Bruinsma, C. (1987) *Systematic errors in survey interviews.* Amsterdam: Vrije Universiteit.

Bryson, S.E. & McDonald, V. (1984) The development of writing posture in left-handed children and its relation to sex and reading skills. *Neuropsychologia, 22,* 91-94.

Bushnell, E.W. (1985) The decline of visually guided reaching during infancy. *Infant Behavior and Development, 8,* 139-155.

Camstra, B. (1981) *Bouwstenen voor onderwijs (Building stones for teaching).* Utrecht.

Carroll, J.B. (1976) The nature of the reading process. In Singer, H. & Rudell, R. (Eds.) *Theoretical Models and Processes of Reading.* Newark: International Reading Association.

Clark, M.M. (1957) *Left-handedness.* London: University of London Press.

Collette, M.A. (1979) Dyslexia and classic pathognomic signs. *Perceptual and Motor Skills, 37,* 1055-1062.

Connolly, A.J., Nachtman, W. & Pritchett, E.M. (1971) *Keymath diagnostic arithmetic test.* Circle Pines, MN: American Guidance Service.

Corbetta, D. (1989) *Le développement de la bimanualité chez l'enfant: symétrie et asymétrie des mouvements (The development of bimanuality in children: symmetry and assymmetry or movements).* PhD Thesis, University of Geneva.

Coren, S. & Porac, C. (1979) Normative data on hand position during writing. *Cortex, 15,* 679-682.

Critchley, M. (1975) Specific developmental dyslexia. In Lenneberg, E.H. & Lenneberg, E. (Eds.) *Foundations of language development, Vol 2.* New York: Academic Press.

Crumbaugh, J.C. & Stockholm, E. (1977) Validation of graphoanalysis by global or holistic method. *Perceptual and Motor Skills, 44,* 403-410.

Crystal, D. (1987) *The Cambridge encyclopedia of language.* New York, NY: Cambridge University Press.

Davies, W.V. (1987) *Egyptian hieroglyphs.* London: British Museum.

Doehring, D.G.(1968) *Patterns of impairment in specific reading disability*. Bloomington: Indiana University Press.

Doorn, R.R.A. van & Keuss, P.J.G. (submitted manuscript) Compensations for visual deprivation in writing short letter sequences.

Driver, G.R. (1976) *Semitic writing: From pictograph to alphabet*. London: Oxford University Press.

Dunham, P. & Reid, D. (1987) Information processing: effect of stimulus speed variation on coincidence-anticipation of children. *Journal of Human Movement Studies, 13,* 151-156.

Dunham, P., Allan, R. & Winter, B. (1985) Tracking ability of elementary school-age children. *Perceptual and Motor Skills, 60,* 771-774.

Eisler, H. (1962) Empirical test of a model relating magnitude and category scales. *Scandinavian Journal of Psychology, 3,* 88-96.

Eisler, H. (1965) The connection between magnitude and discrimination scales and direct and indirect scaling Methods. *Psychometrika, 30,* 271-289.

Eldridge, M.A, Nimmo-Smith, I., Wing, A.M. & Totty, R.N. (1984) The variability of selected features in cursive handwriting: Categorical measures. *Journal of the Forensic Science Society, 24,* 179-219.

Eldridge, M.A, Nimmo-Smith, I, Wing, A.M. & Totty, R.N. (1985) The dependence between selected categorical measures of cursive handwriting. *Journal of the Forensic Science Society, 25,* 217-231.

Elliot, R. (1964) Physiological activity and performance: a comparison of kindergarten children with young adults. *Psychological Monographs,78,* (10, Whole no. 587).

Ellis, A.W. (1984) *Reading, writing, and dyslexia: A cognitive analysis*. London: Erlbaum.

Engen, A. van (1986) *Schrijven in de basisschool (Handwriting in the elementary school)*. Groningen: Jacob Dijkstra.

Enke, W. (1930) Die Psychomotorik der Konstitutionstypen (Psychomotor aspects of constitutional types). *Zeitschrift für angewandte Psychologie, 36,* 237-287.

Enstrom, E.A. (1964) Research in handwriting. *Elementary English, 41,* 873-876.

Eysenck, H.J. & Eysenck, S.B.G. (1975) *Manual of the Eysenck personality questionnaire*. London: Hodder and Stoughton.

Eysenck, H.J. & Gudjonsson, G. (1986) An empirical study of the validity of handwriting analysis. *Personality and Individual Difference, 7,* 263-264.

Eysenck, S.B.G. (1965) *Junior Eysenck personality inventory.* London: Hodder & Stoughton.

Feldt, L.S. (1962) The reliability of measures of handwriting quality. *Journal of Educational Psychology, 53,* 288-292.

Fischer, H.G. (1977) . *The orientation of hieroglyphs. Part I. reversals.* New York: Metropolitan Museum of Art.

Fitts, P.M. (1954) The information capacity of the human motor system in controlling the amplitude of the movement. *Journal of Experimental Psychology, 47,* 381-391.

Freeman, F.N. (1914) Experimental analysis of the writing movement. *Psychological Review Monograph Supplement, 17,* 1-46.

Freeman, F.N. (1921) The scientific evidence on the handwriting movement. *Journal of Educational Psychology, 12,* 253-270.

Freeman, F.N. (1954) Teaching Handwriting - *What Research Says to the Teacher (no 4).* Washington: Association of Classroom Teachers of the National Education Association.

Freeman, N.H. (1980) *Strategies of representation in young children: Analysis of spatial skills and drawing processes.* London: Academic Press.

Furner, B. (1983) Developing handwriting ability: A perceptual learning process. *Topics in Learning and Learning Disabilities, 3,* 41-54.

Furnham, A. & Gunter, B. (1987) Graphology and personality: Another failure to validate graphological analysis. *Personality and Individual Differences, 8,* 433-435.

Gachoud, J-P., Mounoud, P., Hauert, C-A. & Viviani, P. (1983) Motor strategies in lifting movements: a comparison of adult and children performances. *Journal of Motor Behavior, 15,* 202-216.

Galen, G.P. van & Teulings, H-L. (1983) The independent monitoring of form and scale factors in handwriting. *Acta Psychologica, 54,* 9-22.

Galen, G.P. van, Meulenbroek, R.G.J. & Hylkema, H. (1986) On the simultaneous processing of words, letters and strokes in handwriting. Evidence for a mixed linear and parallel model. In Kao. H,S.R., Galen, G.P. van & Hoosain, R. (Eds.) *Graphonomics: Contemporary Research. in Handwriting.* Amsterdam: North-Holland.

Galen, G.P. van, Smyth, M.M., Meulenbroek, R.G.M. & Hylkema, H. (1989) The role of short term memory and the motor buffer in handwriting under visual and non-visual guidance. In Plamondon, R., Suen, C.Y. & Simner, M.L. (Eds.) *Computer recognition and human production of handwriting*. Singapore:World Scientific Publishing.

Gaur, A. (1987) *A history of writing*. London: The British Library.

Gesell, A. (1940) *The first five years of life*. New York, NY: Harper.

Gollnitz, Lenz, Winterling (1957) *Beitrage zur Psychodiagnostik des Sonderschulkindes (Contribution to Psychodiagnosis in Special Teaching)*.

Goodnow, J.J. (1977) *Children's drawing*. London: Open Book.

Goodnow, J.J. & Friedman, S. (1972) Orientations in children's human figure drawings: an aspect of graphic language. *Developmental Psychology, 7*, 10-16.

Goodnow, J.J. & Levine, R. (1973) The grammar of action: sequence and syntax in children's copying of simple shapes. *Cognitive Psychology, 4*, 82-98.

Goodnow, J.J., Sarah, L.F., Bernbaum, M. & Lehman, E.B. (1973) Direction and sequence in copying: the effect of learning to write in English and Hebrew. *Journal of Cross-Cultural Psychology, 4*, 263-281.

Gregory, R. & Paul, J. (1980) The effects of handedness and writing posture on neuropsychological test results. *Neuropsychologia, 18*, 231-235.

Groff, P.J. (1961) New speeds of handwriting. *Elementary English, 38*, 564-565.

Gross, C., (1942) *Vitalität und Handschrift (Vitality and Handwriting)*. Berlin: R. Pfau.

Guiard, Y. & Millerat, F. (1984) Writing postures in left-handers: Inverters are hand-crossers. *Neuropsychologia, 22*, 535-538.

Hammill, D.D. & Larsen, S.C. (1989) *Test of legible handwriting*. Austin, TX: Pro-Ed.

Hamstra-Bletz, E. & Bie, H. de (1985) Diagnostiek van dysgrafisch handschrift bij leerlingen uit het gewoon lager onderwijs (Diagnosis of dysgraphic handwriting for pupils in primary education). In Thomassen, A.J.M.W., Galen, G.P. van & de Klerk, L.F.W. (Eds.) *Studies over de schrijfmotoriek:*

Theorie en toepassing in het onderwijs. Lisse: Swets en Zeitlinger.

Hamstra-Bletz, E., Bie, J. de & Brinker, B.P.L.M. den (1987) *Beknopte beoordelingsmethode voor kinderhandschriften (A brief evaluation method for children's handwriting).* Lisse: Swets & Zeitlinger.

Harris, T.L. & Rarick, G.L. (1959) The relationship between handwriting pressure and legibility in handwriting in children and adolescence. *Journal of Experimental Education, 28,* 65-84.

Harrison, W.R. (1966) *Suspect documents: Their scientific examination.* London: Sweet & Maxwell.

Hauert, C.A. (1980) Propriétés des objets et propriétés des actions chez l'enfant de 2 à 5 ans (Properties of objects and actions in children from 2 to 5 years). *Archives de Psychologie, 185,* 95-168.

Hay, L. (1978) Accuracy of children on an open-loop pointing task. *Perceptual and Motor Skills, 47,* 1079-1082.

Hay, L. (1979) Spatial-temporal analysis of movement in children: Motor program versus feedback in the development of reaching. *Journal of Motor Behavior, 11,* 189-200.

Hay, L. (1981) The effect of amplitude and accuracy requirements in movement time in children. *Journal of Motor Behavior, 13,* 177-186.

Hay, L. (1984) Discontinuity in the development of motor control in chlidren. In Prinz, W. & Sanders, A.F. (Eds.) *Cognition and motor processes.* Berlin: Springer Verlag.

Hearn, R.S. (1969) Dyslexia and handwriting. *Journal of Learning Disabilities, 2,* 39-44.

Heermann, M. (1985) *Schreibbewegungstherapie und Schreibbewegungstest bei verhaltensgestörten, neurotischen Kindern und Jugendlichen (Handwriting tests and therapy for neurotic children).* Munchen: Ernst Teinhardt.

Herrick, V.E. (Ed.) (1963) *New horizons for research in handwriting.* Madison: University of Wisconsin Press.

Hettinga, H. et al. (1988) *Handschrift (Handwriting).* Den Bosch: Malmberg.

Hofsten, C. von (1980) Predictive reaching for moving objects in human infants. *Journal of Experimental Child Psychology, 30,* 369-382.

Hollerbach, J.A. (1981) An oscillation theory of handwriting. *Biological Cybernetics, 39,* 139-156.

Hornsveld, R. J. H. (1983) Schrijftkramp, theorie en behandeling (Writer's cramp, theory and treatment). *Gedragstherapie, 16*, 22-23

Hughes, J.N. (1988) *Cognitive behaviour therapy with children in schools.* New York, NY: Pergamon Press.

Hulstijn,W. & Mulder, T. (1986) Motor dysfunctions in children. Towards a process-orientated diagnosis. In Wade, M. & Whiting, H.T.A. (Eds.) *Themes in motor development.* Netherlands: Nijhoff

Ilg, F.L. & Ames, L.B. (1964) *School readiness.* New York: Harper & Row.

Jack, W.R. (1895) On the analysis of voluntary muscular movements by certain new instruments. *Journal of Anatomy and Physiology, 29,* 473-479.

Jansen, A. (1973) *Validation of graphological judgments: An experimental study.* The Hague, Netherlands: Mouton.

Jeffery, L.H. (1961) *The local scripts of archaic Greece. A study of the origin of the Greek alphabet and its development from the eighth to fifth centuries.* Oxford: Oxford University Press.

Jesness, C.F. (1971) *Manual for the Jesness behavior checklist.* Palo Alto, CA: Consulting Psychologists Press.

Jones, H.E. & Seashore, R.H. (1944) *The development of fine motor and mechanical abilities,* 43rd Yearbook. New York, NY: National Society for Studies in Education.

Kao, H.S.R., Shek, T.L. & Lee, E.S.P. (1983) Control modes and task complexity in tracing and handwriting performance. *Acta Psychologica, 54,* 69-78.

Kao, H.S.R., Galen, G. P. van & Hoosain, R. (Eds.) (1986) *Graphonomics: Contemporary research in handwriting.* Amsterdam: North-Holland.

Kardirkamanathan, M. (1989) A scale-space approach to segmentation and recognition of cursive script. PhD Thesis, Cambridge University.

Keogh, J. & Sugden, D. S. (1985) *Movement skill development.* Macmillan: London.

Kimball, T.D. (1973) *The systematic isolation and validation of personality determiners in handwriting of school children.* PhD Thesis, University of Southern California.

Kirk, U. (1985) Hemispheric contributions to the development of graphic skill. In Best, C. (Ed.) *Hemispheric function and collaboration in the child.* New York: Academic Press

Kolers, P. (1968) Some psychological aspects of pattern recognition. In Kolers, P. & Eden, M. (Eds.) *Recognizing patterns*. Cambridge, MA: MIT Press.

Lacquaniti, F., Terzuolo, C. & Viviani, P. (1983) The law relating the kinematic and figural aspects of drawing movements. *Acta Psychologica, 54*, 115-130.

Lacquaniti, F., Terzuolo, C. & Viviani, P. (1984) Global metric properties and preparatory processes in drawing movements. In Kornblum, S. & Requin, J. (Eds.) *Preparatory states and processes*. Hillsdale, NJ: Erlbaum.

Lally, M. (1982) Computer-assisted handwriting instruction and visual/kinaesthetic feedback processes. *Applied Research in Mental Retardation, 3*, 397-405.

Lasky, R.E. (1977) The effect of visual feedback of the hand on the reaching and retrieval behavior of young infants. *Child Development, 48*, 112-117.

Laszlo, J.I. (1990) Child perceptuo-motor development: Normal and abnormal development of skilled behaviour. In Hauert, C.A. (Ed.) *Developmental Psychology: Cognitive, perceptuo-motor and neurophysiological perspective*. Amsterdam: North Holland.

Laszlo, J.I. & Bairstow, P.J. (1983) Kinaesthesis: Its measurement, training, and relationship to motor control. *Quarterly Journal of Experimental Psychology, 35*, 411-421.

Laszlo, J.I. & Bairstow, P.J. (1985a) *Perceptual-motor behaviour: Developmental assessment and therapy*. London: Holt, Saunders & Winston.

Laszlo, J.I. & Bairstow, P.J. (1985b) *Kinaesthetic sensitivity test and training kit*. Perth: Senkit Pty Ltd., in conjunction with London: Holt, Rinehart and Winston.

Laszlo, J.I. & Broderick, P.A. (1985) The perceptual-motor development of drawing. In Freeman, N.H. & Cox, M.V. (Eds.) *Visual order: The nature and development of pictorial representation*. Cambridge: Cambridge University Press.

Laszlo, J.I., Bairstow, P.J. & Bartrip, J. (1988) A new approach to treatment of perceptuo-motor dysfunction: previously called clumsiness. *Support for Learning, 3*, 35-40.

Lester, D., McLaughlin, S. & Nosal, G. (1977) Graphological signs for extraversion. *Perceptual and Motor Skills, 44*, 137-138.

Luria, A.R. (1932) *The nature of human conflicts or emotion, conflict and will*. New York: Liveright.

Maarse, F.J. (1987) *The study of handwriting movement: Peripheral models and signal processing techniques.* Lisse: Swets & Zeitlinger.

Maarse, F.J. & Thomassen, A.J.W.M. (1983) Produced and perceived writing slant: Differences between up and down strokes. *Acta Psychologica, 54,* 131-147.

Maarse, F.J., Janssen, H.J.J. & Dexel, F. (1988) A special pen for an XY-tablet. In Maarse, F.J., Mulder, L.J.M., Sjouw, W.P.B. & Akkerman, A.E. (Eds.) *Computers in psychology: Methods, instrumentation, and psychodiagnostics.* Lisse: Swets & Zeitlinger.

MacLean, H.B. (1966) *The MacLean method of writing, Teachers' complete manual.* Toronto: Gage.

McCloskey, D.I. (1978) Kinaesthetic sensibility. *Physiological Reviews, 58,* 763-820.

McDonnell, P.M. & Abraham, W.C. (1981) A longitudinal study of prism adaptation in infants from six to nine months of age. *Child Development, 52,* 463-469.

Magnusson, D. (1981) Some methodology and strategy in longitudinal research. In Schulsinger, F., Mednick, S.A. & Knop, J. (Eds.) *Methods and uses in behavioral sciences.* Boston: Martinus Nijhoff.

Meltzer, E.S. (1980) Remarks on ancient Egyptian writing with emphasis on its mnemonic aspects. In Kolers, P.A., Wrolstad, M.E. & Bouma, H. (Eds.) *Processing of visible language 2.* New York: Plenum.

Meulenbroek, R.G.J. (1989) *The study of handwriting production: Educational and developmental aspects.* PhD Thesis, University of Nijmegen.

Meulenbroek, R.G.J. & Galen, G.P. van (1986) Movement analysis of repetitive writing behavior of first, second and third grade primary school children, In Kao, H.S.R., Van Galen, G.P. & Hoosain, R. (Eds.) *Graphonomics: Contemporary research in handwriting.* Amsterdam: North-Holland.

Meulenbroek, R.G.J. & Galen, G.P. van (1988) The acquisition of skilled handwriting: discontinuous trends in kinematic variables. In Colley, A.M. & Beech, J.R. (Eds.) *Cognition and action in skilled behaviour.* Amsterdam: North Holland.

Michel, F. (1971) Etude expérimentale de la vitesse du geste graphique (An experimental study of the velocity of graphic movements). *Neuropsychology, 9,* 1-13.

Mojet, J.W. (1989) *Kenmerken van Schrijfvaardigheid. Procesaspecten van het schrijven bij zes- tot twaalfjarigen. (Characteristics of the developing handwriting skill. Process aspects of handwriting by pupils from 6 to 12 year)*. De Lier: Academisch Boeken Centrum.

Möller, G. (1909-1912) *Hieratische Palaographie I*. Leipzig: J.C. Hinrichs.

Mounoud, P. (1981) Cognitive development: Construction of new structures or construction of internal organizations. In Sigel, I.E., Brodzinsky, D.M. & Golinkoff, P.M. (Eds.) *New directions of Piagetian theory and practice*. Hillsdale, NJ: Erlbaum.

Mounoud, P. (1983) L'évolution des conduites de préhension comme illustration d'un modèle de développement (The development of reading behaviour as an illustration of a developmental model). In Schonen, S. de (Ed.) *Le développement dans la première année*. Paris: P.U.F.

Mounoud, P. (1986a) Action and cognition. In Wade, M.G. & Whiting, H.T.A. (Eds.) *Motor development in children*. Dordrecht: Nijhoff.

Mounoud, P. (1986b) Similarities between developmental sequences at different age periods. In Levin, I. (Ed.) *Stage and structure*. Norwood: Ablex, pp. 40-58.

Mounoud, P., Hauert, C-A., Mayer, E., Gachoud, J-P., Guyon, J. & Gottret, G. (1983) Visuo-manual tracking strategies in the 3- to 5-year-old child. *Archives de Psychologie, 51*, 23-33.

Mounoud, P., Viviani, P., Hauert, C-A. & Guyon, J. (1985) Development of visuo-manual tracking in the 5- to 9-year-old boys. *Journal of Experimental Child Psychology, 40*, 115-132.

Ness, E. van (1989, April 9) As easy as 1-3-2. *The New York Times, 4A*, 47.

Nieuwenhuis, C.W. (1984) *De invloed van "mastery learning principles "op het schrijven: een vergelijkend onderzoek (The impact of mastery learning principles on writing: A comparative study)*. Master's thesis, Vrije Universiteit, Amsterdam.

Nieuwenhuis, C.W. (1988) Criteria voor het beoordelen van handschriften (Criteria for the evaluation of handwriting). In: Orgaan van de Vereniging van leraren in het schoonschrijven *M.O. Stenografie Groote en Machineschrijven*. 79, parts 2 (16-28) and 3 (14-22).

Pang, H. & Lepponen, L. (1968) Personality traits and handwriting characteristics. *Perceptual and Motor Skills, 26,* 1082.

Parreren, C.F. van & Carpay, J.A.M. (1979) *Sovjetpsychologen over onderwijs en cognitieve ontwikkeling (Soviet psycologists on teaching and cognitive development).* Groningen: Wolters-Noordhoff.

Peck, M., Askov, E.N. & Fairchild, S.H. (1980) Another decade of research in handwriting. *The Journal of Educational Research, 73,* 283-298.

Pellizer, G. and Hauert, C-A. (1989) Manual pointing at visually lateralized targets in children and adults. Paper presented at the INS Conference, Ansvers, Belgium.

Pennings, A. & Wiel, J. van de (1980) *Schrijven, praktijkboek voor het schrijfonderwijs aan 4-12 jarigen (Writing, practise book for teaching handwriting to pupils of 4-12).* Den Bosch: Malmberg.

Peters, M. & Pedersen, K. (1978) Incidence of left-handers with inverted writing position in a population of 5910 elementary school children. *Neuropsychologia, 16,* 743.

Pew, R.W. and Rupp, G.L. (1971) Two quantitative measures of skill development. *Journal of Experimental Psychology, 90,* 1-7.

Phelps, J., Stempel, L. & Speck, G. (1984) Children's handwriting evaluation scale. Dallas, TX: CHES.

Phelps, J., Speck, L. & Stempel, L. (1985) The children's handwriting scale: A new diagnostic tool. *Journal of Educational Research, 79,* 46-51.

Piaget, J. & Inhelder, B. (1941) *Le développement des quantités physiques chez l'enfant (The development of physical concepts in children).* Paris et Neuchatel: Delachaux & Niestlé.

Piaget, J. & Inhelder, B. (1969) *The psychology of the child.* London: Routledge & Kegan Paul.

Pijning, H. F. (1969) *Het diagnostiseren en corrigeren van stoornissen in het schrijven (The diagnosis and correction of writing disturbances).* Groningen: Wolters-Noordhoff.

Powell, M.E. (1981) Three problems in the history of Cuneiform writing: origins, direction of script, literacy. *Visible Language, 15,* 419-440.

Prystav, G. (1971) Reliability of interpretation in handwriting psychology. *Schweizerische Zietschrift fur Psychologie und Ihre Anwendungen. 30,* 320-332.

Raven, J.C. (1982) *Mill Hill vocabulary scale.* London: H.K. Lewis.

Reitan, R.M. & Davison, L.A. (1974) *Clinical neuropsychology: Current states and applications.* Washington, D.C: Winston.

Rigal, R.A. (1976) Efficience manuelle et vitesse d'écriture (Manual efficiency and writing speed). *Journal de Neuropsychiatrie Infantile, 25,* 391-400.

Rosenbaum, D.A., Marchak, F., Barnes, H.J., Vaughan, J., Slotta, J.D. & Jorgensen, M.J. (1990) Constraints for action selection. In Jeannerod, M. (Ed.) *Attention and Performance XIII.* London: Erlbaum.

Rosenthal, D. A. & Lines, R. (1978) Handwriting as a correlate of extraversion. *Journal of Personality Assessment, 42,* 45-48.

Rubin, N., & Henderson, S.E. (1982) Two sides of the same coin, variability in instructional practices in handwriting and the problem of those who fail to learn to write. *Special Education Forward Trends, 9,* 17-24.

Rutter, M., Tizard, J. & Whitmore, K. (1970) *Education, health and behaviour.* London: Longmans.

Sassoon R.(1983) *The practical guide to chidren's handwriting.* London: Thames and Hudson.

Sassoon R.(1988) *Joins in children's handwriting, and the effects of different models and teaching methods.* PhD Thesis, University of Reading.

Sassoon, R. (1983) *The practical guide to children's handwriting.* London: Thames and Hudson.

Sassoon, R. (1984) *Children's handwriting.* London: Thames & Hudson.

Sassoon, R. (1986) *Helping your handwriting.* London: Nelson.

Sassoon, R., Nimmo-Smith, I. & Wing, A.M. (1986) An analysis of children's penholds. In Kao, H.S.R., Galen, G.P. van & R. Hoosain, R. (Eds.) *Graphonomics: Contemporary research in handwriting.* Amsterdam: North Holland.

Sassoon, R., Nimmo-Smith, I. & Wing, A.M. (1989) Developing efficiency in cursive handwriting: An analysis of 't'-crossing behaviour in children. In *Computer Recognition and Human Production of Handwriting.* Plamondon, R., Suen, C.Y. and Simner, M.L. (Eds.) Singapore: World Scientific Publishing.

Satz, P. & Van Nostrand, G.K. (1973) Developmental dyslexia: An evaluation of a theory. In Satz, P. & Ross, J.J. (Eds.) *The disabled learner: Early detection and intervention.* Rotterdam: Rotterdam University Press.

Schneider, R. (1987) *Le concept d'unité d'action motrice (The concept of motor access as a unit)*. PhD Thesis, University of Geneva.

Sciaky, R., Lacquaniti, F., Terzuolo, C. & Soechting, J.F. (1987) A note on the kinematics of drawing movements in children. *Journal of Motor Behavior, 19*, 518-525.

Shinn, A.M. (1974) Relations between scales. In Blalock, H.M. Jr. (Ed.) *Measurements in the social sciences*. Chicago: Aldine.

Silk, A.M. & Thomas, G.V. (1988) The development of size scaling in children's figure drawings. *British Journal of Developmental Psychology, 6*, 285-299.

Silver, J.F. (1984) Graphology in the schools. *American Handwriting Analysis Foundation, 17*, 1-6.

Simner, M.L. (1979) *Mirror-image reversals in children's printing: Preliminary findings*. ERIC Document Collection, (ED 174-354).

Simner, M.L. (1981) The grammar of action and children's printing. *Developmental Psychology, 17*, 866-871.

Simner, M.L. (1982) Printing errors in kindergarten and the prediction of academic performance. *Journal of Learning Disabilities, 15*, 155-159.

Simner, M.L. (1984) The grammar of action and reversal errors in children's printing. *Developmental Psychology, 20*, 136-142.

Simner, M.L. (1985) *Printing performance school readiness test*. Toronto: Guidance Centre, Faculty of Education, University of Toronto.

Simner, M.L. (1986) Further evidence on the relationship between form errors in preschool printing and early school achievement. In Kao, H.S.R., Galen, G.P. van & Hoosian, R. (Eds.) *Graphonomics: Contemporary research in handwriting*. Amsterdam: North-Holland.

Simner, M.L. (1987) Predictive validity of the teacher's school readiness inventory. *Canadian Journal of School Psychology, 3*, 21-32.

Simner, M.L. (1988) *Teacher's school readiness inventory*. London, Ontario: Phylmar Associates.

Simner, M.L. (1989) Predictive validity of an abbreviated version of the Printing Performance School Readiness Test. *Journal of School Psychology, 27*, 189-195.

Simner, M.L. (1990) Printing performance school readiness test. *Academic Therapy, 25*, 369-375.

Sirat, C. (1987) *La morphologie humaine et la direction des écritures (Human morphology and the direction of scripts)*. Comptes Rendus; Académie des Inscriptions et Belles Lettres.

Smith, A.C. & Reed, G.F. (1959) An experimental investigation of the relative speeds of left and right handed writers. *Journal of Genetic Psychology, 94,* 67-76.

Smith, D.D. (1981) *Teaching the learning disabled.* Englewood Cliffs, NJ: Prentice-Hall.

Smith, L.C. & Moscovitch, M. (1979) Writing posture, hemispheric control of movement and cerebral dominance in individuals with inverted and non-inverted hand postures during writing. *Neuropsychologia, 17,* 637-644.

Smyth, M.M. (1988) Visual control of movement patterns and the grammar of action. *Acta Psychologica, 70,* 253-265.

Smyth, M.M. & Silvers, J. (1987) Functions of vision in the control of handwriting. *Acta Psychologica, 65,* 65-73.

Solheim, R., Nygaard, H.D., Aasved H. (1984) *II Søkelys på småskolealderen (II Focus on primary level).* Bergen: Universitetsforlaget.

Sommers, P. van (1984) *Drawing and cognition: Descriptive and experimental studies of graphic production processes.* New York: Cambridge University Press.

Sõvik, N. (1975) *Developmental cybernetics of handwriting and graphic behaviour.* Oslo: Universitetsforlaget.

Sõvik, N. (1980) Developmental trends of visual feedback control and learning in childrens' copying and tracking skills. *Journal of Experimental Education,* 106-11.

Sõvik, N. (1981) An experimental study of individualised learning/ instruction in copying, tracking, and handwriting, based on feedback principles. *Perception and Motor Skills, 53,* 195-215.

Sõvik, N. (1984a) The effects of a remedial tracking problem on writing performance on dysgraphic children. *Scandinavian Journal of Educational Research, 28,* 129-147.

Sõvik, N. (1984b) *Utvikling av Skrivedugleik. Teoriar, forsking og pedagogiske retningsliner (Development of writing skills: Theories, research and educational guidelines).* Trondheim: Tapir.

Sõvik, N. (1987) *Learning disabilities in reading, spelling, and writing.* Trondheim: Tapir.

Sõvik, N. & Teulings, H-L. (1983) Real-time feedback of handwriting in a teaching programme. *Acta Psychologica, 54*, 285-291.

Sõvik, N., Arntzen, O. & Thygesen, R. (1986) Effects of feedback trainingon "normal" and dysgraphic children. In Kao, H.R.S., Galen, G.P. van & Hoosain, R. (Eds.) *Graphonomics: Contemporary research in handwriting.* Amsterdam: North-Holland.

Sõvik, N., Arntzen, O. & Thygesen, R. (1987 a) Relation of spelling and learning in writing disabilities. *Perception and Motor Skills, 64*, 219-236.

Sõvik, N., Arntzen, O. & Thygesen, R. (1987 b) Writing characteristics of "normal", dyslexic, and dysgraphic children. *Journal of Human Movement Studies, 13*, 171-187.

Sõvik, N., Flem Mæland, A. & Karlsdottir, R. (1989) Contextual factors and writing performance of normal and dysgraphic children. In Plamondon, R., Suen, C.Y. & Simner, M.L. (Eds.) *Computer recognition and human production of handwriting.* Singapore: World Scientific Publishing.

Stelmach, G.E. & Teulings, H.L. (1983) Response characteristics of prepared and restructured handwriting. *Acta Psychologica, 54*, 51-68.

Stevens, S. S. (1975) *Psychophysics: Introduction into its perceptual neural and social prospects.* New York: Wiley.

Stott, D.H. Moyes, F.A. & Henderson S.E. (1985) *Diagnosis and remediation of handwriting problems.* Guelph, Ontario: Brook Educational.

Suen, C.Y. (1983) Handwriting generation, perception and recognition. *Acta Psychologica, 54*, 358-362.

Surwillo, W.W. (1974) Speed of movement in relation to period of the electroencephalogram in normal children. *Parapsychology, 11*, 491-496.

Tait, W.J. (1987) *Demotic paleography: Styles and dates.* Paper presented to the Third International Conference for Demotic Studies, Cambridge, U.K., 8-12 September, 1987.

Tait, W.J. (1988) Rush and reed: the pens of Egyptian and Greek scribes. *Proceedings of the XVIII International Congress of Papyrology Volume II.* Athens: Greek Papyrological Society.

Teulings, H-L. & Maarse F.J. (1984) Digital recording and processing of handwriting movements. *Human Movement Science, 3*, 193-217.

Teulings, H-L. & Thomassen, A.J.W.M. (1979) Computer-aided analysis of handwriting movements. *Visible Language, 13,* 218-231.

Texas Education Code. House Bill 157. (1985) Austin, TX. Texas State Legislature.

Thelen, E. & Fisher, D.M. (1983) The organization of spontaneous leg movements in newborn infants. *Journal of Motor Behavior, 15,* 353-377.

Thomas, G.V. & Tsalini, A. (1988) Effects of order of drawing head and trunk on their relative sizes in children's human figure drawings. *British Journal of Developmental Psychology, 6,* 191-203.

Thomassen, A.J.W.M. & Teulings, H-L. (1979) Computer-aided analyses of handwriting movements. *Visible Language, 13,* 299-313.

Thomassen, A.J.W.M. & Teulings, H.-L. (1983) The development of handwriting. In Martlew, M. (Ed.) *The psychology of written language. Development and educational perspective.* Chichester: Wiley.

Thomassen, A.J.W.M., Keuss, P.J.G. & Galen, G.P. van (1983) Motor aspects of handwriting. *Acta Psychologica, 54,* 1-3.

Touwen, B.C.L. (1982) Groei en ontwikkeling van het centrale zenuwstelsel (Growth and development of the central nervous system). In Beekhuis, H. & Eeuwnea, J. (Eds.) *Leerboek voor de Jeugdgezondheidszorg.* Assen: Van Gorcum.

Trites, R.L. & Fiedorowicz, C. (1976) Follow up study of children with specific (or primary) reading problems. In Knights, R.M. & Bakker, D.J. (Eds.) *The neuropsychology of learning disorders.* Baltimore: University Park Press.

Undheim, J.O. (1989) Lese- og skriveutvikling fra 4. til 6. klasse (Development of reading and spelling from the 4th to 6th grade). *Norsk Pedagogisk Tidsskrift,73,* 16-23

Ure, D. (1969) Spelling performances of left-handed school children as affected by the use of a pencil modified to increase visual feedback. *Journal of Experimental Child Psychology, 7,* 220-230.

Vellutino, F.R. (1978) Towards an understanding of dyslexia: Psychological factors in specific reading disability. In Benton, A.L. & Pearl, D. (Eds.) *Dyslexia.* New York: Oxford University Press.

Vinter, A. (1988) Perception of facial movements in infancy: some reflections in relation to speech perception. *Visible Language, 1,* 78-111.

Vinter, A. (1990) Manual imitations and reaching behaviors: an illustration of action control in infancy. In Bard, C., Fleury, M. & Hay, L. (Eds.) *Development of eye-hand coordination across lifespan.* Columbia: The University of South Carolina.

Viviani, P. & Cenzato, M. (1985) Segmentation and coupling in complex movements. *Journal of Experimental Psychology: Human Perception and Performance, 11,* 828-845.

Viviani, P. & McCollum, G. (1983) The relation between linear extent and velocity in drawing movements. *Neuroscience, 10,* 211-218.

Viviani, P. & Terzuolo, C. (1980) Space-time invariance in learned motor skills. In Stelmach, G.E. & Requin, J. (Eds.) *Tutorials in motor behavior.* Amsterdam: North-Holland.

Viviani, P. & Terzuolo, C. (1982) Trajectory determines movement dynamics. *Neuroscience, 7,* 431-437.

Viviani, P. & Terzuolo, C. (1983) The organization of movement in handwriting and typing. In Butterworth, B. (Ed.) *Language production, Vol. II: Development, writing and other language processes.* New York: Academic Press.

Viviani, P. & Zanone, P.G. (1988) Spontaneous covariations of movement parameters in 5- to 7-year-old boys. *Journal of Motor Behavior, 20,* 5-16.

Vygotsky, L.S. (1979) *Mind in society.* Boston: Harvard University Press.

Wann, J.P. (1986) Handwriting disturbances: Developmental trends. In Whiting, T.A. & Wade, M.G. (Eds.) *Themes in motor development.* Dordrecht: Nijhoff.

Wann, J.P. (1987) Trends in the refinement and optimization of fine-motor skills: Observations from an analysis of the handwriting of primary school children. *Journal of Motor Behavior , 19,* 13-37.

Wann, J.P. (1989) The appraisal of the velocity-curvature relation in children's hand movements: a research note. *Journal of Motor Behaviour, 2,* 145-150.

Wann, J.P. & Jones, J.G. (1986) Space-time invariance in handwriting: Contrasts between primary school children displaying advanced or retarded handwriting acquisition. *Human Movement Science, 5,* 275-296.

Wann, J., Nimmo-Smith, I. & Wing, A.M. (1988) Relation between velocity and curvature in movement: Equivalence and divergence between a power law and a minimum jerk model. *Journal of Experimental Psychology: Human Perception and Performance, 14*, 622-637.

Warren, W.J. (1989, April 12) Middle schools grow in academic importance. *The New York Times.* Education, p. 17.

Watts, M. L (1965) *Curriculum guide for handwriting* Calgary: Department of Education.

Wechsler, D. (1955) *Wechsler adult intelligence scale.* New York, NY: Psychological Corporation.

West, P.V. (1957) *Manual for the American handwriting scale.* New York: A.N. Palmer.

West, P.V. & Freeman F.N. (1950) *Handwriting. Encyclopedia of educational research.* London: MacMillan.

Wing, A.M.(1979) Variability in handwritten characters. *Visible Language, 13*, 283-298.

Wing, A.M. (1980) Response timing in handwriting. In Stelmach, G.E. & Requin, J. (Eds.) *Tutorials in motor behavior.* North Holland: Amsterdam.

Wing, A.M. & Baddeley A.D. (1978) A simple measure of handwriting as an index of stress. *Bulletin of the Psychonomic Society, 11*, 245-246

Wing, A.M. & Nimmo-Smith, I. (1987) The variability of cursive handwriting measure defined along a continuum: Letter specificity. *Journal of the Forensic Science Society, 27*, 297-306.

Wing A.M., Nimmo-Smith I. & Eldridge M.A. (1983) The consistency of cursive letter formation as a function of position in the word. *Acta Pychologica, 54,* 197-204.

Woodcock, R.W. (1974) *Woodcock reading mastery tests.* Circle Pines, MN.: American Guidance Service.

Zanone, P-G. (1987) *La poursuite visuo-manuelle chez l'enfant et l'adulte (Visuo-manual tracking in children and adults).* PhD Thesis, University of Geneva.

Zazzo, R. (1962) Considerations sur l'enfant gaucher (Thoughts on the left-handed child). In Zazzo, R. (Ed.), *Conduites et consciences: Vol 1.* Paris: Delachaux et Niestlé.

Ziviani, J. (1984) Some elaborations on handwriting speed in 7- to 14-year-olds. *Perceptual and Motor Skills, 58*, 535-539.

Ziviani, J. & Elkins, J. (1986) Effect of pencil grip on handwriting speed and legibility. *Educational Review, 38*, 247-257.

Index